TAKING CONTROL OF YOUR OFFICE RECORDS:

A Manager's Guide

edited by
Katherine Aschner

Illustrations by Kerry Leimer/ Creative Services
Cartoons by Fred Birchman/Salmon Graphics

Knowledge Industry Publications, Inc.

Information and Communications
Management Guides

Taking Control of Your Office Records:
A Manager's Guide

Library of Congress Cataloging in Publication Data
Main entry under title:

Taking control of your office records.

    (Information and communications management guides)
    Bibliography: p.
    Includes index.
1.   Records—Management—Addresses, essays, lectures.
I.   Aschner, Katherine.   II.   Series.
HF5736.T34   1983   651.5   83-6133
ISBN 0-86729-057-9
ISBN 0-86729-058-7 (pbk.)

Printed in the United States of America

10   9   8   7   6   5   4   3   2   1

Table of Contents

List of Tables and Figures

Foreword

I don't think I know anyone whose favorite subject is records. And yet we all live with them, some more willingly than others. Those of us who find coexistence difficult usually voice the same basic complaint: we accumulate more and more files in which we can find less and less information. If this complaint sounds familiar, then this book is for you.

The trouble in most offices is easily traced: there is no records system to work with and no files space to work in. You defend yourself by making an extra copy of everything and squirreling it away in your own personal filing system. Your best defense is that 80% of filed records are never called for again. Your worst fear is that one day you'll have to rely on someone else's personal filing system, and that it will be just as antiquated and difficult to unravel as your own.

HOW THIS BOOK CAN HELP

Files don't have to be a problem. What it takes is a systematic approach to organizing your records. It starts with making sure your paper files are under control. You need a classification scheme that everyone can understand and use. Your filing scheme must also work for you in other ways, such as keeping outdated files from cluttering up your office.

Organizing your records means more than just straightening out your file cabinets, however. It also means taking advantage of the full array of modern methods for handling information. For instance, you may need to microfilm certain records, either to simplify retrieval or to duplicate valuable files. Even small businesses can employ this technology, by using service bureaus to produce their microfilm.

There may also be situations in which you need to automate your record-keeping. Desktop systems make it affordable to computerize paperwork in ways that weren't possible 10 years ago. Today's office technology is also much simpler to use than before.

Not all of your records problems will require technological solutions. Some categories of records present special control problems, such as maps, drawings and engineering documentation. Large technical reference files also require careful management if they are to be used to their fullest.

Other types of records require special protection, because your business would be lost if they were inadvertently destroyed by a fire or other disaster. For older records, you may need to set up an archive, or an inactive records center.

A good records program deals with all of these situations. And whether you are working in a large corporation, a medium-sized city or a small professional firm, the approach and the techniques are the same. (For simplicity's sake, the text refers to business records; however, it applies equally to government records.)

Offices, like people, are prone to a form of mid-life crisis. Those in the know say it begins with this desperate cry: "We've got to do something about the files!" That's what this book is all about: doing something about the files. It is written on the assumption that you have a limited budget, that you don't want to hire a consultant and that your records are more or less out of control. The book outlines a step-by-step methodology for taking charge of your files and assuring your access to information.

Katherine Aschner
May 1983

1

A Strategy for Taking Control

by Katherine Aschner

Before launching yourself into the unfamiliar territory of records, it's important to have a good roadmap of where you're going. You will need it to develop a sound system for dealing with your company's files. You will also need it to convince other managers and co-workers that your system will work.

Don't assume just because people complain about their files that they will welcome your help. Whether workable or not, most people regard their files as gold mines of information and are very protective of them. In order to persuade people to share this wealth, you will need to present them with a well-designed system and some pretty cogent reasons for going along with it.

While we're on the subject, it is worth noting that sharing the wealth is not the same as giving it up. A good records system establishes centralized control over files and other information resources. This is accomplished through the development of uniform classification systems and uniform standards for deciding when to use microfilm or computers (among other things). However, centralized control most emphatically does not require that the files and other records be physically centralized as well. The records themselves are best kept with the people who work with them, as long as this is done in a manner that meshes with the company's overall records system.

THE FUNDAMENTALS OF A GOOD RECORDS SYSTEM

What Records Should Your System Include?

That's simple: all your records. Just because some are in cabinets and others are rolled in map files, stored in boxes or recorded on floppy diskettes does not mean that any one group is more important than the others. They are all part of your company's information resources. All of these resources cost something to collect and maintain. All of them should be scrutinized to make sure that useful information is accessible and that obsolete information is purged before it costs you even more money.

Defining the term "records" is not quite as easy. For our purposes records include, but are not limited to: files, maps, drawings, indexes, photographs, microfilm, computer files and disks, sound and video tapes, reference materials and other sources of recorded information. Your records system should include any company records received from outside organizations, as well as all internal records.

The Principles of Records Management

A records system has three basic objectives. First, it documents your organization's policies, operations and transactions. Second, it does this in such a way that you can find information quickly when you need it. Third, it ensures that long-term information is preserved, so that you can draw on it as long as necessary. A good records system establishes the controls needed to ensure that all three of these objectives are met.

Cost Controls

The cost of maintaining one four-drawer file cabinet is about $800 per year. On the average, 68% of these costs (about $550) is for labor. The remaining 32% is the cost of supplies, equipment and space.

A records system introduces cost controls by eliminating duplicate files and removing nonessential records from valuable office space. This increases the efficiency of the files clerk, who no longer has to rummage through obsolete records to find the right file.

Most files personnel spend about 25% of their time searching for the 1% to 3% of files that are misfiled. A well-designed system can significantly reduce such non-productive filing labor costs.

However, maintenance is only a small portion of your labor costs. The real costs are incurred before the files ever reach the cabinet. These are the costs of collecting, reading and processing the information. That is why it is so important to consider all the options open to you, including microfilm and automation. No matter how well-organized your files are, if the records should not be on paper in the first place, you are wasting time and money. A systematic analysis of your records ensures that cost controls are applied to the collection and processing of information, as well as to its maintenance.

Quality Controls

Using inaccurate or obsolete information is often worse than not being able to find the information at all. For instance, using the wrong version of a contract in a negotiation, or using the wrong version of a drawing to install a heating system, can have disastrous results. However, these situations easily arise when there is no records system to mandate how current and superseded documents are handled. A properly designed system ensures the quality of the information you are working with.

Management Controls

Good management is virtually impossible without good information. In an increasingly competitive business environment, accurate reporting and cost accounting are essential both in day-to-day operations and for strategic planning. In an increasingly regulated environment, good records are essential for ensuring compliance and avoiding costly lawsuits. And in an era of restricted budgets, managers must still be able to draw on information without delays or unnecessary expense.

Incorporating management controls in a records system implies selectivity. It means keeping all the information you need, not everything you can. The principle also recognizes that all records are not of equal value. You do need to evaluate all your records, however, in order to decide which are worth concentrating your resources on. Then you can establish systems to make sure management receives the information it needs on a timely basis and in a usable format.

MANAGING A RECORDS SYSTEM

The balance of this book tells you how to set up a good records system. However, your information requirements are going to change over time. If you want to go through mid-life crisis only once, you will need to stay on top of your new system. In other words, taking control of your records is not a one-time project. To keep your system in order will require some ongoing management attention.

Establish a Records Policy

The most trustworthy employee in the company, who wouldn't pad a penny in an expense account, will take your files without a second thought. The problem isn't dishonesty or even carelessness. On the contrary, it's the conscientious employees who assume personal custody of their files, taking them with them when they change positions. However, as their replacements usually find out, the office that gets left behind also gets left in a lurch: its most important records are often missing.

Most employees simply don't understand that their files and records are *company* property, not their own personal property. One of the most important components of a records program, therefore, is a company policy that clarifies the custodianship of all information resources. (Appendix 2 includes a sample policy statement that can be included in a company files manual.)

Once you have established company ownership of records, you should also adopt another policy: official files do not belong in individuals' desks. Desk files make it too hard for other people to get at the records, because of a natural reluctance to open a private desk. Desk filing also promotes the feeling of personal rather than company ownership of records. Only working files should be housed in desks rather than in official file cabinets.

Another problem of desk files is that they often mean managers are doing their own filing. This is a poor use of skills, to say the least. Filing is a clerical function. If the system is too complicated or unreliable for the support staff, then the answer is to design a better system. Managers and professionals should not be involved in this task.

Put Someone in Charge

Whatever records system you design, it will change. It is this factor that makes central control so important. The purpose is not to stifle change, but to make sure that changes are appropriate and uniformly applied. Otherwise, if each office starts revising the filing system or setting up a technical library on its own, in a very short time you will be back where you started: with son of mid-life crisis.

Putting someone in charge of the records system ensures centralized control. This does not necessarily imply a full-time position. The level of commitment required depends entirely on the size of your company and the complexity of its records. However, the management function is the key to a good records program. The records manager must be assigned sufficient authority to carry out this critical responsibility. (Appendix 2 includes an outline of the basic responsibilities and tasks of the records manager.)

Conduct an Annual Review

One of the primary tasks of the records manager is to conduct an annual audit of your records system. Even if no one has suggested changes and additions, chances are that some will be needed. It is also likely that some offices will be more lax than others in following the system. Passive management, waiting until problems come to the records manager, is not good enough. At least once a year, the records manager has to search out the problems and deal with them.

HOW TO USE THIS BOOK

For Managing Files

In spite of all the talk about the "paperless office," files are still what most of us have to work with. Introducing some organization into the files is thus the first step in setting up a comprehensive records system. Chapter 2 of this book explains the basic theories of files management. These provide the framework upon which your files system will be built.

Chapter 3 describes the process of the files inventory. This essential step collects the information you need to develop your filing system. Unfortunately, there is no standard system that can be plugged into every office. A files inventory tells you what kinds of files you have. It also focuses your attention on records problems that may require special handling, such as microfilm or automation. And don't assume you already know all about your files. If you did, you wouldn't be having such a hard time finding information in the first place. Chapter 3 includes a sample records inventory form. Complete instructions for using the form are provided in Appendix 1.

Chapter 4 describes the process of working your inventory into a files classification scheme. This groups related records, such as finance or personnel records, into categories by their function or purpose. Within categories, files are arranged hierarchically into sub-categories, which makes the system logical and easy to use.

Chapter 5 explains how to integrate records retention schedules into your files classification scheme. A wise manager once said, "It's the records you keep that get you in trouble." But trouble can also come if you throw away records you are legally required to have. Retention schedules protect you by specifying how long records must be kept for each files classification. You will learn how to develop records retention schedules, and what resources are available for determining legal retention requirements.

The next step is to write procedures to make your filing system work. Appendix 2 is a complete policy and procedures section that you can adapt for your own files manual. Then you need to convert your old files into your new system and train people in how to use it. Appendix 3 outlines procedures for managing the conversion of your old files to your new system. Appendix 4 contains useful information about filing equipment. As long as you're setting up a new system, you should also take a look at how your files are housed.

For Managing Maps and Drawings

Large-format records, particularly maps and engineering documentation, usually require special handling. For one thing, they are more awkward to store. They also are more complex to index and retrieve. Moreover, there are often several generations of a drawing, and procedures are required to make sure current and obsolete files are adequately controlled. Chapter 6 provides useful guidance on categorizing these types of records and on organizing them efficiently.

For Using Technology

Microfilming is often an attractive solution to difficult records problems. It can speed retrieval, reduce distribution costs and ensure better control over files. However, filming paper records can involve very high labor costs. Microfilming is no substitute for applying basic records retention schedules. Microfilming decisions should be made carefully, and on the basis of complete information about the technology.

Chapter 7 introduces you to the various types of films, formats, processing and retrieval systems available, and discusses their relative advantages and uses. It also presents criteria for determining whether or not to microfilm a given set of records.

Chapter 8 explains the process of establishing and monitoring a microfilm program, should you decide one is needed. Special emphasis is placed on deciding how to choose between in-house and service bureau operations, and on what to expect from your service bureau.

One of the most critical decisions you will make is whether to automate your record keeping. Even if you cannot put all of your information on magnetic media, it may be advantageous to set up an index on a word processor or small computer. And for paperwork systems that involve extensive clerical operations, automation offers substantial benefits.

Chapter 9 describes the uses and advantages of word and data processing, and explains how they can be integrated efficiently on personal computers. You will learn about computer software and how to find the right commercial or custom programs for your needs. The uses of data bases, computerized indexes and modeling programs are discussed. Finally, there are sections on developing a program specification and on choosing the right size system for your needs.

For Protecting Your Records

Whether you are in business or government, about 1% to 2% of your total records are considered vital records. These are the files you would need in order to restore operations in the event of a major disaster. Typical records in this category include contracts, stockholder records, accounts receivable and other documents needed to reestablish your financial position and legal obligations. Because the total volume is usually small, it takes very little extra care to ensure that these records are adequately protected. As Chapter 10 explains, that protection may be the best investment you ever made.

Not all records can be protected from disaster. One of the most common problems is general water damage as the result of a fire. Water typically causes far more destruction than the fire itself. And while the damaged records may not be vital, the cost of recreating all your files can still be very high. There are steps you can take to minimize the damage, but it is essential that you be prepared and that you act quickly. Chapter 10 outlines basic recovery procedures that you should be aware of well before a fire starts.

For Managing Your Inactive Records

Inactive records are those you need to keep, but to which you do not refer on a regular basis. Last year's accounts payable files and closed personnel files are typical examples. While active records are organized with the emphasis on fast retrieval, inactive records are organized with emphasis on efficient storage. Specifically, they are usually held in low-cost warehouse-type space, where they can be accommodated in high-density shelving.

The fact that retrieval plays a secondary role in inactive storage does not mean that it should be ignored altogether. Too often, files are consigned to the second basement storeroom without any thought being given to why they are being saved, how a particular file is to be found if needed or whether the space is really suitable for records storage.

Chapter 11 tells you how to deal with these issues and explains the mechanics of establishing inactive records storage areas. It also explains how to choose a commercial records center if you do not have the volume or facilities for an in-house operation.

Chapter 12 offers another idea for the storage of some special inactive records: a company archives. An archives is a repository for your company's history. Typically about 5% or less of your total records will be of historical significance. These include founding documents, information about important decisions and contracts, trademarks, and other records that trace the growth of your business.

A company archives need not be elaborate, although it can be, since special methods of protecting and displaying old records may be involved. Many businesses find an archives invaluable, however, not just as a source of information but also as an excellent public relations tool. This chapter will help you evaluate your need for an archives and will provide guidance on how to set one up.

For Managing Technical and Outside Information Resources

If your firm uses extensive technical reference materials, especially outside resources, you may want to consider a special library (as in-house libraries are usually called). But a library can be expensive, and a badly organized library can be worse than none at all. Chapter 13 gives you an overview of what's involved in setting up a special library. It identifies several levels of service to choose from, explaining when each is used and what advantages are gained as the range of services (and costs) increases. A basic plan for organizing your library and determining what it will cost is presented. If your needs are extensive, you will require the services of a professional librarian. This chapter can help you decide if you need a library (and a librarian) or not.

2

The Principles of Files Management

by Katherine Aschner

Files serve two basic functions: documenting your organization's policies and transactions, and doing this in such a way that you can find information again when you need it. Thus, a good filing system means getting the right information to the right person on time and at a reasonable cost.

Your files are your organization's memory. It is important to keep that memory sharp and uncluttered, so that you can draw upon it easily. Thus, eliminating obsolete files is as important to good files management as identifying and maintaining your long-term records.

FILING SYSTEM OBJECTIVES

Files management is distinct from information management. Information systems are large collections of data, typically stored in computers or technical libraries. Files systems, to oversimplify a bit, consist of files and other documents dispersed throughout an organization. Although there is some overlap between the two, information systems deal with discrete units of information; files systems deal with complete files—usually incorporating incoming and outgoing correspondence, internal and external supporting materials, working papers and other types of records. Efficient management of files systems is governed by some very specific objectives.

Preserving the Order of Records

The essential difference between an information system and a records system is one of significant order. In other words, units of information have no set organization. They are intended to be sorted, extracted, compared. Records, however, do have a set order: their sequence is significant (as anyone who has ever dealt with a misfile knows). Certain records belong with other records, and their meaning would be destroyed were they to be separated. One of the principal objectives of a good filing system, therefore, is to preserve this important order.

Simplified Retrieval

Getting information to people in a timely manner requires files classifications that aid retrieval. The most important feature in deciding how to file a record is how it is likely to be asked for again. This is easy to figure out for yourself, if you are the only person who will have to work with your files, and if the information in your files applies to you alone. However, few of us have that luxury.

Efficient filing depends on uniform files classifications that make sense to a broad number of people. This means people not just in your own department, but in all departments company-wide.

Continuity of Information

The hallmark of a well-designed system is that it continues to function regardless of personnel and organizational changes. When staff turnover occurs, or when departments reorganize, the files classification system remains constant, although individual offices' holdings may change. In everyday terms, this means that you can find information in another department's files (and your own), even if the regular files clerk is out.

Uniform filing also helps when one department must turn over files to another. For example, product development files may become manufacturing files, or design files may become construction files and eventually operations files. A standard system based on files classifications that fit in all departments greatly simplifies this process.

UNIFORM FILES CLASSIFICATIONS

Fine, you say, but how to come up with these uniform files classifications? That, of course, is the purpose of the files inventory, which is explained in the next chapter. One of the principal goals of the inventory is to reduce the terms used for files classifications to their lowest common denominator. This means three things:

- Identifying the smallest groupings of records that are used, filed and retired in the same way. These are called *records series*.

- Describing records series according to the function they perform. This is called *functional filing*.

- Identifying related records series so that classification codes can be developed to link them together. This is called *hierarchical filing*.

Records Series

This basic files unit may be a single record, such as a purchase order, or it may be a set of different types of records, such as one person's official personnel folder. In either case, records series are the building blocks of the files classification system. Each unique series has its own files classification code. For instance, all personnel records might be coded PER. As is explained in Chapter 5, each series also has its own unique retention period.

Functional Filing

Records series are identified according to their purpose or function. How records are used, not who created them, is the key. Thus, a personnel record is a personnel record whether generated in the personnel office or in the branch sales office. A budget document is a budget document whether found in the finance office or the maintenance shop. In short, the records series title must be descriptive enough to work wherever a particular record is found. This method of filing is called functional filing.

Hierarchical Filing

Certain records series are related to one another. For instance, hiring and employee benefit records both relate to personnel management. When files classification schemes are developed, these series should be grouped together in a way that aids retrieval and promotes efficient office procedures.

In a typical company or city, records series will fall into from 18 to 25 primary classifications. Examples of common administrative primaries, as these classification groupings are called, are Personnel Management, Financial Management and Public Relations. Examples of specialized primaries include Mining Operations, Nursing Administration and Business Development. These groupings are obviously dependent upon the type of organization involved.

Within primaries, secondary and tertiary classifications are established. Chapter 3 lists a sample primary with all its secondary and tertiary classifications. For instance, under Personnel Management, a secondary classification is Separations, and two tertiary classifications under that are Resignations and Involuntary Terminations. This method of filing is called hierarchical filing.

Setting Up Case Files

This is a good time to bring up case files. A case file relates to a specific person, company, client, project, event, geographic area or other unique entity. Thus, case files *are* filed by proper name. However, this does not violate the principle of functional filing established above. A case file is first identified according to its functional classification. Within that classification, it is then filed alphabetically or numerically by the name of the case.

Let's use official personnel files to illustrate. These might be filed under PER-10-1, a code developed for that particular personnel records series. (Chapter 4 explains how to set up codes for files classifications.) In our example, each personnel folder would be labeled with the code PER-10-1 and an individual's name. The folders would then be arranged in the file in alphabetical order by employee name.

The files system you develop should identify functional classifications only. Case files are not included, because they change all the time. If case names were included in a published files manual, the manual would go out of date before it could be distributed.

Offices may create case files whenever they are needed, at any level of the files classification outline. For instance, vendor case files may be established within an accounts payable classification. In this instance, there is a simple relationship between a classification code and the case files set up for it: the same classification code is used for each case file.

It is also possible to use many files classifications in a single case file. If you are managing several large construction projects, for instance, each project may generate the same types of records. Accounts receivable and accounts payable files are good examples. When you are setting up the project files, you basically have two choices. You can file all accounts receivable and payable records together, regardless of project. Or, you can separate these records by project and file them with other records pertaining to a given project. If you choose the latter method, you have established a case file incorporating multiple files classifications.

Whichever way you choose to organize your case files, accounts receivable and payable records will use the same files classifications whether they are arranged in a case file or not. They still serve the same function, and the basic classification does not change.

The distinction made here about case files may seem a fine point. However, it is a point worth mastering, because it is the key to setting up a workable files manual. There is a real tendency during an inventory to list case files by name and to try to work these into the classification system. Not only does this program your system for obsolescence, but it also makes for a large and unwieldy classification scheme. As you proceed with your files manual development, test your proposed classifications. Are they functional (e.g., professional associations) or case files (e.g., American Medical Association)? Make sure you weed out the case files as early as possible.

RECORDS RETENTION SCHEDULES

The other major principle of filing you will have to concern yourself with is retention. It is very expensive to keep records in prime office space. This practice should be limited to records you refer to frequently enough to warrant the cost. For most records, this means a period of one or two years after they were created. Thereafter, they can be transferred to a lower-cost inactive storage area or even be destroyed, depending upon the type of records.

Several factors determine records retention requirements. Federal and state law govern most decisions. Users' needs and common business practice are also very important. Chapter 5 provides more complete guidance on setting up proper retention schedules, as these lists of retention periods are called.

The key point to remember here is that you will have to establish one retention period for each records series in your classification scheme. In order to do this, each records series must be designed so that all of the documents in it have the same retention requirement. What this means is that function and ease of retrieval are not the only factors to consider in defining a records series. The retention period of the records is equally significant.

When this rule is not followed, outdated files are usually allowed to accumulate in current files. The problem is that the labor cost of purging the files on a record-by-record basis is prohibitive. It is easier to do nothing, or to wait until all of the records are obsolete.

To avoid this situation, it is critical that files be set up properly to begin with, so that records naturally sort themselves into groups with common retention periods. Take official audits, a common financial record, as an example. You can lump all audit documentation, including both the final audit report and the working papers, in the same series. However, you will probably end up keeping all the records for seven years, since that is how long audits must be retained.

If, on the other hand, you separate these records into two different series, you can dispose of the working papers as soon as the audit has been approved, usually at the end of one year. In this way, you can conserve files space and still be sure that you are retaining essential records for the required period of time.

Once retention periods are established for your records series, the specific dates can be noted on file folders at the time the files are created. This makes it very simple to scan a file drawer, identify those folders that are eligible for transfer or destruction and pull them out. The labor expended in the initial phase of filing systems design will be more than recovered here.

These principles of basic filing systems are not just theoretical. You can rely on them to guide your entire process of filing system development. Keep them in mind and the detailed procedures in the following chapters will make sense. Apply them to your own records and your files manual should fall into place.

3

How to Do a Files Inventory

by Katherine Aschner

To manage your files, you need to develop a systematic classification scheme. To develop your classification scheme, you need to do a files inventory. The reason is simple: you can't organize your records until you understand what they are. This means more than knowing that accounting has accounting records and engineering has engineering records. During the inventory, you will acquire a working knowledge of all your company's information resources and how they are used.

WHAT IS A FILES INVENTORY?

An inventory consists of a complete cataloging of all your files holdings. At the end of your inventory, you will have all the information you need about the types, volume and age of your records to begin to set up your classification scheme and retention schedules. The process involves filling out one records inventory form (see Figure 3.1) for roughly every current records series found in your file cabinets. Obsolete files are also cataloged, but in less detail. This data collection has three basic objectives:

- To identify individual records series;

- To determine how records series are used and how they relate to each other; and

- To determine how long records series must be kept in active and inactive storage.

A files inventory is probably easier to do than to explain. In other words, the explanation inevitably makes the inventory sound more complicated than it actually is. In preparing for your inventory, you should read this chapter and the inventory form instructions given in Appendix 1. Then, before you begin the actual project, do a sample inventory of one or two cabinets that are close

Figure 3.1: Records Inventory Form

RECORDS INVENTORY

File Code

LOCATION

Department	Office	Cabinet
Contact	Title	Phone

IDENTIFICATION

Working Records Series Title

Contents/Case Files

☐ continued on reverse

Use/Retrieval Terms

☐ continued on reverse

DESCRIPTION (Check All That Apply)

Arrangement
- ☐ subject   ☐ geo
- ☐ alpha   ☐ org
- ☐ numeric   ☐ other
- ☐ chron

Format
- ☐ < letter   ☐ dp printout   ☐ mag media
- ☐ letter   ☐ bound vols   ☐ on-line
- ☐ legal   ☐ maps dwgs   ☐ photos
- ☐ > legal   ☐ microfilm   ☐ A/V media

Storage
- ☐ cabinet/shelf   ☐ boxed
- ☐ desk drawer   ☐ mechanized
- ☐ flat   ☐ other
- ☐ rolled

Finding Aids

type   arrangement

Volume	Inclusive Dates	Activity
total cubic feet	from	☐ multi/daily ☐ other
		☐ daily
annual accum rate	to	☐ weekly
	☐ present	☐ monthly

User Reference (Yrs after creation)
☐ < 1   ☐ 1   ☐ 2   ☐ 3   ☐ 4   ☐ 5   ☐ 6   ☐ 7   ☐ other   ☐ while current

User Retention

in office   in inactive storage

STATUS   (Check All That Apply)

Legal Status
- ☐ official records
- ☐ supporting files
- ☐ reference materials

Restrictions
- ☐ vital record   Public Disclosure
- ☐ confidential   ☐ required
- ☐ archival   ☐ prohibited
- ☐ subject to audit

File Integrity
- ☐ file breaks/missing items
- ☐ related files elsewhere
  explain

Information Duplicated Elsewhere

Information Summarized Elsewhere

ANALYSIS

Official Records Series Title

Retention Period

in office   in inactive storage   authority

Microfilm Recommendations

Automation Recommendations

Surveyor	Date	
		☐ add ☐ change ☐ delete

Arcadia Associates

AA RM Form 1 7/82

at hand. This hands-on experience will help you plan the rest of the task with confidence.

What to Include

When you conduct an inventory, remember to include *all* of your company's records. Desk files, map files, reels of microfilm and photographic collections are as important as the records in traditional file cabinets.

Computer records must also be included. For some reason, there is a tendency to stop classifying or scheduling a records series as soon as it moves from paper to an electronic state. However, it is still a part of your company's information base, and there are operational and legal requirements that govern its retention. This does not mean you have to catalog the contents of every disk, but you should incorporate major data processing systems, files and output reports in your inventory and in your files classification manual.

Other Considerations

Although the primary reason for an inventory is files classification and retention scheduling, the process also provides an excellent opportunity to collect other important data. For instance, you can begin to identify vital records that might require microfilming or other means of special protection. You may come across records that have historical value to your business. These can be earmarked for potential inclusion in a company archives.

You should also take time to find out what problems users are having with their records. For instance, several people may need access to the same file at once. Or, some files may be so heavily used that important documents get damaged or even lost. Situations like these require a second look: microfilming or even automation may be in order.

The inventory is a unique opportunity to look at all your information handling practices. Be sure to use it to full advantage.

PRELIMINARY SURVEY

A company-wide files inventory is often a major undertaking. Therefore, most inventories start with a preliminary survey so that you plan for enough time and people to complete the entire task.

The preliminary survey is not mandatory. It is a planning aid that may not be necessary in a smaller company. However, even if you skip the process, you should still read through the following material. Some of the information applies to the actual records inventory as well.

In conducting a preliminary survey, you are looking for three things:

- The volume of records (expressed in cubic feet);

- The length of time it will take to inventory them; and

- Where the records are located.

Records Volume

Computing your records volume is the first step in determining how many days your inventory will take. The volume is expressed in cubic feet. The chart in Figure 3.2 shows you how to convert your holdings into cubic feet.

Figure 3.2 Cubic Feet Conversion Chart

1 letter-size file drawer holds	1.5 cubic feet
1 legal-size file drawer holds	2.0 cubic feet
1 desk-drawer file holds	2.0 cubic feet
15 linear inches of letter-size files is	1.0 cubic feet
12 linear inches of legal-size files is	1.0 cubic feet
12 linear inches of computer printout is	1.5 cubic feet
A commercial records storage box, letter or legal size, holds	1.0 cubic feet

Always estimate to the nearest cubic foot. Use the linear measures for lateral filing cabinets (the modern files that run lengthwise rather than the traditional drawer files) and for open-shelf files. For microfilm or computer tapes, simply count the number of items. The same applies to maps, drawings and other odd-size documents. Converting these to cubic feet has little meaning other than coming up with one composite volume figure for management.

Inventory Time Projections

The next step is to compute the number of days required to inventory your total cubic footage. The total volume tells only part of the story, however.

You also need to determine to mix of current and obsolete records, because the rates at which they can be inventoried are quite different.

Current vs. Obsolete Records

Current records are those created in the current year, or possibly even the last two or three years. Typically, they are still in active use. Obsolete records are inactive files to which you no longer refer, or to which you refer very rarely. Most often, they have been superseded by more current editions of the same series. For instance, the 1983 correspondence files are current, while the 1976 files are probably obsolete.

Not all current records are active, of course. Older records still in effect, but not consulted very often, are considered current and inactive. For instance, engineering drawings, titles to real property and contracts may be current for many years—as long as what they document is in force. However, they may be stored in a vault or other inactive area for safekeeping. Care must be taken to ensure that these records are treated as current records during your records inventory.

In-depth and Bulk Inventory Techniques

Current records must be surveyed in detail. These are the files for which records series must be identified in your classification scheme. Surveying of obsolete records is usually done in bulk. The primary purpose is to catalog records holdings, so that you can determine how much longer these files must be kept. The difference in survey techniques recognizes that only records series in current use need be included in the new files classification system.

Another category of records that can be inventoried in bulk is reference files. These are technical and other source materials, usually originating from outside organizations. Examples are technical publications, vendor catalogs, and airline and hotel books. Since reference materials can be incorporated in your files manual as a single records series, there is no need to examine these records in detail.

The procedure for a bulk inventory is simpler than for current records. It is enough to note that there are six drawers of correspondence files, spanning the years 1972 to 1978. It is not necessary to review all the folders in the file, as would be done for current records.

Records Inventory Rates

Once you have established the volume and mix of current and obsolete or reference records to be inventoried, you can use these figures to determine your projected survey times. On the average, one person can expect to inventory about 20 to 30 cubic feet of current records, and as much as 80 cubic feet of obsolete or reference records, per day.

If your current files consist of many different types of records, you will probably want to project 20 cubic feet per day (10 to 13 file drawers) per surveyor. This rate is typical for alphabetically arranged subject files, which usually take the most time to inventory.

If, on the other hand, your files contain voluminous records series, such as purchase orders, maintenance shop records or customer files, then the survey will go much faster. Once the basic function and contents of the series have been established, it is not necessary to look at all the folders in the file. This rule applies to most large collections of case files. You will probably want to use 30 cubic feet per day to develop your survey time estimates (about 15 to 20 drawers per day).

Bulk inventories are usually done at the rate of 80 cubic feet per day (about 40 to 50 file drawers). If you do plan a bulk inventory, be very careful first to segregate inactive files that are still current from truly obsolete files. Because all inactive records tend to be stored together, it is easy to miss the ones that are still in force.

Records Location

You need to identify records locations in order to ensure that everything gets included in the inventory. This step is especially important if you are going to parcel out the actual inventory among several people.

One trick you may find useful is to code each files location, and within each code to further identify file cabinets and even drawers. One of the most awkward parts of an inventory is describing the location of the records: the third cabinet from the water cooler in room 511. If you have to write that down more than once, the process becomes very tedious. Assigning codes to rooms, cabinets and drawers allows you to refer to files locations much more easily. You can even stick a coded label on each drawer during your preliminary survey.

CONDUCTING THE RECORDS INVENTORY

The success of your inventory depends upon two things: good survey personnel and good survey tools.

Survey Personnel

Who should conduct the inventory depends upon how many files you have and how much time you can allocate to the project. Ideally, the fewer people surveying, the better. For instance, if you do the inventory yourself, you will begin to recognize common records series as they turn up in various offices. You will be able to start developing uniform terms for these as you go along, which greatly simplifies the final classification process.

If files are surveyed by different people, they lose this common thread. Individuals may actually develop different terms for the same things. A well-designed inventory form and a well-supervised survey can reduce this risk, but it does tend to increase as the number of surveyors expands.

Becoming a good surveyor is more a question of time and comprehension than special skills. You may want to ask one secretary or clerk in each office to inventory that group's files. This approach has the advantage of spreading the work. It also means that the people who inventory the files understand how they are used. Another alternative is to assemble a special project team. As outsiders, the team members may have to ask more questions, but you often get better standardization by concentrating the inventory in fewer hands.

Whoever conducts the inventory, it is important that they understand the survey objectives. This means more than handing out the inventory form and asking people to fill in the blanks. Your surveyors need to be familiar with the basic principles summarized at the start of this chapter. Initial orientation and training are essential. You should also stay on top of the inventory, reviewing the surveyors' work on a daily basis and coordinating the use of common terms as much as possible.

The Inventory Form

Good inventory tools basically means having a good inventory form, supplemented with clear instructions. The form shown in Figure 3.1 is the form I have developed in my own consulting practice. There may be better forms, but I doubt it: I think I've plagiarized them all. In any case, this form does have two advantages: it is well-tested in the field, and it seems to fit almost every situation. You are welcome to adopt it if you wish.

Appendix 1 contains complete instructions for using the form. A copy of the instructions should be given to each member of the team. In some cases, supplementary material is added in the Appendix to explain the correct entry for a particular item on the form. The instructions and the explanations are a good source of material for developing training for your inventory team.

General Procedure

The basic procedure consists of filling out one form for each type or set of records in your files. The one-to-one relationship makes it much easier to start sorting the forms into primary, secondary and tertiary classifications.

In some instances, of course, you will have to group different kinds of records on a single form. The records may be badly arranged, and you cannot always make records series decisions on the spot. When you do lump records together like that, it is very important to identify them fully in the contents and retrieval terms sections, as described in the instructions to the inventory form (see Appendix 1). This procedure is commonly used for alphabetically arranged subject files that may include many series in a single drawer.

You may be able to shortcut the inventory process somewhat by asking files personnel to submit copies of any files indexes, lists or classification guides that they are presently using. You should check these against the actual files during your inventory. If the lists accurately represent files contents, they can simply be attached to the inventory forms.

Not all of the information required on the inventory form can be gleaned from the files folders themselves. You will have to talk to the users of the files. You will also have to perform some analysis on your own. Although files personnel may understand the importance of a record to their own operations, they may not appreciate larger organizational requirements. In other words, one person's working file may be another person's vital record. You will have to use your accumulated knowledge about files management in general and your company's records in particular to ferret out all the answers.

When you complete your files inventory, you will undoubtedly know more about your company's records than you were ever tempted to ask. The stack of inventory forms is higher than you imagined possible. The idea that a systematic classification scheme lies buried in those forms is probably the craziest idea you ever heard. Well, take heart. All the information you need to put together a files manual is sitting in front of you. And it is not nearly as hard to unscramble as it seems.

4

From Inventory to Filing System

by Katherine Aschner

The process of working an inventory into a files classification scheme is somewhat like putting together a jigsaw puzzle. Virtually all the pieces (the individual inventory forms) count. However, many are duplicates. In other words, the same records series appears on several forms. Therefore, the first step is to eliminate as many of the duplicates as possible, working toward a single list of unique records series. Then you work these series into their correct places in the classification scheme. In a puzzle, the picture helps you group like pieces together. In an inventory, your knowledge of how the records are used is your guide.

PRELIMINARY PROCEDURE

Immediately upon completion, your inventory forms should be roughly in organizational order. That is, all the forms from a given office are still grouped together. If you develop your classification scheme manually—by physically sorting and reorganizing the forms—the forms will be rearranged and the final order will be very different. Even if you use word processing or a computer to aid your sorting, it is likely that some reordering of the forms will occur.

Having your inventory forms in organizational order is of no value in terms of developing a classification scheme. However, once the classification scheme is designed, it is sometimes handy to be able to return your inventory forms to their original arrangement. For instance, this may help in coordinating the removal of obsolete files eligible for immediate destruction.

Before you start working with your inventory forms, take a moment to number them in sequence. Use organizational codes, and start a new sequence of numbers for each organization. For example, the Finance Department's inventory forms might be numbered F-1 through F-58. Personnel's forms might be numbered P-1 through P-12. This number should appear in the very upper right-hand corner of your inventory forms, just above the box for the classification code.

If you're lucky, you may never need to refer to this sequential order again. However, if you do, it will be much easier to recreate if you take the time to number your forms now.

MANUAL VS. AUTOMATED SORTING

At this point, you have two choices. You can sort your inventory forms manually, grouping them into like categories, eliminating the duplicates and then arranging the remaining forms in an appropriate order. Or, you can enter key information from each form into a word processor or computer, relying on the power of the machine to sort like records together. (Either a word processor or computer will do, provided the system has sorting capability. However, word processing is preferred because of the subsequent need to type the files manual.)

Manual Sorting

The manual approach has some advantages, at least in the early stages. It is often easier to visualize how inventory forms relate to one another by spreading them out and looking at a large part of the collection at once. With a word processor, your scope of vision is more or less limited to the contents of your video display. This may not be enough to begin to perceive patterns and differences.

Manual sorting also makes it somewhat easier to spot duplicates. a quick scan of two forms with different series titles may reveal that they are actually the same. If both series titles happen to be entered in the word processor, however, the duplication may be more difficult to discover.

Automated Sorting

Using word processing does have its advantages. A classifiction scheme does not always snap into place the first time. You are very likely to arrange and rearrange, especially as you begin to work in the retention requirements for each records series. At this point, the ability to manipulate an experiment with classifications on the screen before commiting them to print is very useful indeed.

Using word processing becomes even more useful when you start to prepare the files manual itself. The basic scheme is already entered; all you have to do is reformat it for the manual. When you're ready to create the alphabetical cross-index, most word processors can handle that, too. That's where the sort capability comes in especially handy.

Finally, you can use the same classification listings to generate file folder labels. When you do your initial files conversion (see Appendix 3) and thereafter when you create new folders at the beginning of a fiscal year, running the labels off on a word processor saves considerable time. (Chapter 9 discusses automation in greater detail.)

Combination Approach

For all of the above reasons, a hybrid approach is probably best. Your initial sort should be done manually. At the end of your first sort, most duplicates should be eliminated and your primary classifications (see Chapter 2) established. Your inventory forms will now be in order by primary classification. When you begin to work within primaries, to further identify secondary and tertiary classifications you should move to a word processing system if at all possible.

SORTING OUT A CLASSIFICATION SCHEME

Whether you work manually or on a word processor, the basic steps to developing a classification scheme are the same:

- Sort records into primary classifications based on function. In other words, focus on what the records are used for, not who originated them. You should end up with somewhere between 18 and 28 primary groupings for a company-wide files classification scheme.

- Screen out multiple titles for the same records series. In other words, eliminate duplicates from each of the above primary groupings. Continue this process when working with secondary and tertiary classifications, below.

- Within each primary, arrange records series into secondary and tertiary classifications. (Some realignment of primary classifications will probably occur during this phase.) You should have between 10 and 20 secondaries within each primary, and no more than five or 10 tertiaries within a given secondary. If you have more than that, your classification scheme is probably too detailed to be practical. Do not use fourth level classifications. Avoid setting up records series titles for case files (see Chapter 2).

- Some records series, such as policies and procedures, studies and reports, regulations and reference materials, really pertain to all records primaries. In other words, there are policies pertaining to personnel management and policies pertaining to financial management. For these records, it is often most efficient to set up standard secondary categories that are repeated for each primary. The arrangement is always the same, which makes these records easy to locate, and they are located with the other files they pertain to. The first four secondaries established for personnel management in Figure 4.1 show how this is done.

- Establish retention requirements for each records series (i.e., each primary, secondary and tertiary classification). This process, which is explained in full in Chapter 5, may again require some adjustment of your classification scheme. All records in a series should have the same retention period. Your retention schedule will identify how long records should be kept in active files, how long in inactive storage and when destroyed.

• Establish an alphanumeric code for each records series. Primary classifications should be identified by a three-letter mnemonic code. Secondary and tertiary classifications should have numeric codes that identify their hierarchical positions within the primary (and consequently within a file drawer).

• Develop an alphabetical cross-index to your files classification scheme. This should list the records series in alphabetical order, cross-referenced to the above alphanumeric code. (It is not necessary to cite page numbers in the files manual; the alphanumeric code is a sufficient reference.) You should also include formerly used names for each records series, again cross-referenced to the correct alphanumeric code. In other words, if you have screened out multiple names for a given records series, be sure these names get picked up in the cross-index. This makes it much easier for people to adjust to the new system.

If a picture is worth a thousand words, an example ought to be worth at least five hundred. Figure 4.1 is a files classification sampler. It includes some typical primary classifications, ones that are common to many businesses. One of the most common primaries, Personnel Management, is listed out completely. Note the alphanumeric coding structure, the hierarchical arrangement of secondary and tertiary classifications, and the retention periods for each series. The retention period codes are defined in the footnote on the first page of the figure. A sample of an alphabetical cross-index concludes the sampler.

ALTERNATIVES TO ALPHANUMERIC CLASSIFICATION SCHEMES

The alphanumeric classification scheme presented here is not your only choice; there are many others. Some people advocate using numbers only, typically arranged into some kind of Dewey-decimal-like format. Others use alphabetical or even chronological filing.

Any classification scheme can be made to work, providing two conditions are met. First of all, people must understand how it works. And second, it must be uniformly applied. However, after examining all the options, the alphanumeric scheme still looks the best. The alpha part of the code is easy to remember and work with. The numeric part is relatively short and preserves hierarchical relationships (which, in turn, make the system logical and understandable). Furthermore, like the inventory form, the alphanumeric structure appears to fit almost every situation. Thus, while other classification systems can be made to work with the inventory and classification procedures outlined in this book, they are not discussed in detail.

Figure 4.1: A Files Classification Scheme Sampler

Some Typical Primary Classifications

Facilities and Equipment Management	FEM
Financial Affairs	FIN
Legal Affairs	LEG
Personnel Management	PER
Public Relations and External Affairs	PRE
Purchasing Management	PUR

A Complete Primary Classification
PER - Personnel Management

FILING CODES		RETENTION CODES*	
PER-1	Policy and Procedure	C/P	
PER-2	Legislation/Regulations	C/O	
PER-3	Special Studies	1/5	
PER-4	Reference Materials	C/O	
PER-5	Official Personnel Folders	C/20	V
PER-6	Manpower Management	1/2	
PER-6-1	Personnel Forecasts	1/2	
PER-6-2	Staffing Allocations	1/5	
PER-7	Position Adminstration	1/2	

---

*Explanation of Records Retention Codes

C = retain while current   M = microfilm

V = vital record   P = retain permanently

/ = numbers before a slash indicate years in office space; numbers after a slash indicate years in inactive storage before can be destroyed.

Figure 4.1: A Files Classification Scheme Sampler (cont.)

FILING CODES		RETENTION CODES*	
PER-7-1	Classifications	C/3	
PER-7-2	Position Descriptions	C/3	
PER-7-3	Personnel Rosters	C/6	
PER-8	Salary Adminstration	1/2	
PER-8-1	Surveys and Studies	1/5	
PER-8-2	Schedules	C/P	
PER-8-3	Seniority Registers	C/6	
PER-9	Hiring and Appointments	1/2	
PER-9-1	Job Announcements	1/0	
PER-9-2	Applications	1/5	after terminate
PER-9-3	Exams and Interviews	1/5	after terminate
PER-10	Orientation and Training	1/2	
PER-10-1	Materials	C/0	
PER-10-2	Training Programs	1/2	
PER-10-3	Skills Registers	C/0	
PER-11	Benefit Plans and Participation	1/2	
PER-11-1	Medical Insurance	C/6	
PER-11-2	Dental Insurance	C/6	
PER-11-3	Life Insurance	C/6	
PER-11-4	Stock Option Plans	C/6	
PER-12	Leave Adminstration	1/2	
PER-12-1	Leave Requests	1/2	
PER-12-2	Leave Reports	1/2	
PER-13	Pension and Disability Programs	1/2	
PER-13-1	Pension Programs	C/P	
PER-13-2	Disability Programs	C/P	
PER-13-3	Participants' Files	C/6	after terminate
PER-14	Labor Unions	1/2	
PER-14-1	Union Negotiations	6/M	V
PER-14-2	Union Agreements	6/M	

Figure 4.1: A Files Classification Scheme Sampler (cont.)

FILING CODES		RETENTION CODES*
PER-14-3	Grievances and Appeals	6/M
PER-14-4	Arbitration	6/M
PER-14-5	Membership Rosters	C/6
PER-15	Evaluations and Investigations	1/2
PER-15-1	Performance Evaluations	1/5
PER-15-2	Disciplinary Actions	1/5
PER-15-3	Awards and Commendations	1/5
PER-16	Employee Activity Programs	1/2
	Program Materials	C/0
PER-17	Separations and Terminations	1/2
PER-17-1	Resignations	1/5
PER-17-2	Involuntary Terminations	1/5
PER-17-3	Layoffs	1/5
PER-17-4	Exit Interviews	1/5

Partial Alphabetical Cross-Index

Accounts Receivable Ledger	FIN-7-5
Application for Employment	PER-9-2
Associations—Personnel Management	PER-4
Associations—Purchasing Management	PUR-4
Audits	FIN-9
Budget Requests	FIN-2-9
Collision Reports	LEG-3-3
Deeds	LEG-5-4
Equipment Leases	FEM-6-1

COLOR CODING AND TERMINAL DIGIT
FILING OF CASE FILES

An alphanumeric scheme classifies records series. However, within a given records series, you may find a very large collection of case files that are arranged alphabetically or numerically. For instance, a medical clinic will have a large collection of patient files, typically filed alphabetically by name. The same records in a hospital might be filed by patient number, since alphabetizing tends to break down in very large files.

Classification of these records is no particular problem. The difficulty comes from having to work with them. Misfiles occur easily and are almost impossible to uncover. Straight sequential filing also tends to bunch all the most recent files, and therefore the most active files, in one small part of the available storage space.

Color coding and terminal digit filing are techniques that have been developed to address these problems. If you have large collections of case files, especially if they are housed in open shelving, you may want to consider one of these solutions.

Color Coding

Color coding works with either alphabetical or numerical files. Colored labels are affixed to the tops or sides of individual files folders. When the folders are filed in the appropriate sequence, bands of uniform colors are created on the shelves. When a given folder is misfiled, the nonmatching colors quickly flag it as out-of-place. Several manufacturers of filing supplies sell color coding systems, complete with pre-coded folders or labels, and a color-coding key. If misfiles are your problem, one of these standard color-coding systems may well be the solution.

Terminal Digit Filing

Terminal digit filing, which is often used in conjuction with color coding, actually addresses a different problem: the distribution of individual folders in a large file. If folders are stored in straight sequential order, all the most recent ones will be bunched together. This means files personnel will be tripping over one another in one area of the files room, while the other is empty. Furthermore, as older files are removed from the shelves, a large gap is opened up in one place. Typically, this means shifting all the other files back a shelf or two, which wastes time and effort.

Terminal digit filing is a system of arranging folders so that numbers *ending* in the same last digits are filed together. In order to set up a terminal digit filing system, folder numbers are divided into groups. For instance, the number 120397 is divided as follows:

tertiary or final	middle or secondary	terminal or primary
12	03	97

Within a terminal digit system, folders are broken into 100 primary groupings: 00 through 99. Within each primary grouping, records are further filed according to their secondary and then final groupings. Of 100 new numbers assigned to the file, one will fall in each of the 100 primary groupings. Thus, the file is distributed evenly. Furthermore, older files, which typically have lower folder numbers, are easy to identify and remove from the shelves.

There are many variations on the above theme, including middle digit filing and triple digit filing. Each of these has its place, and each is somewhat specialized. Since case numbers are assigned in sequence, it is even possible to obtain folders with the numbers and color coding imprinted at the factory. Your filing system supplier is a good source of information about specific coding systems.

5

Records Retention Scheduling

by Katherine Aschner

Retention scheduling is one of the most significant components of your records program. Good classification schemes and procedures make sense and save your company time and money. However, good records retention schedules can do even more than that. In the event of a legal challenge, they can also save your company's business. For instance, a major soft drink manufacturer estimates it saved $3 million by being able to produce records in just one lawsuit. An electronics manufacturing firm was able to maintain its market position by being able to prove an old patent claim.

Underlying the use of records retention schedules is a very simple rule: your company cannot be held liable for records that were discarded according to a proper records retention schedule in the course of normal business practice.

REASONS FOR KEEPING RECORDS

Before you assign retention schedules to your records, it is important to understand what you are keeping them for. There are five "values" (as professional records managers use the term) that affect records retention: operating, administrative, fiscal, legal and historical requirements.

- *Operating* requirements usually pertain while the record is current. For instance, a purchase order has an operating value to a manufacturing or sales company until the order is filled.

- *Administrative* uses often follow after operating requirements are satisfied. For instance, all purchase orders may be summarized to analyze sales and to project inventory and other resources needed for the next quarter.

- *Fiscal* requirements pertain to financial transactions. Once the purchase order has been filled, it still is required for invoicing, and in support of sales and income tax returns.

- *Legal* values are often related to the other records values. For instance, the purchase order may be used as evidence in the event of nonpayment. Or, it may be used to substantiate the terms of the order if there is a dispute over the delivered product. Litigation support is one of the chief reasons for setting up good retention schedules.

- *Historical* values are important, but typically apply only to about 5% of your records. A purchase order would qualify only if it were unique in some way, such as the first or the largest. It might also be assigned a historical value as a "typical" purchase order for your company archives. Aside from pure historical interest, records in this category may also have long-term research value.

When you are developing retention schedules, concentrate your efforts on those records series that are important to your business. Typically, these are the ones that have fiscal or legal value. High volume records also fall in this category.

REASONS FOR NOT KEEPING RECORDS

Cost, obviously, is the primary factor. If you have never purged your inactive records, the results of your first clean-up campaign may surprise you. Most

companies find that they can move one-third of their office records to inactive storage (see Chapter 11) and throw one-third away outright. The savings in equipment and space are dramatic. The State of California was able to avoid buying any file cabinets for 10 years as a result of implementing a records retention program.

An even greater benefit is streamlined access to your current files and information. Files personnel are more efficient and users get the information they need faster.

Liability is another reason for not saving records. Even if your company is innocent, defending a lawsuit is expensive. Being able to demonstrate that you no longer have the records, and that you are no longer required to have them, can save you the time and expense of producing and defending them in court. However, the test here is that the records were disposed of as part of your normal business procedure (see below). If it can be proved that certain records were selected out and destroyed for the specific purpose of concealing them, you are out of luck.

PROPER RECORDS RETENTION SCHEDULES

"Proper" implies that your records schedules are in compliance with applicable federal and state laws. However, there are two problems with this. The first is that only a part of your records will be covered by any law. For the rest, you have to come up with some other standard for what is proper. However, as will be described below, there are some guidelines you can follow.

The second problem is that the laws are very difficult to locate and, once located, even more difficult to apply. For example, one review identified nearly 900 federal regulations that mentioned record-keeping requirements. Yet less than half of these identified what specific records were to be kept or for how long.

Interpreting the Laws

Even when laws can be found, they are subject to interpretation. For instance, in one state the statute of limitations regarding an architect's liability for building design problems runs six years. However, there is disagreement as to whether the six years begin when the building is turned over to the owner or when the problem is discovered. Considering the life of a major office building, this is a considerable discrepancy.

Given the inherent vagueness of the situation, you may not be able to satisfy your attorneys, your accountants or yourself that your schedules are in complete compliance with the law. However, you should be able to show that they are in compliance with the intent of the law, as much as possible. This means being able to demonstrate that legal research was conducted and that you have a justification for the interpretations you have made.

Documenting Your Program

Researching retention schedules is not enough. Your schedules must also be documented in writing and incorporated in a published statement of procedure (such as a files manual). One reason for this practice is making sure that all employees are aware of the schedules, so that they are not inadvertently violated. However, there is also an important legal requirement. Only when your program is documented and distributed company-wide, can you meet the legal test of destroying records as part of your normal business practice.

LAWS ON RECORDS RETENTION

Federal Laws

For records governed by federal laws, the Code of Federal Regulations (CFR) is the primary source of information. As a general rule, federal laws apply to two categories of records. The first is standard records that all businesses and even government employers are required to maintain. The major types include reports on income, taxes and employment. The retention requirements for these records are fairly easy to identify.

The other category is regulated industries and processes. Utilities, banks and hospitals are examples of regulated industries. Record keeping in each of these businesses is controlled, at least in part, by one or more federal agencies with oversight responsibility.

In addition, many nonregulated businesses engage in some processes that are subject to federal laws. Disposing of hazardous wastes is a good example. Again, the agency with oversight responsibility for the process usually mandates some record-keeping requirements.

Another way in which companies may become subject to federal record-keeping requirements is to work as government contractors. Contractors often are subject to laws that otherwise only affect federal agencies, such as the Freedom of Information Act and the Privacy Act. The requirements of these two acts are particularly stringent, and should be adhered to with care.

The Code of Federal Regulations is organized into titles by agency. You will have to use an index to get at the regulations affecting your particular business. Both the CFR and its index are usually available in most business and law libraries. Aside from the CFR, you can also query the agencies that you deal with directly.

State Laws

For records governed by state law, your state code is the source of information. State laws apply to many types of records. In some cases, they expand on federal legislation. For example, state environmental regulations may be stricter than those imposed by the federal government.

State laws also govern matters that are left to the discretion of the states, such as statutes of limitations and other civil actions. Most states have their own taxation systems, with their own record-keeping requirements. And many states have regulations that affect selected businesses only, such as hotels or food establishments.

As with federal laws, state codes are summarized in an index. These, too, are typically found in business and law libraries. Remember, if you do business in more than one state, different regulations may apply in each case.

Sources of Information

As a preliminary to conducting extensive legal research on your own, you might consider whether someone else in your industry has already done it for you. A like business, perhaps larger or older than yours, may be a good source of reference. If you belong to a professional association, you should ask if any schedules have been developed. Many organizations do this as a service to their members.

There are also some publications that list major federal and state agencies and the regulations that affect retention requirements. These sources also list retention periods for common business records for which no legal retention requirement has been established.

SCHEDULING RECORDS FOR WHICH NO LEGAL REQUIREMENT CAN BE FOUND

For records that are not covered by government-mandated retention schedules, there still are some guidelines to follow. The first is quite simple: how long the records are used. The preliminary information you collected during the inventory will help you here: look at how long users refer to their files and at how long they keep them. You should also give weight to your own understanding of your company's need for the information. You have to balance the possibility of the records being called for against the cost of maintaining them.

When the law is silent, the status of records as official or supporting files can be very useful in setting retention requirements. This is especially true when you further categorize the records according to one or more of the five values described earlier in this chapter.

If you used the inventory form and procedures outlined in Chapter 3 and Appendix 1, you noted the status of records series as being either official records or supporting files and memoranda. Official records are originals that document policies, operations, property, employment, financial transactions, and fiscal and legal obligations. Originals of correspondence also fall in this category. Supporting files include duplicates of official records, as well as other working papers and reference materials.

Retaining Official Records

As a general rule, official records that have operating or administrative value *only* are held for three years. Official records that have legal value are held for six years, those with fiscal value for seven. Remember that some fiscal records, such as vouchers and journals, are temporary in nature. Once they have been posted to the general ledger, they do not need to be kept seven years. The general ledger, on the other hand, must be kept much longer: it is a permanent record.

For records series that remain in force for a long period of time, such as contracts or official personnel folders, the retention period typically starts to run when the record is no longer current. For instance, this occurs when the contract is completed or the employee leaves your company.

Truly archival records, of course, are permanent. However, as indicated above, no more than 5% of your total records holdings should be assigned to this category.

Retaining Supporting Records

Supporting files are usually kept only as long as they are current. If these records have some continuing reference value, they may be retained longer, usually about three years. One thing to watch out for is duplicate files or working papers that are annotated in the course of business. If the annotations have value to your company, then these copies become official records and must be treated as such.

It cannot be overemphasized that the above guidelines are general rules only, to be applied only when no other guidance is available. There are many, many exceptions to these rules, especially with regard to operating and legal records. However, the law is silent in so many cases that some framework for dealing with the remaining records is essential.

Although your legal research should be thorough, at some point you will have to rely on your own judgment. Your protection in this case is to develop a schedule that introduces as much uniformity as possible into your system, to have it approved by both users and management, and to document it in writing. This process gives your schedule legal standing even when legal citations cannot be found.

RETENTION SCHEDULE CITATIONS

In those instances where legal requirements are cited, it is important to make note of the statutory authority. Ideally, this should be included in the files manual, along with the listing of the retention period. However, it is usually easier to list the citations separately. You should create a master retention schedule listing all records series, their retention requirements for both original and duplicate copies, and the authorities used for determining those retention periods. Where extensive duplicates of a record exist, perhaps because of varied operating requirements, it is also useful to identify the office of record. This is the office designated as holding the official record copy.

With regard to listing retention schedules for duplicate copies of official records, you have two choices. Ideally, your files manual should list retention periods for both primary and secondary copies. However, this clutters the manual with information that is often redundant. A better choice may be to establish a standard policy for all secondary copies, listing only exceptions in the files manual itself.

Although you do not have much flexibility in deciding how long to keep records, you do have considerable latitude in deciding how long to keep files in office space. Depending on the availability of space, most offices keep one year's inactive files before sending them to a records center. As with most processes in records management, you will have to balance convenient access against storage costs in order to come up with the best solution.

6

Managing Maps and Engineering Drawings

by Frederick Klunder

Maps, engineering drawings and supplementary documents are among the most valuable records in many organizations. Companies with building and plant facilities need these records for documentation purposes. In engineering and architectural firms, they are essential to ongoing operations. These special materials represent considerable labor and expense for the organization involved.

In spite of their importance, however, maps and drawings are often poorly managed. Staff may neglect procedures for careful indexing and purging of drawing and map files. Files become saturated with obsolete material and redundant copies. Current records are difficult to locate, and resulting searches and redrawing are costly. In some cases, production and construction delays may result. Since many of these records must be kept for a period of years, the problem steadily worsens as volume increases.

Good files management is important in this area, and providing it requires familiarity with the four areas to be discussed in this chapter. These include the basic types of maps, drawings and supplementary documents; the media, processes and methods used to produce and copy them; preferred systems of arrangement and indexing; and standard drawing sizes and available filing equipment.

Because maps and drawings are most commonly encountered in engineering and architectural firms, this chapter will concentrate on their use in that context.

TYPES OF DRAWINGS, MAPS AND SUPPLEMENTARY DOCUMENTS

Maps

For the most part, managing maps will be easier than managing drawings.

Maps have less graphic and written detail to update, generally involve fewer supplementary documents to keep track of and can follow relatively straightforward principles of arrangement.

Maps show boundaries, distances, elevations, depths and specific features of given pieces of land or bodies of water. They include a wide variety of types, ranging from common geographical and road maps, to topographic and hydrographic maps, large scale cadastral maps of municipal areas for tax purposes, city utility plats and plats documenting ownership of specific tracts, subdivisions and parcels. Most drafting handbooks will give you sufficient information to recognize the types involved.

Drawings

Managing your drawings and related documents is more complex. Because they must contain all the information necessary for construction, engineering drawings are usually more detailed and interrelated records than maps, and are more frequently revised. The basic kinds of records you will deal with fall into the following categories.

Preliminary Design Records

These records are produced at the start of the design process to explore the general idea and feasibility of an engineering project. They include lists of requirements and general sketches and calculations. Finished design drawings also fall into this category. Engineers develop them to obtain the go-ahead for final design and construction. You may also hear them called design layouts, layout sketches, presentation drawings or sketch plans.

All of these records are superseded by more detailed information for construction once approval is obtained. You may want to file them separately so you can purge them when they are no longer needed.

Working Drawings

Final or working drawings are developed once approval is obtained. These provide all the information needed for construction and production, and therefore have long-term value. They are often revised to reflect design changes.

Each drawing is identified in a title area, or title block. This is generally in the bottom, right-hand corner.

The title block area usually includes the following as a minimum: name and numbers of the drawing, sheet number if the drawing has more than one, the scale and drawing size. It may also include dates and approval information, and list composite drawings to which the drawing is related as a part. Figure 6.1 shows the drawing sheet format.

Drawings also have blocks for information about drawings revisions, as shown in the bottom left strip of Figure 6.1. The revision block includes descriptions of changes, authorization signatures, dates and symbols tying revision notation to the parts of the drawing which were revised.

Working drawings fall into two categories: detail drawings or assembly drawings. Detail drawings depict parts, such as bearings, or components, such as stairs. Assembly (and sub-assembly) drawings, on the other hand, show how the individual parts form a whole. Examples of assemblies include building floor plans and basic machine drawings.

Detail drawings may be presented individually or combined on large sheets with other details. One detail may relate to several assemblies, and even to several projects.

Supplementary Documents

In a sense, every other engineering document connected with the project supplements the drawing. On simple projects, a drawing can contain all of the written explanatory notes about materials and workmanship necessary for construction. On more complex projects, where the notes are detailed and extensive, this technical information is often presented separately. Listings used in production or construction are called parts lists, bills of materials or separate schedules. Specifications prepared for contracting purposes also contain a large amount of information which falls into this category.

Drawings and supplementary documents are often issued with engineering releases or changes attached. You can think of these basically as authorization and transmittal documents. They state the reason for and nature of the new documentation; list all records, parts, models and facilities affected; and note special distribution and other relevant information. They ensure that changes are orderly and thorough, and are an important audit trail.

All these supplementary documents generally have the same long-term

Figure 6.1: Drawing Sheet Format

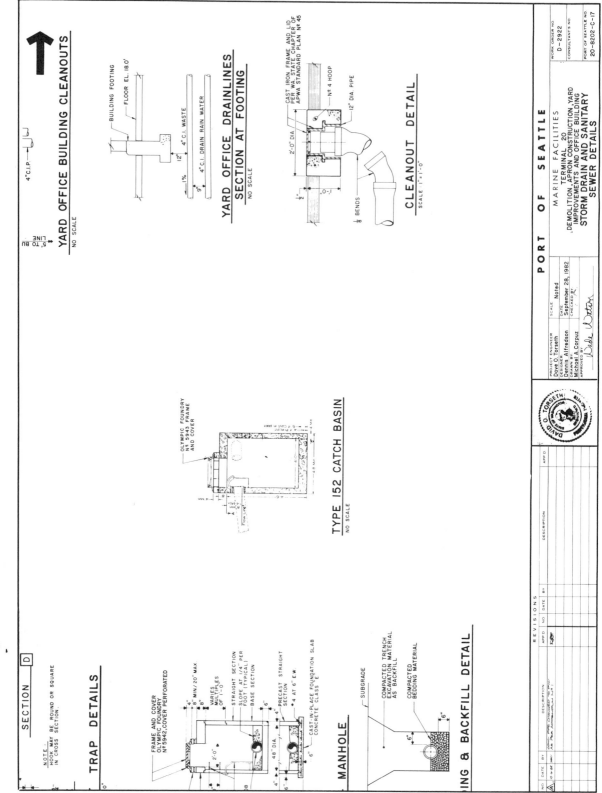

retention value as the related drawings. Like the drawings, they require effective systems of filing and indexing.

DUPLICATION MEDIA, PROCESSES AND METHODS

In order to manage maps and drawings, you need a basic knowledge of how they are duplicated. Engineering professionals refer to this subject as "reprographics," and most of the systems used are unique to the area of maps and drawings. Understanding them is important. As with any kind of records, drawings must be duplicated in order to communicate what they contain. In addition, however, duplication serves as a method for revising drawings without having to redraw everything. Avoiding redrafting may easily save several thousand dollars on a single drawing.

Media

The most significant thing to understand about drawing duplication is the division of media into reproducibles and nonreproducibles. Reproducibles are drawings on translucent material; nonreproducibles are produced on opaque media. As a general rule, reproducibles are the more important drawings because they are suitable for inexpensive reproduction using either the flexible diazo process or the earlier blueprint process (see below). In addition, only reproducibles can be used for overlay drafting, a process which saves a lot of time.

Because reproducibles are so important, access to them should be controlled. They should only be used for reproduction, revision or precise measurement. When drawings need to be referred to for other purposes, you should use a drawing index, and paper or microfilm working copies.

Mylar

Most reproducibles nowadays are produced on polyester. This is popularly referred to by the Du Pont tradename of "Mylar."

Mylar, introduced in 1951, has gradually replaced the translucent cloths and papers which used to be popular. It is much more durable and not subject to expansion or contraction. As a result, many companies have converted all cloth and paper reproducibles still in active use to the Mylar medium.

Mylar comes in three basic types: for drafting, diazo reproduction and photographic reproduction. Drafting Mylar is meant for original drawing in ink or pencil, on one or both sides. The second type, diazo Mylar, is used for diazo duplication. When you buy it with a matte surface on one or two sides, it is also good for subsequent drafting. It comes in brown-line (sepia) or black-line stock. The third type, photographic Mylar, is used for photographic duplication. Like diazo, it is also good for subsequent drafting.

Other Media

In addition to diazo and photographic polyester, you may encounter older brownprint copy reproducibles. These are produced in a blueprint-like process on a translucent paper.

There are a number of opaque, nonreproducible media. They include the various papers used in the blueprint, diazo, photographic and copier technologies.

Reprographic Processes

Diazo Reproduction

As we mentioned, today most drawing reproduction uses diazo technology. Diazo is an ammonia-based process that produces positive copies with dark lines on a light background. Lines can be black, sepia (brown) or blue. Sepias are generally preferable as reproducibles in the diazo process. Copies are inexpensive and of high quality, and can be made on both translucent and opaque media. The major drawback is that they are not permanent, since the image deteriorates when exposed to heat, light or ammonia fumes.

There are two kinds of diazo duplication equipment: rotary and contact printers. Rotary machines are most common, and use a rotating belt to carry the reproducible and the copy pages past the light source, back to back. When the copy emerges, it is fed through a built-in developing unit to bring out the image. Machines cost anywhere from $2000 and up, depending on features.

Rotary machines have the advantage of being compact and easy to use. However, they do not give you a perfect match between reproducible and copy image. This is especially important with overlay drafting (see below). Figure 6.2 illustrates a rotary machine.

Contact printers avoid this problem. They place the reproducible and copy

Figure 6.2: Diazo Rotary Duplicator

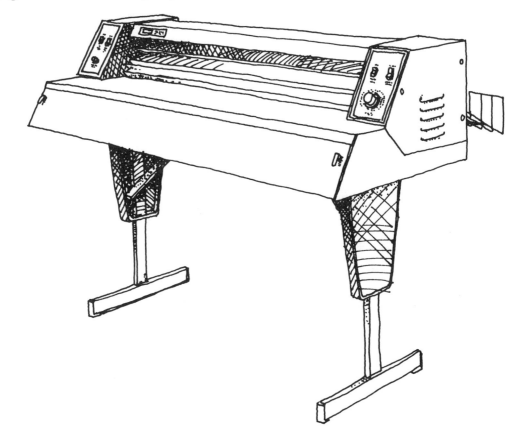

paper on a fixed glass copyboard with sub-surface illumination, covered with a hinged flap. Development occurs in a separate ammonia processor.

Blueprinting

Although blueprinting is largely obsolete, you will still find the prints in many files. They are negative-image copies, with white lines on a blue background. The image is relatively permanent. Brownprints use an analogous process.

Photographic Reproduction

Photo reproduction is the most flexible method of reproduction. It is also the most costly, and is often overused. Costs can be five to 10 times more than diazo. However, sometimes photo reproduction is the only way to do the job.

There are two methods of photographic reproduction. The simplest one uses a machine somewhat similar to the diazo contact printer. Photosensitive, silver-coated paper or polyester takes the place of diazo paper or Mylar. As with diazo reproduction, the original must be reproducible. However, unlike diazo, the silver process gives you a potentially permanent or "archival" image. It is also less likely to pick up shadows when using overlay drafting.

The more complex method of photographic reproduction begins with a large engineering camera. Original drawings are photographed onto camera negatives. Once these are developed, the image is projected onto light-sensitive paper or polyester and developed.

The camera process has two major advantages over the contact process. In the first place, you can reduce or enlarge originals. A detailed floor plan, for example, can be reduced for use as a summary construction plan. Entire drawing sets in reduced size are becoming increasingly popular for purposes of convenience. Second, unlike photographic contact reproduction, and also unlike blueprint and diazo processes, camera reproduction works with nonreproducibles. Therefore, camera reproduction is essential when you need to make reproducibles or paper copies of old prints.

Copier Reproduction

Copiers will be used increasingly in drawing reproduction because they can do many of the things cameras can do at a fraction of the cost. First of all, they can create copies of nonreproducibles. Moreover, machines with reduction capabilities that can copy onto plain paper and polyester transparencies are increasingly available. Image permanency with some machines is quite good. The traditional problems of copier reproduction—high costs, inferior quality and limited copy size—are decreasing with the introduction of improved equipment.

Microfilm

Chapters 7 and 8 discuss the use and production of microfilm in detail. The space, retrieval, duplication and distribution cost advantages of microfilm are especially relevant in the case of copies of drawings. Microfilm is an excellent substitute for traditional files of reference drawing prints, especially when the number of drawings and print requests is large. Aperture cards and 35mm rollfilm are most commonly used. The cost of an aperture card duplicate is one fifth of the cost of the traditional diazo print, and there are added savings from reduced handling. Wear on the master reproducible is also reduced.

Microfilm can make it economically feasible for you to maintain an off-site drawing file for protection against a potential disaster. And you can retain copies of superseded drawings as a design history file in situations where it would be extremely costly to keep full-size records.

Experience in the utility sector (public works, power plants, etc.) shows that, when they are referred to, screen images of microfilm generally suffice for at least 90% of the time. When screen images are not suitable, prints from microfilm can usually take the place of reproducibles or traditional prints from full-size drawings. Engineering organizations of major manufacturing firms report that at least 80% of all the prints they produce are from microfilm rather than from full-size drawings.

One of the advantages of printing from microfilm, especially when large volumes are involved, is lower cost. Supply costs for microfilm paper prints are half those of diazo prints, and production speed is more than double. Increased speed means reduced labor requirements and faster response to user requests.

Users tend to prefer reproducibles or copies from full-size drawings in two situations. First, when they need to revise a drawing, and second, when they have to calculate precise distances from scale. The reason is that in the process of reducing drawings to microfilm and subsequently enlarging them for reading or printing, the resulting image may diverge slightly from the original drawing. One alternative is to film a ruler at the bottom of each microfilm image, or to have drafters draw on special grid paper. In situations where redrafting is required, some organizations use microfilm camera-enlargers which can enlarge from microfilm back to full-size photographic drafting media in a very precise fashion.

Successfully introducing microfilm for engineering filing applications depends in large part on educating users about what microfilm can do. In addition, a good program generally requires modified drafting standards. Letter height for documents you want to microfilm should be at least ⅛-inch; space between lines of lettering should be at least half of letter height; and all lines should be of uniform darkness. The National Micrographics Association (NMA) publication R003, listed in the bibliography, will give you more information. Film quality should conform to standards discussed in Chapter 8.

Systems Drafting Methods

The following drafting methods have become increasingly popular because they save time through reproducing standard material instead of redrawing it. These methods usually require special files and indexes, and using them makes it especially important to clean house and establish sound drawing management practices.

Composite and Overlay Drafting

Composite drafting resembles what graphics people call "pasteup." Commonly used materials such as standard details are combined side-by-side on a carrying sheet and then duplicated. Diazo and photographic contact printers are used when reproducibles are involved, while cameras and copiers are used with nonreproducibles.

Overlay drafting involves generating repetitive information, such as a building floorplan, as a base reproducible. Separate overlay reproducibles can then be generated. These may represent, for example, electrical and heating, ventilating and air conditioning (HVAC) systems. Each of these overlays can then be aligned in turn on top of the base, and reproduced as a final working drawing using a contact printer or camera.

Composite and overlay drafting can save from 20% to 40% in project design and drafting time. Standard material can be reused and requires revisions can be limited to certain composite elements or specific base or overlay sheets, without having to redraft the entire drawing. Composite and overlay drafting have therefore become very popular. However, proper management is a must. This required that you do a good deal of advance planning and carefully identify and file each of the separate layers that go into a final working drawing. *Pin Graphics Manual*, listed in the bibliography, discusses appropriate classification and filing methods.

Computer-aided Design and Drafting

Computer-aided design and drafting (CADD) is also called automated drafting (AD). It involves storing standard material, such as that on base sheets in overlay drafting, on magnetic media for subsequent reuse and modification. With CADD, you can call up this material and then change scales, merge in standard details, make modifications and additions, and file and print out the final product. In a sense, CADD is simply a quicker and more flexible way of doing composite and overlay drafting. As such, it also builds on the ways you would organize your drawings for these methods of drafting.

In practice, CADD usually supplements rather than replaces manual methods. Graphics are generally input to the computer using a digitizer, which is essentially an electronic pointer with a switch. The digitizer is placed on an existing drawing while the switch is turned on and off to read the line positions into the computer. When the graphics concerned involve a limited number of standard elements, drawings may be composed directly on a computer screen.

Only a limited number of drawings are usually stored on magnetic disk. Current computer media are a very expensive way of storing information, and long-term data reliability is questionable. Until long-term computer media are developed which have a lower price per unit of information, the usage of traditional storage media such as paper, Mylar and microfilm is unlikely to be affected.

Getting into automated drafting involves significant costs and planning. Systems themselves begin at about $60,000 for the simplest equipment, although this will probably come down. Digitizing is a very labor-intensive process. And CADD requires a lot of thought in the area of files organization. Because revisions are stored in machine-readable form and are so easy to make, keeping track of them and of standard details becomes especially important.

When should you consider CADD? In many cases, composite and overlay techniques will be the best way to handle drafting and revision. They are also the best way to prepare for automated methods. It makes sense to push beyond into CADD when your revision level is high, when you use many standard details and when your repertoire of characters and standard shapes is relatively limited. It will probably be easier to find good software for relatively simple drawings, such as those for printed circuit board drawings, than for more varied designs such as those in the architectural field.

CADD is especially attractive when you have additional computer applications and can merge it with other information processing requirements. Examples include producing three-dimensional drawings from two-dimensional views, doing simulated tests of designs and using data from drawings and supporting documents to produce reports such as cost estimates and materials and manpower schedules. In many cases, the best way to get into CADD will be to start with a service bureau.

SYSTEMS OF ARRANGEMENT AND INDEXING

Arranging and Indexing Maps

Arranging maps or map indexes is generally straightforward. You can usually group them by type of map, and further, by mapping project. Arrangement for larger series is generally geographical. You can use street address, section numbers and coordinates to set up these files. Maps for subsections commonly follow those for the areas that include them.

Arranging Drawings

Major Project Categories

The principles for arranging drawings are the same as those you use in classifying any records: hierarchy and function. When organizing drawings for a large variety of projects or products, initial grouping or indexing should generally be by type of project or product. A municipality, for example, might define categories for municipal buildings, schools, sewage treatment facilities, sewers, water supply, parks, and streets and highways.

Drawing Set Organization

Each project type should include current drawing sets for the various projects. Each project, in turn, is usually assigned a unique number. This number generally represents the first section of the drawing numbers for all drawings in that set.

Drawings for specific projects or products are usually subdivided into those for specific systems or functions. The drawing set for an office building, for example, might include separate subgroupings for architectural drawings, structural drawings, mechanical drawings and electrical drawings. A drawing set in the aircraft industry might include categories such as power plant, wings and tail assembly, and electronics and instruments.

Many organizations assign each kind of system a standard number or letter. This often forms the second section of each drawing number. There may be a third section for the standard type of drawing within each system. This added element of hierarchy makes it easier to come along later and add numbers for additional drawings of a given type. Otherwise, you may not be able to file drawings of the same type next to each other within a given system. And the number always has a section for the specific drawing itself. This is usually the last section of the drawing number.

Revised drawings usually assume the number of the drawing they replaced. The old version is stamped "superseded," then destroyed or placed in a separate history file. The specific drawing numbers may be standardized when a specific kind of drawing is always included for a given type of project. Figure 6.3 illustrates the method of numbering discussed.

You'll find that some organizations use much simpler systems. On the other hand, certain firms add extra sections to incorporate information about paper size, job number, procurement specification and security level. What is appropriate depends largely on the situation. However, in general, it's best not to burden your numbering system with unnecessary detail.

Assembly drawings come before detail drawings within each systems category or subgroup. The first sheet of each drawing set often contains an index which lists each drawing's title and number. In the case of large projects, drawings for specific systems may be subordinated to a chrono-logical arrangement according to construction phases.

Figure 6.3: Example of Hierarchical Drawing Numbering System

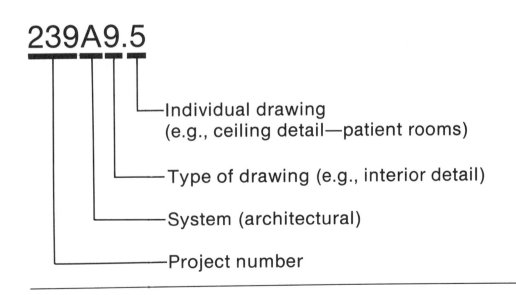

Organizing Detail Files and Supporting Documents

Standard details are often used in connection with more than one project or product. Firms specializing in the design of a specific kind of building, for example, reuse drawings of standard elements on a regular basis with only minor changes. They often establish separate standard detail files, in addition to filing details by project with assembly drawings. Firms that use standard parts, such as some manufacturing firms, may only use separate detail files—standard details are not filed with the drawing set.

There are various ways of arranging standard detail files. Construction details can be arranged according to a system similar to that used for grouping and numbering project drawings. Another option is using a system keyed to the Construction Specification Institute Masterformat classification scheme. Details are classified according to material types and functions, such as concrete, wood and plastic, and thermal and moisture protection. Corresponding indexes are sometimes established based on construction phases. Two books listed in the bibliography, *Systems Drafting* and *The Guidelines Standard Detail Management and Indexing Manual*, will give you examples of both methods. In manufacturing firms, details are often arranged or indexed by the main physical characteristics of the part.

It is best to arrange supplementary documents such as parts lists and engineering releases or changes in a manner similar to that used for the drawings themselves. The same is true of specifications.

Indexing Drawings

All drawings should be indexed. In the first place, indexes provide a simple way of browsing through the files. As a result, there is no need to look at extensive paper or microfilm copies of actual drawings until you find exactly what you want.

If your operation is small, you can use loose-leaf ring binders with lined sheets (see Figure 6.4). A binder is established for each project or product type. Each binder contains a front summary section and a following detailed section. Drawing set titles are listed line by line in numeric order in the front section. The following section lists specific drawing titles in drawing number order for each drawing set.

Indexes can also serve as retrieval aids for pulling together related drawings and supporting documents such as parts lists, specifications and engineering orders and changes, and for retrieving drawings filed in random sequence. Random filing will probably be unavoidable if you have large records volumes associated with major projects or products. Indexing will also help you if you want to integrate old drawings into a new system of arrangement without physically reordering them. This saves time and can be an easy way to improve control.

Because of the large amount of repetitive index data and the need to do lengthy searches, drawing indexes are very appropriate for computerization.

Drawing Control

Drawing files must be systematically controlled to ensure that users work from current information. When new revisions are created, old drawings must be stamped "superseded" and removed from the active file. The same is true of obsolete drawings. These drawings should be destroyed or filed in a separate records series or "history file."

In large operations, it can be very important to track and document the use of each drawing. When drawings have been inactive for some time, and where your retention schedules permit, you can use this information to draw up a list of records proposed for destruction or transfer to inactive storage. The list can then be circulated throughout your organization for review.

Usage information is recorded on a drawing control card. It often includes when reproducibles are charged out for revision, by whom and possibly by what authority and for what purpose. In addition to ensuring that drawings will be returned, use of the control card guards against unauthorized and haphazard revisions. Distribution information is often included so the organization will know to which files stations to send revisions. In this way, everyone in the organization will be using current information. Further, drawing status information can include notations about authorized revisions which are pending. If staff members check drawing status before responding to print requests, they will be able to hold off until revisions have been made so as to avoid distributing obsolete information.

When drawing management has been neglected, purging obsolete records and establishing current and coherently organized drawing sets can be a

Figure 6.4: Loose-leaf Drawing Index

Project No.	Project Title	Remarks
	Table of Contents - TERMINAL 20	
20-7202	Terminal 20 Demolition and Yard Improvement	
20-7203	Shoreline Management Act Permit	
20-7204	Shed 5 Additional Office & Recoop Area	
20-7205	Temporary Floodlight Service & Relocation	
20-7206	Lunch Room Building	
20-7207	North Tank Farm Refining Vessel & Filter	
	Press Addition	
20-7208	Bonded Tallow Lines	
20-7301	Tallow Line Extension to Berth 4 & 5	
20-7302	Deve. Unit #1 Demolition, Dredging Fill & Apron	
20-7303	Warehouse #3 - Customs Area - Security Locker	
20-7304	Recoop Office with Locker	
20-7305	Hydrocarbon Lines	
20-7306	Relocate Existing Office Building from	
	Anchor Marina to T-20	
20-7307	Survey - TOPOG	
20-7308	Tank Farm Power Service	
20-7309	Warehouse No. 1 - Dry Sprinkler System	
20-7310	Warehouse No. 1 - Cold Storage Facility	
20-7401	Tallow Loading Area	
20-7402	Battery Charger Installation with 1 Freeze Fac.	
20-7403	Install Additional Tank at Tallow Farm	
20-7404	Shed #3 Office Sound Attenuation	
20-7405	Warehouse No. 1 Installation of Roll Up Door	
20-7406	Term. 20 (U.S. Gypsum Prop.) North Yard Improv.	

major undertaking. In this case, you may have to begin with a detailed records inventory.

STANDARD DRAWING SIZES AND FILING EQUIPMENT

Standard Drawing Sizes

Drawings occur in the standard sheet sizes given in Figure 6.5.

Figure 6.5: Standard Sheet Sizes

American National Standards Institute (ANSI) Format submodule: 4.25 × 5.5″	International Metric Format
	A6 size: 105 × 148mm
	A5 size: 148 × 210mm
A size: 8.5 × 11″	A4 size: 210 × 297mm
B size: 11 × 17″	A3 size: 297 × 420mm
C size: 17 × 22″	A2 size: 420 × 594mm
D size: 22 × 34″	A1 size: 594 × 841mm
E size: 34 × 44″	A0 size: 841 × 1189mm

You will notice that both the U.S. and international formats are essentially multiples or sub-units of a standard letter-size sheet (8½ × 11-inch or 148 × 105mm). As always, however, expect exceptions. The more popular American off-sizes include 24 × 36-inch and 30 × 42-inch.

Filing Equipment

Filing equipment holds drawings and maps either horizontally or vertically.

Horizontal Filing Equipment

Horizontal equipment consists of bin units for rolled drawings and drawer units for flat filing. Both allow you to stack multiple modules to fully use available space. However, flattening out rolled drawings is difficult. For this reason, try to avoid bin units except when they are necessary, as in the case of older rolled drawings. Drawer units are only somewhat better. Leafing through maps and drawings in drawers is slow, and also very hard on the records.

Vertical Filing Equipment

Vertical or hanging filing equipment is preferable. It comes in several types. Some units suspend drawings from rods, and others use hanging folders.

There are generally two ways to hold your reference prints. One of these is inexpensive stick files. These are similar to units used for current newspapers in libraries. Accordian-folding for placement in standard file folders is another method. Because this makes access more difficult, it is only appropriate for drawings which have a low reference rate. Drawings are placed in folders so that the top edge has a single fold, and so that the title block is in the lower right-hand corner.

Official reproducible copies and prints which require better protection should be hung in cabinets. Drawings are suspended from rods which move apart to permit filing and retrieval when the cabinet is opened.

7

Using Microfilm

by Frederick Klunder

Microfilm is a way of handling information in the form of photographically reduced images. If you use it for the right kinds of applications and stay on top of your program, it can help you increase efficiency and cut costs.

The next two chapters will tell you what you need to know to do just that. This chapter discusses using microfilm. It explains when you should consider microfilm, and goes on to talk about the various kinds of systems and when they are appropriate. Chapter 8 will discuss how to implement and manage a microfilm program.*

ADVANTAGES OF MICROFILM

Microfilm systems offer you four potential advantages over other methods of information handling:

1.) Inexpensive duplication of information for distribution and backup files;

2.) Rapid retrieval;

3.) Maximum reduction of required space and associated equipment; and

4.) Permanence and admissibility as evidence in court.

Whether you already have microfilm or are considering a program, you will probably want to consider whether these advantages are relevant for any records series in your organization.

---

*In this chapter and the one following, the terms "microfilm" and "microform" are used interchangeably.

Inexpensive Duplication

Microfilm is presently the most inexpensive way for you to produce multiple copies of large volumes of information. A card-size (105mm x 148mm) sheet of microfiche, for example, can hold images of up to 270 pages. The commercial cost for each duplicate microfiche after the first master is created is as low as $.20, which equals one tenth of a cent per letter-size image. By contrast, computer paper is at least five times more expensive, and copier costs are even higher.

The minimum number of pages per report, per number of copies, needed to justify microfiche duplication is given in Figure 7.1.

Figure 7.1: Pages per Report Required to Justify Microfiche over Paper Printouts in Four Copy Duplication Categories

One copy:	250 pages/report
Two copies:	103 pages/report
Three copies:	68 pages/report
Four copies:	59 pages/report

Microfilm can be attractive if you have to mail or distribute large volumes of information. Postage costs for information in microfilm form are a fraction of what they would be for heavier paper packages. Reference copies can be printed much less expensively from microfilm than from full-size drawings. Once information has been microfilmed, it becomes economically feasible to produce an extra copy for off-site storage as protection against a disaster. And it becomes possible to protect the completeness of your files by providing copies instead of loaning out the master.

However, whether you can justify microfilm in terms of reduced duplication costs depends on three conditions. First, savings for subsequent copies must be sufficient to cover the high cost of the initial microfilm master copy. The first copy of a card-size sheet of computer-produced microfiche, containing up to 270 pages, may cost about $3 if produced commercially. This is because of the initial labor involved in filming each document, and because of the special film and chemicals required for the master. Since subsequent copies are only $.20, microfilm becomes more attractive as your copy requirements increase.

The second condition concerns whether you will be able to use the majority of the piece of microfilm. For example, many users like to limit each sheet of microfiche to the contents of a specific file folder or report, regardless of whether it fills the fiche or not. However, if most of a sheet of microfiche remains blank, paper copies will probably be cheaper. Of course, you do have the option of combining different files or reports on one piece of microfilm. Whether it is practical to do so depends on the preference of users, and whether this will complicate the retrieval process.

Third, savings must be enough to cover the cost of the equipment needed to retrieve and view the film. As we will see, cost depends greatly on the sophistication of the hardware. Prices can range from $200 to hundreds of thousands of dollars.

Rapid Retrieval

Rapid access to information is a second advantage to consider. Microfilm can allow you to locate information in a million-document file in seconds, whereas retrieving the same information from a paper file might require several minutes. Distributing firms and purchasing organizations often use microfilm for this reason.

Simple systems speed retrieval by placing large quantities of information close at hand. More sophisticated systems incorporate mechanized film advance and computerized indexing so you can go directly to the record you want.

Rapid retrieval has two advantages: it saves labor and improves your responsiveness to enquiries. Typically, this is important for organizations that have large groups of records with high reference rates. Online computer systems are, of course, another option. However, for large files of information, the cost of automating the entire system is often prohibitive. (See Chapter 9 for a discussion of automation issues.)

Space Reduction

Space saving is probably the advantage most frequently associated with microfilm. Microfilm is first of all an image reduction technology. Film can take as little as 2% of the space and equipment needed for paper-based systems. Given the high annual costs of floor space, converting large units of records can mean sizable savings.

Whether or not the space-saving feature of microfilm is important to you depends on two factors: how long you must keep the records, and whether they are suitable for storage in an inactive records center. Generally speaking, it does not pay to microfilm records which are inactive enough after several years to be transferred to a full-service, high-density records center. Various studies show that you can use good in-house records centers for 25 years before the cost involved equals the cost of microfilming.

Some major groups of files, of course, must be kept in office space for more than several years. They have to be available in offices for immediate access. This is true, for example, of major series of records in the areas of insurance underwriting, property registration, medical care and purchasing. In addition, some records must be retained for longer than 25 years. Engineering documentation, personnel registers and plant and general ledger information fall into this category. And finally, you may not have access to a good records center that can provide inexpensive storage, security and rapid retrieval of requested records. (For more about records centers, see Chapter 11.) If any of these factors apply to your activities, you should consider microfilm.

Permanence and Admissibility in Court

The permanence of microfilm and, to some extent, its general acceptability as evidence in court, sets it apart from computer-based magnetic storage media such as disk and tape. Microfilm will last as long as paper records if you are careful about proper production and storage. (Chapter 8 discusses how proper management of a microfilm program can ensure permanence and admissibility.)

Other Considerations

You'll have to weigh these advantages against other considerations. Cost is obviously a major one which we will discuss extensively in this chapter and the next one. In addition, as we will see, courts and regulatory agencies may not accept microfilm as evidence in certain situations.

It may also be that what you need is some technology other than film. Microfilm records information in final form. Computers record it on magnetic media as data meant to be processed in one or more ways before being used. As Chapter 9 will explain, computer systems will probably be appropriate the more you need to manipulate information. They may also be right if you need very rapid access to information, or if it is revised frequently.

However, for simple storage and retrieval of large volumes of information, computers are expensive (although this may change in the future). Because of the advantages discussed above, microfilm may be the best bet for many organizations.

TYPES OF MICROFILM AND USER EQUIPMENT

If you think microfilm seems appropriate for your organization, the next step is to understand the kinds of microfilm available, equipment alternatives and associated costs.

KINDS OF MICROFILM

There are basically four kinds of microfilm, or microforms, you can use. The basic microforms are:

1.) Roll types such as reels or cartridges;

2.) Microfiche;

3.) Microfilm jackets; and

4.) Aperture cards.

They are illustrated in Figure 7.2. They are usually produced from rolls of film in one of three widths. These include 16mm, 35mm and 105mm as shown in Figure 7.3.

Figure 7.2: Basic Kinds of Microfilm

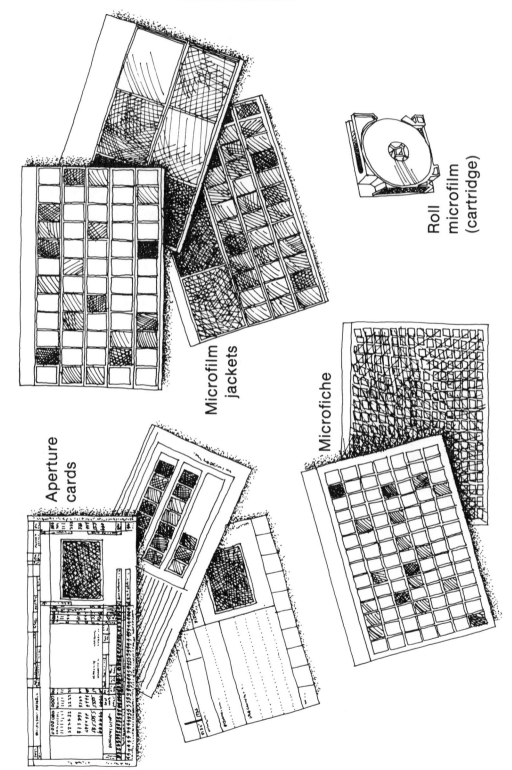

Roll microfilm (cartridge)

Microfilm jackets

Microfiche

Aperture cards

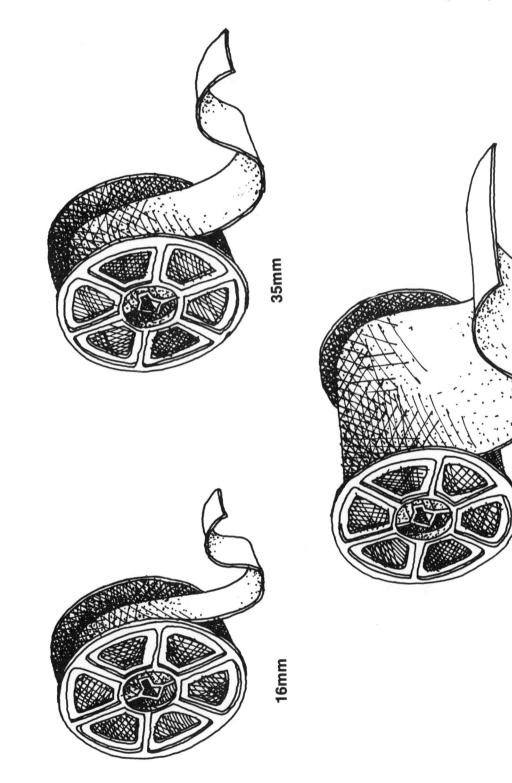

Figure 7.3: Three Microfilm Sizes

35mm

105mm

16mm

Rollfilm Microforms

The most inexpensive microform is simply film wound onto a reel, in much the same form as it comes out of the camera. Film sizes are usually 16mm or 35mm, with the second generally reserved for larger documents requiring a very sharp image. You are probably most familiar with the use of 35mm roll film on reels for newspapers in libraries. Engineering drawings are another application.

Advantages and Disadvantages

A disadvantage of rollfilm on reels is that you must thread it into the viewer by hand. The time involved may be acceptable for library use or for information that you rarely look at. However, it is unacceptable for doing rapid and multiple retrievals in a business environment.

Fortunately, in the case of 16mm film, there is an excellent alternative. You can load the reels of film into cartridges, as illustrated in Figure 7.4. Cartridges allow automatic threading for rapid retrieval, and also protect the film. As we will see, they are the heart of many computer-assisted retrieval units.

Figure 7.4: Reels and Cartridges

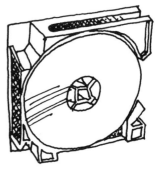

Reel   **Cartridge**

A 215-foot roll of film for use in a cartridge will hold at least 6000 letter-size images, depending on the size of your documents and how you film them. The National Micrographics Association (NMA) publication MS23-1979 listed in the bibliography will give you more information about the capacities of reel microforms with various size documents.

There are three problems with all roll microforms, regardless of whether you use reels or cartridges. In the first place, documents that you film later cannot be inserted between those filmed earlier. Simply put: you cannot interfile. It is possible to cut an existing roll and to splice in new images.

However, doing so is inconvenient, weakens the film and may make the roll inadmissible as legal evidence. Second, because units of information are so large, rollfilm is usually not a good way to distribute information. And third, you cannot combine 16mm and 35mm images on the same roll.

Costs

Commerical costs for producing rollfilm from paper documents depend on the characteristics of the job and local market conditions. Typical costs as of early 1983 are $.03 per image for the first 16mm master, and $.25 for the first 35mm master. Duplicating charges are approximately $.003 per image for 16mm film and $.02 for 35mm film. Per-image costs for 16mm rollfilm in cartridges are a fraction of a cent higher.

Microfiche

Microfiche, or simply "fiche," are pieces of 105mm film containing images filmed on a grid pattern as illustrated in Figure 7.2 above. They are cut in 148mm lengths. Older 4×6-inch formats are also available. A standard microfiche has anywhere from 98 to 270 images, and the top strip contains title information which you can read without magnification. Per-image costs for fiche from paper originals are somewhat more than those for 16mm rollfilm.

Advantages

Fiche are a convenient distribution medium because they contain considerably fewer images than rollfilm microforms. As previously noted, you can quickly copy the fiche you want for as little as $.20. By contrast, with rollfilm you would have to duplicate an entire 6000-document roll containing much information you are not interested in.

Fiche also provide a degree of interfiling capability. For example, assume that you have a records series of case files on microfiche, with no more than one case per fiche. If new documents come in which pertain to an existing case, you can film them and file the new fiche behind the existing fiche. Interfiling in this sense is impossible with roll microforms. In addition, fiche use the most inexpensive viewing equipment of any microform.

Disadvantages

Standard fiche do retain two of the disadvantages of rollfilm microforms. In the first place, you cannot mix 16mm and 35mm size images on a single microform. In addition, with traditional systems, you cannot add to or update an individual fiche. Adding additional information means adding a new fiche. Since only a portion of the new fiche is usually used, this adds cost, and it also splits information. However, there are alternative microfiche systems on the market which do allow updating. Updatables make it possible to add images to an existing fiche, and greatly reduce the need for skilled labor and facility modifications. However, they also involve high equipment cost, and proprietary supplies which lock you into the pricing, support strategy and economic viability of a single company. Questions have also been raised about the image permanency of certain products.

Microfilm Jackets

Microfilm jackets overcome all the drawbacks of traditional fiche systems, but involve somewhat greater cost. A jacket consists of two pieces of clear plastic bonded together to create channels into which you can slip pieces cut from a roll of microfilm. The most common format is similar in size to standard microfiche. Maximum capacity for standard jackets is about 60 images.

Advantages

The advantages of jackets are that you can both interfile them as you would traditional fiche, and add to or update them. You can insert more images wherever and whenever you want, just as you would add pages to a paper file. This is especially attractive for case files such as personnel folders, hospital medical charts and policy files. Jackets can also accommodate a variety of needs. They can hold 16mm film, 35mm film or both. They are made in various sizes, and with areas for handwritten notes. While offering these advantages, jackets retain all the attractive features of microfiche. These include inexpensive duplication and user equipment.

Disadvantages

The price you pay for this flexibility is greater media cost and processing time. Costs per microfilm image are generally one and one-half times that of rollfilm cartridge systems. This is because of the cost of purchasing jackets and inserting film. Since you generally fill them only partially, jacket costs can be significant.

Aperture Cards

Aperture cards are essentially computer punch cards with one or more windows or apertures to hold frames of microfilm. A newer fiche-size card is also available. Like jackets, the cards will accommodate 16mm, 35mm and mixed sizes of film. The most common type is 35mm cards with a single opening, traditionally used for engineering drawings, and illustrated in Figure 7.2. Aperture cards have ample space for adding identifying information manually and by keypunching.

Advantages

You will want to consider aperture cards if you have to interfile and purge very small units of information, usually a single image. This is very important with engineering drawings, which are revised frequently. Aperture cards are also attractive if you need the ability to annotate on the microform. Like fiche, the aperture card is easy to duplicate.

Disadvantages

As with jackets, the primary disadvantage of aperture cards is cost. Because of the need for card supplies and mounting, per-image costs are more than two times that for simple rollfilm. Since there are fewer images per microform, costs are also higher than jackets. Duplicates cost approximately $.20 per card when produced commercially. Filing space requirements are at least five times those of a rollfilm file.

KINDS OF VIEWING AND RETRIEVAL EQUIPMENT

By now you should have some idea of applications and types of microforms which are appropriate for your organization. The next step is to look at equipment for retrieving and viewing the film. Each of the microforms works with specific kinds of equipment. Depending on whether or not the pieces of equipment perform viewing, printing, or viewing *and* printing functions, they are called "readers" and "viewers," "printers," "enlarger-printers," or "reader-printers." This section will give you a general idea of what is available and what to look for.

Rollfilm Microform User Equipment

Retrieval equipment for roll microforms fall into one of three categories: visual, photo-optical and computer-assisted retrieval equipment. They are illustrated in Figure 7.5.

Visual Retrieval Equipment

Visual retrieval equipment is the simplest type. To operate it, you thread the film and advance it with a hand crank or motorized film drive. You generally watch the viewer screen until the appropriate location image flashes by: usually an oversize number or letter. You then stop the film and search slowly, image by image, until you find what you want.

The equipment is relatively flexible and inexpensive. With minor adjustments, it can usually handle both 16mm and 35mm rolls, and certain systems can be modified to accept some or all of the other microforms as well. Some readers are portable. Prices for units without paper print capability range from $300 to $1000.

The problem with visual systems is speed. Film advance has to be relatively slow for you to recognize where to stop, and subsequent image-by-image searching is also slow. This is generally unacceptable for reasonably active information in a business environment.

Photo-optical Retrieval Equipment

The next step up from visual retrieval equipment is to photo-optical units. Based on user instructions, they can advance directly to the desired document at very high speeds by sensing prerecorded codes. Photo-optical units use self-threading cartridges. You should consider this equipment when you need fast retrieval, especially when a limited number of readers are involved. Each retrieval unit costs approximately $6000 to $7000 for standard equipment with print capability, so it is expensive to equip many workstations. Production units—i.e., the cameras used to film the documents—vary much more widely in price.

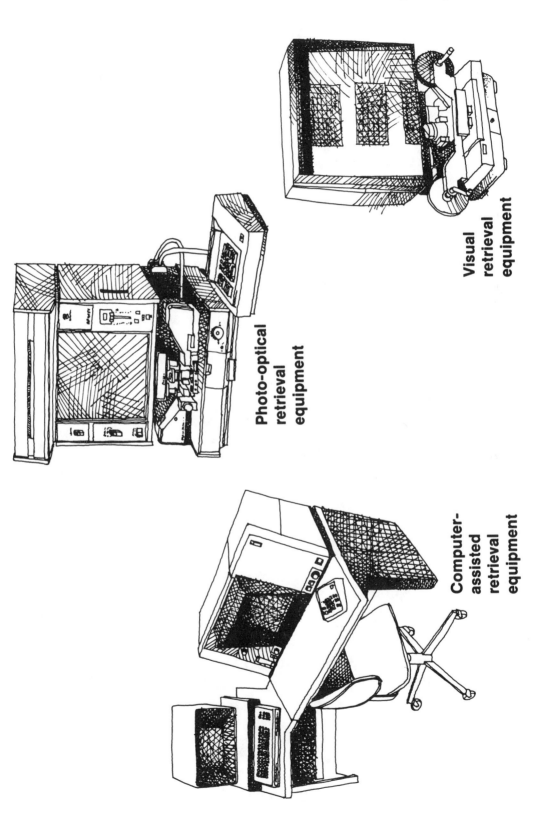

Figure 7.5: Rollfilm Retrieval Equipment

Visual retrieval equipment

Photo-optical retrieval equipment

Computer-assisted retrieval equipment

Bar code systems

Photo-optical equipment comes in two basic types. One uses cameras which encode each image with a bar code type symbol. These symbols look like the product code on items in a grocery store. The codes correspond to any eight-digit number your camera operator chooses, usually a case number or other file code. To use the film, you insert the appropriate cartridge into the retrieval unit and key in the desired number. The unit advances at high speed until it recognizes and stops at the required code.

Blip systems

The second type of photo-optical retrieval equipment uses blips. In their simplest form, blips appear as identical rectangular spots placed below each image at filming. To use the blip film, you insert the appropriate cartridge as you would with a bar code system. However, you then look at an index to discover the location number of the desired document. This number is the sequential position which the document occupies on the roll of film, and does not usually correspond to a file number. When you key in the number, the unit advances, counting blips until it stops at the document you want to see.

Traditionally, each system has had its advantages. Essentially, bar code systems cost more in time and money at the filming or production stage; blip systems are slower at the retrieval stage. Bar code units let you use a number from the document itself to instruct the retrieval unit. Since you don't necessarily have to consult an index as with blip systems, this simplifies and speeds retrieval. This is not to say that you will never have to use an index. Even with a bar code system, if some files in a numerical sequence are still open when you film the closed ones, you will need some way to indicate the roll they are on when you film them later.

Blip systems have the advantage of using standard cameras costing a fraction of bar code camera equipment. In addition, because the camera operator producing blip film doesn't have to tell the camera which number to encode, the film production rate can at least double. Blip systems are also the easier of the two to upgrade to computer-assisted retrieval. This is important, since, as we will see, computer assistance makes the whole issue of index reference time irrelevant.

Computer-assisted Retrieval Equipment

A computer-assisted retrieval (CAR) system for roll microforms usually consists of a computer connected to a blip retrieval unit. It is a hybrid which offers the best of two worlds: computer speed and flexibility tied to low-cost microfilm storage. Specifically, the computer gives you three advantages: it makes it easier to maintain and find index information, reduces the need to sort before filming and eliminates the need to key location addresses into the retrieval unit.

With regard to indexing, you can key information on a computer terminal much faster than you can post it to a manual index. And you can greatly expand the number of cross-reference terms for each document. For example, depending on the situation, you might want to retrieve a document by author, recipient or date. Or you might want a document that fits the criteria of several index terms—for example, all documents by a particular author to a particular recipient in a given month. With more ways to search, document retrieval becomes faster. And if you include enough descriptive information in your index, it may be unnecessary in most cases to refer to the microfilmed document at all. Many information searches can be satisfied from the index alone.

CAR systems also eliminate the need to key the document address into the retrieval unit. The computer transfers it automatically when you touch a key on the terminal keyboard after you complete the search of the index and insert the correct cartridge. More expensive systems will load the appropriate cartridge as well.

Retrieval units come complete with their own separate computers and disk storage units, or as peripheral units to attach to already existing computers and magnetic storage hardware. Complete, ready-to-run systems cost anywhere from $30,000 to $55,000. The price includes programs and microform print capability, and varies depending on how much disk storage you want. Usage reporting, password security and features that make it easy to index film directly from the screen instead of from an original paper document are available as options. Units to attach to an existing computer cost $15,000 plus programming. They can be attractive if you want to cross-reference supporting documentation on microfilm directly from existing computer files. The better units will allow you to tie a number of modules to a single computer port.

CAR is definitely a valuable option for all roll-based systems. For this reason, having blip marks placed on all rollfilm you produce is well worth considering. This is true even if you plan to begin with simple visual retrieval systems. Although the tradeoff is that less area is available on the film for images, blip marks give you the flexibility of easy conversion to CAR if you should ever want to.

Microfilm Jacket and Microfiche Retrieval Equipment

The important thing to realize here is that good equipment is inexpensive. You can buy simple viewers for $250, desk space required is minimal and the units are easy to use and maintain. As a result, jacket and fiche systems are very attractive if you plan to distribute microfilm files and readers to a number of users.

The simplest equipment is generally adequate. The number of images on a jacket or fiche is usually small enough for you to find what you want just by looking. To make it easier, though, whenever possible, you'll want to provide microforms with interspersed, eye-readable titles or targets. These will subdivide the microform so your user will know which section to examine under the viewer.

More expensive, automated CAR units are also available. The more highly automated units can handle files of more than one million documents. Both manual and automated retrieval units for jackets and fiche are illustrated in Figure 7.6.

Aperture Card Retrieval Equipment

Aperture card equipment is usually comparable to jacket and fiche hardware in terms of simplicity and low cost. Many units can handle 35mm rollfilm as well. Figure 7.6 illustrates the equipment. Highly automated units are available which use computer technology to track information such as revision level and distribution lists, and to provide access control. Some also incorporate integral diazo duplicating modules and remote access to microfilmed documents on high-resolution terminals.

EQUIPMENT FEATURES TO WATCH FOR

There are several general considerations to keep in mind when you evaluate specific models of readers and reader-printers. Screen size is probably the most obvious. Dimensions close to original document size are nice, but are not always essential. If you are an infrequent user, or only need to be able to look at part of an image at a time, a smaller screen may be enough. You may be able to settle for an image two-thirds or three-quarters the size of the original. And some readers have multiple lenses. With large documents like

Figure 7.6: Retrieval Equipment for Jackets, Fiche and Aperture Cards

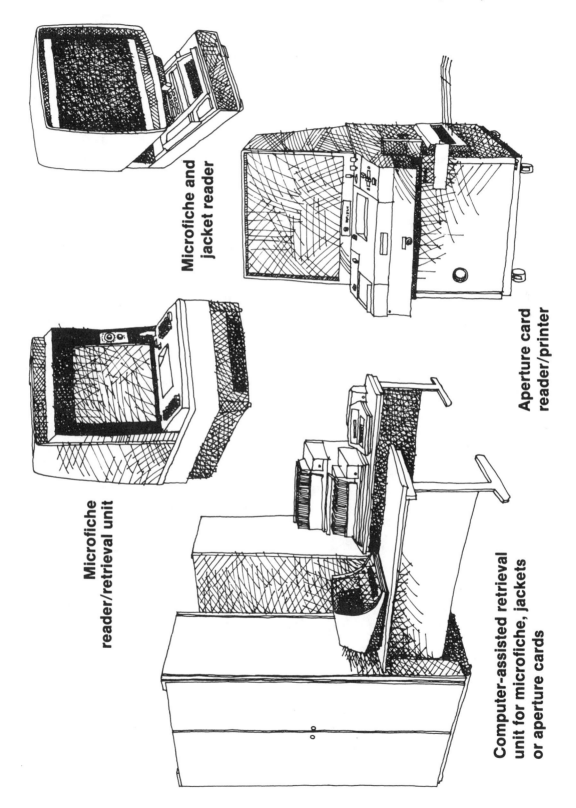

Microfiche and jacket reader

Aperture card reader/printer

Microfiche reader/retrieval unit

Computer-assisted retrieval unit for microfiche, jackets or aperture cards

drawings, multiple lenses let you view a full document at low magnification, and then switch to a higher magnification to look at the section you are interested in.

Interchangeable Lenses

Always make sure that a variety of interchangeable lenses is available. Different groups of documents are often filmed using different camera reduction ratios. You will probably need a different lens for each group. Otherwise, you may wind up with surplus equipment that is too limited. Microfiche, for example, is often produced on cameras that reduce the original document 48 times, but cameras that reduce the document 24 times are also used. If your reader lens magnifies about 48 times, it will usually be right for the first kind of fiche. However, if you decide you also want to read the second kind some years later, the lens will enlarge the documents so much that you may see only part of them on the screen.

Although you don't want to buy more lenses than you will use, it is important to know that you can buy others when you need them. Lenses should be able to be changed by the operator instead of only at the factory. To check all these factors, you can ask for an equipment demonstration with the kind of microfilm you plan to use now, plus whatever you may possibly use in the future.

Image Rotation

Image rotation is another feature to watch for. It allows you to rotate the image 180 degrees on the screen. Sometimes, camera operators have to film source documents in unusual ways to make them fit. As a result, they occasionally appear sideways on the screen, and being able to rotate an image gives you a way to compensate.

If you are looking at jacket or fiche readers, make sure the carrier that holds the fiche moves easily but has enough drag to allow you to center your image and make it stay put. Also check that the image selection index is appropriate for the image reduction ratio and magnification you plan to use.

User Comfort and Convenience

User comfort and convenience should always be a major consideration, both when you install a system and on an ongoing basis. How you handle this will probably have a big impact on employee productivity and morale, especially for users who spend much of their day looking at microfilm. Tiltable screens and revolving bases, for example, can help reduce neck strain. Contrast is also important. You need some for a clear image, but too much can be hard on your eyes. Certain readers allow you to adjust contrast or may provide a switch with two light intensity levels. Depending on the light in your room, hoods and anti-glare or tinted screens can be very important. Also, make sure that there is no evident distortion. The image should be as clear at the edges of the screen as it is at the center.

Projection Method

Projection method is another factor you should consider. There are two different methods of putting images on a reader screen—from the front or the rear. Front projection readers focus images down on an opaque screen, while rear projection machines focus the image on a translucent screen from behind, much like a computer terminal. Although image quality differs very little, there are other differences that may matter. Bifocal wearers, for example, sometimes prefer front projection equipment, but rear projection units may give you a wider viewing angle.

Maintenance

Look for equipment that is easy to get into for simple maintenance. Ask how to do things like changing bulbs, and cleaning mirrors, screens and lenses. Initial maintenance for more complex needs should be covered in your warranty. A year for parts and 90 days for labor is usual.

SPECIFIC READER-PRINTER FEATURES

There are reader-printers that will produce paper prints from each of the microforms. Although many of the considerations are the same as those for selecting a reader, there are some additional ones.

Printer Technologies

Basically three printer technologies are in use. The most popular are direct electrostatic or "electrofax" systems. They use special coated paper plus powder or liquid toner. Supplies are relatively costly. However, the machines give you greater adjustment flexibility when printing from microfilm of poor quality. Powder toners are better because they produce sharper copies and do not have to dry when they come out of the machine.

The second technology uses coated paper as the only supply. Dry silver is probably the most popular type of paper. Since you don't have to add toner, user maintenance is simpler than with electrofax. However, images tend to fade and discolor over the course of time.

The third and preferred technology is xerography. It is essentially the plain paper copier process. Print quality is the best of any technology, and since the machines usually use ordinary paper, they have the advantage of flexibility and low supplies cost. Xerography has traditionally been limited to high-volume printers meant for centralized operations, and costs have been relatively high. However, this is beginning to change.

Speed and Flexibility

In addition to costs, image quality, permanence and user convenience, you should consider your requirements for speed and flexibility. Speed is usually expressed in number of copies per minute. Flexibility involves factors like variety of print media, paper sizes and whether you can make prints of your film in the polarity you want (white on black and/or black on white). Certain equipment, for example, will produce permanent prints at high speed on a range of media, including plain paper and Mylar, and on various paper sizes up to 18 × 24-inches. It may also have automatic exposure, automatic adjustment for the condition of the toner, automatic focus and stack feeders for microforms such as aperture cards. However, the price can be upward of $25,000, and the equipment may require considerable maintenance. On the other hand, you can purchase good reader-printers for as little as $2000 if you are able to sacrifice some features and flexibility.

IMPLEMENTING A PROGRAM

If microfilm sounds as if it might be appropriate for your organization, or if you want to improve an existing program, Chapter 8 will give you information about managing a microfilm program. It will discuss whether to produce film on a contract basis or in-house, and methods and standards you should insist on to ensure quality and permanence.

8

Managing a Microfilm Program

by Frederick Klunder

If you are using or considering the use of microfilm for your records management, you should know something about how microfilm is produced. You will have to evaluate whether to produce your microfilm in-house or have it done on a contract basis. And wherever you do it, you'll have to know what to expect in terms of quality, certification, service and long-term permanence. Microfilm programs often fail because managers assume that film production is as simple as operating an office copier. This does not mean that you need the highly detailed knowledge of a microfilm production technician, but you should know enough to supervise one.

PRODUCTION STEPS

Different production steps are involved depending on the basic kind of camera you use to produce your microfilm. There are two kinds: source document cameras and computer output microfilm (COM) cameras or "recorders." The first type photographs paper documents. The second photographs images from a special computer screen (VDT) or laser (which writes onto film directly) and is used as an alternative to paper printouts for computerized information.

Source Document Microfilm Production

Producing good source document microfilm is a labor-intensive process. In fact, labor accounts for at least 70% of the total cost involved.

Much of this goes for copy preparation. Someone has to remove unnecessary records, such as duplicates, place records in the right order, obtain missing items, remove staples and folder clips, and repair damage and creases which might obscure information.

Targets

After this, targets must be inserted. Targets are sheets of paper that are filmed to provide additional information related to the original documents. They may, for example, give roll numbers, note the absence of oversize documents that will be filmed on other cameras and identify retakes that must ultimately be put together with images from other rolls of film. In addition, targets contain test charts to monitor camera and film processor performance, and declarations of authenticity by responsible officials. When all the targets are inserted, staff must divide the documents into groups large enough to fill a roll of film.

Filming and Processing

The next step is to run tests to determine the correct exposure before filming the documents. Properly selected exposure is more critical with microfilm than with normal photography. It is basic to microfilm legibility, and decides whether you can make good microfilm and paper duplicates. Traditional processing requires strict control to ensure legible and permanent images. It involves monitoring various chemical and water tanks for the correct temperature and potency, and ensuring that equipment in the processing laboratory is clean. (A simpler processing form, possible in some circumstances, will be discussed later in this chapter.)

Film Inspection

This process includes visual inspection for obvious defects such as blank film, scratches and overlaps. In addition, there are technical tests for level of detail reproduced, or "resolution"; degree of contrast between image and background, or "density"; and image permanence (methylene blue test). Film that does not meet standards must be redone. If microfiche, jackets or aperture cards are involved, you also have to cut the film into individual pieces, strips or images. With jackets you need to insert film on machines called "reader-fillers."

Duplicates

If you want duplicates, additional processes and inspections are required. Basically, you can use two kinds of film: diazo film or vesicular film. Diazo film is processed with ammonia, and it reproduces the polarity of your master copy. If your master has clear letters on a black background, as is often the case, your diazo copy will also be clear on black. In general, a dark background is preferred because it is easier to read on a viewer. Vesicular films are developed with heat and light, and generally reverse the polarity of the master microform. Most inspection processes are the same as with camera master film, although the sampling frequency can be less.

Publications listed in the bibliography will give you more information on microfilm production. These include the National Microfilm Association (NMA) MS23-1979, and the more detailed *Microfilm and the Courts: Reference Manual*.

COM Production

COM production differs from source document microfilming in that no copy preparation is involved. This makes it cheaper to produce and easier to justify, assuming your data are already computer-readable. COM recorders are sold with computer programs which reformat data intended for paper printouts into micrographic format. This happens in the recorder itself, and special programming is available from the vendor.

Filming itself can occur in online or offline mode. Online mode involves transmission of data from your main computer to the recorder via communications cables, and is most appropriate for short reports. In offline mode, you take magnetic tapes off the main computer and mount them on the tape drives of the recorder, to transfer the data into that unit.

Regardless of which you use, putting information on film is faster than printing it on paper, and requires much less operator involvement during and after printing than with the usual computer line printer. As discussed in Chapter 7, COM can also be considerably cheaper than computer printouts in terms of media cost. Film used can be 16mm or 105mm (microfiche) size.

The basic principles of processing and quality control are similar to those for source document microfilming. In practice, because the COM unit is generally operated in a computer environment rather than in one specifically oriented to micrographics, and because long-term retention is not usually required, inspection is sometimes more cursory. Ideally, however, all operations should conform to the recommendations set forth in the NMA technical report MS1-1980 (see bibliography). Duplication procedures are also the same as for source document microfilming.

COM production equipment is expensive. However, as the next section explains, you do not have to own this equipment to take advantage of the technology.

IN-HOUSE OR SERVICE BUREAU

In general, if you're new to microfilm, you are probably best off having it produced at a service bureau. This is the easiest way to start up a program. And even if you're an experienced user, your volume will have to be very high before in-house production becomes economically feasible. The following case studies illustrate this point.

Case Study: Source Document Microfilming

The example of an engineering department of a municipal utility shows what it takes to bring source document filming in-house. This organization was sending out drawings and supporting documents for production of rollfilm and aperture cards. The costs for filming, processing, mounting and producing occasional paper prints of 3600 documents was $800. Annual cost of one 35mm camera alone, amortized over five years, would have been several times more. Total annual costs for labor, maintenance, equipment, supplies and facility modifications would have been in excess of $60,000 per year.

This does not mean that it never makes sense to produce small volumes of microfilm in-house. The municipal engineering department was fortunate enough to have a reputable service bureau close by. Similar organizations in other cities may not be as fortunate, and even if there is a good service bureau, an in-house operation may be the only way to ensure acceptable turnaround time and confidentiality. For example, if you want to film incoming correspondence before distributing it, service bureau production probably isn't feasible. If confidential documents that may not be removed from your office are involved, you may also have to go in-house. Some service companies will set up shop on your premises, but they may be reluctant if volume is small.

Some combination of service bureau and in-house production is also an option. For example, some companies contract out the initial conversion to film, but handle the rest in-house. This avoids over-investment in equipment that the company won't need later. Other organizations film all documents in-house and send out the exposed film for processing. However, splitting responsibility for filming and processing can make a microfilm program hard to manage. If quality problems develop, it may be difficult to decide what went wrong and who was responsible.

Case Study: Computer Output Microfilming

Another example from the utility mentioned above illustrates the considerations involved in deciding where to produce COM. In this case, the utility was producing COM using a service bureau, and was considering whether to move the operation in-house. The production rate was 200,000 original frames per month, at an annual cost of $40,000. The utility calculated that bringing the operation in-house as cheaply as possible would have cost $67,000 per year.

Since there were no other requirements, such as confidentiality, the utility correctly decided to continue its use of the service bureau, and postpone any reexamination of its COM operation until production volume had doubled.

Although general guidelines are difficult to provide, it generally does not make sense to consider in-house COM until your volume approaches 500,000 frames per month, or until the other considerations mentioned above warrant it. Unless you are a large user, a reputable COM service bureau will probably be the most cost-effective way to produce your microfilm. Price reductions could lower this threshold in the future. However, reductions would have to be major to have significant impact.

COST OF AN IN-HOUSE PRODUCTION OPERATION

If you think you may be close to the point where you should be producing microfilm in-house, you will want to figure out the costs of your options. This section offers general information on the labor, supplies, facility and equipment costs of in-house operations. When you've made your in-house calculations, you can compare them with quotations obtained from local service bureaus.

Staffing Requirements

The number of in-house staff required will depend in large part on the type, condition and number of documents you have to film. Table 8.1 will give you an idea of the man-hours needed to produce microfilm from average source documents, using trained and properly managed staff. You should also allocate personnel for management and training, maintenance, handling user requests and developing and testing new systems.

Table 8.1: Average Man-hours Needed to Produce Finished Microforms of 1000 Documents Using Standard Equipment

Equipment	Original Copies	Duplicates
16mm roll film or cartridges:	2 hours	5 minutes
35mm roll film:	5 hours	12 minutes
16mm microfilm jackets:	3½ hours	50 minutes*
Source document microfiche:	2 hours	50 minutes*
COM microfiche:	6 minutes**	15 seconds**
Aperture cards:	9 hours	50 minutes*

*Assumes 20 frames/fiche and low-volume duplicating equipment.
**Assumes 250 frames/fiche, 48:1 reduction, 40 lines/frame.

Equipment Considerations

You have several options when choosing film processing equipment and cameras. Without getting into technological details, there are some things you will want to be aware of, since they directly affect the cost and ease of producing microfilm in-house. (Costs are listed in Table 8.2, following this discussion.)

Simplified Processing Equipment

The major equipment consideration concerns the acceptability of several simplified kinds of microfilm processing. Using them can lower the point at which you can justify producing film in-house. However, they are not always appropriate.

A traditional microfilm processor is separate from the microfilm camera, and requires a trained operator. It consists of rollers which transport the film up and down through at least four tanks: a developer tank, wash tank, fixer tank and final wash tank. The processor requires an adjacent sink, with hot and cold running water. It generally has auxiliary chemical tanks which automatically replenish the internal developer and fixer tanks.

Some segments of the microfilm industry have promoted a simplified form of traditional processing. The intent is to make microfilm easy to produce in an office environment.

Mono-bath systems

These simpler units are often mono-bath systems, which reduce the number of traditional baths, and possibly eliminate chemical and water replenishment. Certain processors may also use straight-path designs. Instead of having tanks through which film passes up and down over a series of rollers, these processors use a system in which solutions are quickly sprayed up onto the film and then wiped off before the film goes on to the next solution. Some processors are included in the same unit as the camera. In this case, unexposed film is loaded into the unit at one end and removed in processed form at the other end.

Although generalizations are difficult, there are two potential problems you should be aware of. The most important is the limited wash which the film may receive in these systems. As a result, it may be difficult to thoroughly remove the fixer from the film. Since remaining fixer will gradually erode the recorded image, you should be careful about this kind of equipment whenever you need to keep your film for a long period of time, possibly in excess of 10 years.

In addition, without automatic replenishment and running water, these systems require you to change and add solutions more often; this increases costs. It may also encourage operators to forego chemical changes, resulting in poorer quality of the microfilm image.

Thermal processing

The second simplified and relatively new form of processing uses thermally developed films. Processing involves no chemicals—only heat, and possibly toner. Because of the simplicity, the camera and processing units are usually housed in the same unit. Camera-processors for thermally developed films are available for both traditional and updatable microfiche. They are especially popular for COM recorders, since recorders are generally operated by computer personnel who are unaccustomed to the laboratory environment associated with traditional processing.

Because thermal processing is relatively new, there are still some questions about the long-term image permanence associated with it. As a result, if you do decide to use it, stringent annual sampling of your film is recommended. If deterioration becomes evident, you can create inexpensive duplicates on traditional diazo copy film, or consider more expensive silver duplicates.

A disadvantage of thermal processing is that a particular brand of machine can only use that same brand of film. Thus, buying such equipment locks you into the marketing and support strategies of a single company. By contrast, there are many suppliers of traditional microfilm, and the market is more competitive.

Cameras

Cameras are another area where you have options when you cost out an in-house operation. The simplest types are planetary and rotary. The first type uses fewer moving parts. As a result, planetary cameras produce the highest quality images and are the most maintenance-free. They consist of a camera head positioned on a column above a copyboard.

Rotary cameras derive their name from the rotating belt which carries documents past the lens. They are somewhat faster than planetary cameras, and have the ability to film both sides of a document simultaneously. However, document size is considerably more limited, and base price is also higher. Because of the number of moving parts, the cameras need more maintenance and break down more often than planetary cameras, and do not produce images of the same clarity. Strict copy preparation is required to avoid jams. As a result, rotary cameras are not recommended unless maintenance support is readily available and your documents are of standard size and in very good condition.

Equipment, Supplies and Other Costs

Equipment and Supply Costs

Table 8.2 presents approximate 1983 costs for equipment and supplies. Local vendors will provide exact figures if you tell them what you need. You'll probably want to amortize equipment costs over five years.

In general, except at very high volumes, the number of images you plan to produce will affect the number of cameras needed, but not the number of machines in the processing, duplicating and inspection areas.

Additional Costs

Maintenance charges for major equipment generally run 10% of purchase price per year. However, if your local vendor has qualified support staff, it may be cheaper to pay them (if they can be relied on to come out quickly when you need help), than to pay for a maintenance contract.

You will need furniture to accommodate copy preparation and to put

Table 8.2: Equipment and Supply Costs for Microfilm Production

Cameras

16mm planetary camera	$ 3,500
16mm planetary processor camera	4,000
16mm rotary camera	10,000
Microfiche camera	20,000
Microfiche camera/processor	19,000
16mm updatable microfiche camera/processor	25,000
35mm planetary camera	23,000
35mm planetary camera/processor	24,000
COM recorder	100,000

Processing, Unitizing and Duplicating Equipment

Traditional, medium-volume processor with chemical and water supply attachments	$ 10,000
Jacket and aperture card loaders	3,000
Diazo rollfilm duplicator	13,000
Diazo jacket and fiche duplicator (low volume)	3,500
Diazo fiche duplicator (high volume)	35,000
Diazo aperture card duplicator	15,000

Inspection Equipment

Equipment for visual inspection	$ 500
Microscope for resolution inspection	350
Densitometer for density inspection	2,000

Supplies

100 ft. roll 16mm silver film	$ 6.00
100 ft. roll 35mm silver film	11.50
100 ft. roll 105mm silver film (210 fiche)	30.00
100 ft. roll 16mm diazo film	1.50
100 ft. roll 35mm diazo film	2.50
100 ft. roll 105mm diazo film	9.00
100 microfilm jackets	12.00
100 35mm aperture cards	5.00
Processor chemicals per 16mm roll	.25
Processor chemicals per 35mm roll	.40
Processor chemicals per 105mm roll	1.25+
Diazo duplication chemicals (210 fiche)	.50

equipment on. Surplus furniture is appropriate as long as it meets the needs of the workers using it (i.e., incorporates the proper ergonomics). The working surface should be approximately 26 inches off the ground, and should allow at least 6 inches of knee clearance. Chairs for preparation stations should allow elbow height of several inches above the working surface. In addition, you will need a refrigerator for storage of unprocessed film.

Also allow for space and facility modification costs. Your production area will need ample hot and cold running water, and a sink. You will probably need lighting modifications and partitions, and may have to provide for exhaust venting, air conditioning and environmental monitors.

CHOOSING A SERVICE BUREAU

If you have more than one service bureau in your area, be sure to shop around before contracting with a specific firm. Present your needs, and ask what type of microfilm program each would suggest. In the process, try to gather enough information to draw up a standard specification for the various companies to bid on. Without a specification, their bids may not be comparable.

The specification should describe the number, size, format and condition of the materials and media you will submit to the service bureau for microfilm production. Note whether you will submit the documents ready for filming or not—with all paper clips removed, all damage repaired, etc. If not, the service bureau will prepare the documents for filming, but at considerable expense.

If computer output microfilm is involved, you should mention how the magnetic tapes are formatted. The specification should also include your requirements, such as film size, type of microform, degree of reduction, how you want the documents arranged on the film, and the type of identification and certification you need. Quality requirements are also essential. As will be explained below, these include standards for resolution, density and image permanence.

You will obviously want to include your copy needs. If you require a duplicate security copy for retention longer than 100 years, you should specify that the copy be on silver film. Also state any packaging requirements you may have, such as cartridge types, envelopes and other containers. Include special needs relating to confidentiality, turnaround time, pick-up and delivery, and disposal of records.

You might also require vendors to submit a sample of microfilm produced from your documents with their bids. Choose 20 or 30 documents of varied image quality. Each vendor should film the same documents. Indicate that the samples will be used to choose a vendor and ultimately to evaluate the finished product for acceptance and payment.

Factors to consider in evaluating the responses include cost, quality, and reputation and anticipated responsiveness. At some stage in the evaluation process, you should tour the facilities of potential contracting firms. This will give you a feel for the people you'll be dealing with, and for the general cleanliness and orderliness of the operation. Your contract should include the requirements you stated in your specification. If turnaround time is vital, you may want to specify penalties for failure to meet agreed-upon deadlines.

SETTING QUALITY STANDARDS

Regardless of whether you use a service bureau or produce film in-house, you need to establish standards. Some people mistakenly assume that microfilming is no more demanding than photocopying. However, there are several important differences. With microfilm, there is less margin for error, and when you do make a mistake, it may be a while before you find out. Poor quality film may only show up when you try to duplicate it, or when the image begins to fade seriously some years later. In addition, microfilm may be inadmissible as evidence in court unless you follow certain procedures.

Source Document Quality Standards

Appropriate standards for microfilming differ depending on the documents involved. In general, however, you should require that film be free of visual defects which impair information. Your original microfilm should be able to withstand technical inspections. This is an area where you will need technical knowledge. A good place to start is with the NMA technical report MS23-1979, which sets forth the recommended practice for microfilm production (see bibliography).

Your film should generally have a background density of from 1.0 to 1.2, a minimum density of no more than 0.1, and a resolution of between 80 and 135 lines per millimeter. Specific resolution requirements will depend on document contrast and the size of the lines and letters filmed.

Appropriate requirements should be determined using the method outlined in MS23-1979, and keeping in mind possible requirements of regulatory agencies. For permanent retention of all except thermally processed films, you should also require a methylene blue test for residual fixer on at least a monthly basis, with results below .7 micrograms per square centimeter. This will give you a reasonable guarantee of image permanence. Less stringent requirements of 2 micrograms can be enough for film which will not be kept longer than 10 years. However, multiple standards may be confusing from the point of view of microfilm production management.

If you use a service bureau, you should consider requiring that it furnish a certificate of acceptability for each roll or batch of film, stating resolution and density test results. Methylene blue test results should be included once a month.

COM Quality Standards

Quality areas for original COM are the same as those for source document film: image permanence, density and resolution. Specific standards for image permanence using the methylene blue test are identical to those already discussed.

Density and resolution standards differ because you have more control over the image photographed with COM than you have with source document microfilm. Testing COM film for density and resolution is somewhat more difficult than it is for source document filming. It is also more limited: resolution and density tests do not measure the quality of the image generated in the recorder by the screen or laser. However, it is important to enforce standards.

Background density for negative-appearing original microfilm should be at least 1.8, with a corresponding minimum density of no higher than .05. As with source document film, resolution requirements will differ with the size of the characters filmed. One method of measuring involves the use of a test slide. Depending on size, the pattern read should generally be between 2.2 and 2.8.

ADMISSIBILITY OF MICROFILM EVIDENCE IN COURT

There are various grounds for justifying the admissibility of microfilm as evidence in court and before government agencies. First, there are statutes that expressly permit it in certain situations and under certain conditions. You may be able to have microfilm admitted even if you don't comply with these statutes, but it's obviously better to be safe.

Compliance with UPA

The Uniform Photographic Copies of Business and Public Records as Evidence Act (UPA) is probably the strictest and most straightforward piece of legislation on admissibility. This federal law governs evidence presented in federal courts. It has been adopted with only minor modifications by at least 44 state legislatures, and has influenced the regulations of federal and state agencies. As a result, UPA is a good place to begin.

In order to comply with UPA, you must meet several conditions. First of all, you must be able to show that the original record and any copy, whether paper or film, was made in the regular course of business. Second, the microfilm copy must be satisfactorily identified. And third, the microfilm process used must result in accurate and durable reproductions.

The last condition can be met by proving that your film was produced in compliance with the quality standards outlined above. The first two conditions are satisfied by documenting your microfilm program. To begin with, this means maintaining logs which document the microfilm production process. It also means completing certificates and statements about the identity of the records and the intent of your microfilm program for each microform. Various formats are available. One option is the form recommended by the American National Standards Institute (ANSI) in MS19-1978 (see bibliography). It is usually filmed at the beginning of microforms produced on source document cameras. In the case of COM film, the paper copy is usually simply filed.

In addition, it is important to document the general outlines of your microfilm program. Signed mission statements and microfilm production manuals and contracts fall into this category.

Compliance with Regulations

Before starting a microfilm program, you'll also have to check specific state legislation and regulations of relevant government bodies. Although UPA is basic to most of these, there are deviations. Many states, for example, consider microforms inadmissible when the record involved is a negotiable instrument, such as a stock or bond. The compilation of regulations and laws in *Legality of Microfilm* (see bibliography) is a good place to begin your research.

STORING MICROFILM

Once you've produced microfilm, you'll want to make sure it's stored correctly. Microfilm can last as long as paper. This is a significant advantage over all current forms of computer magnetic storage media. However, in order to make it last that long you must provide a carefully controlled environment. And the longer you want your microfilm to last, the stricter the environmental requirements.

Environmental Requirements

Environmental requirements for microfilm begin with temperature and humidity. You should store microfilm that has a permanent retention period at a maximum temperature of 70° Fahrenheit and 30% to 40% humidity, with no more than 5% change within any 24-hour period.

Monitoring these conditions usually means installing a recording themometer-hygrometer in the storage area and inspecting it daily. Reels and paper enclosures for your film, as well as all other materials in the storage area, should be of special paper, and free of acids and peroxides which can trigger destructive chemical reactions. If film is not stored in sealed containers, air in the storage room must be carefully controlled. It should be free of abrasive particles and gaseous impurities which can harm the film. In urban or industrial areas, you will need an air filtration system. For large microfilm files, you should conduct a 1% random sample every two years. As much as possible, you should carry out the same visual, density and resolution inspections which are performed immediately after processing.

Outside Facilities

As you have probably already gathered, the costs involved in providing the required environment will probably be prohibitive unless you have a major microfilm operation in your organization. In most cases, you are probably better off using an outside facility if you can arrange it. Service bureaus are one possibility, since many of them provide this service. For records of historical importance, local archives or historical societies may be another possibility.

Requirements for microfilm with a relatively short retention period are considerably less demanding. Film needed for a maximum of 10 years can be kept in areas with temperatures as high as 77° and humidity of up to 60%. You generally will not need special atmospheric controls.

Film with an even shorter retention period is even easier to provide for. You can obviously afford to be harder on working copies than on your original. As long as you're careful with your master, you can always create new copies.

The pamphlet "Practice for Storage of Processed Safety Photographic Film, ANSI PH1.43-1979," or Harold Dorfman's "Film Storage," in *Microfilm Shop Talk*, will give you more detailed information about storage conditions. These materials are listed in the bibliography.

9

Automating Your Records Systems

by Katherine Aschner

Most companies start the automation process by trying to decide which word processor or computer to buy. However, equipment choices are the last part of the decision-making process. It is far more important to decide if automation is appropriate and, if so, whether word or data processing (WP or DP) makes the most sense. When a computer is required, choosing the software (the programs) is what guides the selection of the right system. If the programs don't fit your needs, the best computer in the world won't help you.

WHEN TO CONSIDER AUTOMATION

Automation addresses two interrelated office requirements: improving productivity and enhancing capabilities. Poor productivity typically manifests itself in two ways: important work doesn't get done on time; low priority work (such as filing) doesn't get done at all. Assuming that individual employees are working to capacity, you have two choices. You can add more staff or you can provide existing staff with new tools, such as automation, to get the work out faster. In more and more business situations, automation is proving the more cost-effective solution.

Enhancing capabilities is a more subtle advantage of automation. Word processing permits correspondence, reports, resumes and proposals to be quickly tailored to specific situations. Often, this can mean the difference between a successful or marginal operation.

Using data processing, you can gain access to valuable information in your files that would be impractical to retrieve in a manual system. For example, customer sales history cards arranged in alphabetical order make it easy to review manually any *one* sale; all you have to do is scan to the right customer name. However, if you want to analyze *all* sales—perhaps by product, salesperson or area—you must thumb through the entire file, manually tabulating the products sold by each salesperson in each area. The result is rarely worth the considerable effort. Instead, you make do without the figures.

This is not the only problem associated with card files. As your card file grows, misfiles become more common, simply because there are so many more cards to work with. For the same reason, access to any particular card is slower. Finally, as long as your card file is manual, creating a duplicate is difficult and costly. This is especially true for files that are very active. It's hard enough to keep the master up to date without worrying about a security copy.

On the other hand, if certain items of information about each customer's sales history are stored in a computer, you can retrieve this information in a variety of ways, depending on your needs at the time. One month you might choose to review a new salesperson's performance. Next month, you might choose to focus on the sales of a new product.

The computer makes it practical to retrieve, and therefore to use, more information. It ensures your ability to satisfy a wide range of information requests with a single, fast, flexible system. Finally, the creation of a duplicate security copy becomes a simple operating procedure that significantly reduces your company's risk.

Of course, not all information gathering problems can be improved by automation. If you are spending too much time or taking too long to process information, automation will help. If you are collecting the wrong information, or inaccurate information or gathering information in the wrong sequence, automation will only compound the problem. It has been said before, but it bears repeating: make sure your manual systems are in order before bringing in a computer.

CHOOSING BETWEEN WORD AND DATA PROCESSING

If you think automation is what you need, the next step is to decide between word and data processing. The distinction is not really one of technology, but of function. In fact, a word processor is nothing more or less than a computer designed to run a highly specialized kind of program: one that processes text. Before discussing how to choose between WP and DP, a review of what each does and how they fit together is in order.

What Word Processing Does

Word processing stores keyboarded information (both text *and* format) for two kinds of applications: repetitive and revision typing. Repetitive typing refers to the reuse of either standard text or standard format over and over. While this saves considerable time, most offices do not tend to do the same thing over and over with any great volume. Therefore, the actual value of this feature may be somewhat limited.

Revision typing, on the other hand, is very practical for drafting correspondence, editing long documents, updating monthly reports, preparing and redoing budgets, and handling complex technical typing. Advanced word processors have the ability to generate outlines, create tables of contents and alphabetical cross-indexes, and manage the placement of footnotes and charts automatically. This saves time for both authors and typists.

Many word processors offer advanced file management and mathematical capabilities. They can maintain and sort large mailing lists or store a sequence of mathematical calculations (such as might be required to produce an invoice or update a report). Some systems will even execute a further sequence of operations, based on the result of a calculation. For instance, the system can be set up to check for negative column totals and double-underline them automatically.

This linking of automatic procedures begins to look very much like data processing. However, as long as these capabilities are an integral part of a word processing system, they are considered word processing functions. Nevertheless, one reason WP can be considered for your automation requirements is that it performs many DP functions quite well.

What Data Processing Does

Reduced to its simplest terms, data processing performs two functions: managing files of information and performing computations. (This discussion is limited to office-based systems, and does not consider uses of data processing in manufacturing, engineering or scientific applications.)

Computerized information files are called data bases. Some are as simple as the customer sales history file described above. Others are large and complex; for example, a data base for a large manufacturing firm may contain complete customer information. In either case, the role of data processing is to make information available to users in a variety of formats.

Performing computations, often referred to as number-crunching, is what computers do best. Applications range from producing a simple purchase order to processing the financial transactions of a *Fortune* 500 company.

In many computer applications, both functions exist together. For instance, the manufacturing firm's customer data base may be part of an accounts receivable computer program. When an order is processed, the customer's sales history file is automatically updated. The same information is also used to debit inventory, produce an invoice and bill of lading, and update the sales journal and general ledger.

The above descriptions provide a general idea of how word and data processing are used. Now it's time to take a closer look at how each might fit with your applications. But first, in case you are not familiar with all the jargon, a short course in computer terminology.

THE COMPONENTS OF A COMPUTER

All computers (including word processors) are divided into two parts: hardware and software. The hardware is the machine: it's what you see. The most basic component is the computer itself, usually referred to as the central processing unit or CPU. Actually, to say that you see the CPU is not entirely accurate: what you really see is the cabinet that houses your finger-nail-sized microprocessor(s).

Bits and Bytes

In order to understand computer technology, it is important to understand bits and bytes. A bit is the smallest unit of information recognized by a computer: an electric pulse that is either on or off. In most office computers, 8 bits in various combinations of on and off patterns are required to represent a single character, or byte. A byte refers to the amount of storage required for a single character (letter, number, symbol, space).

CPU Technology

The size of the CPU, which determines the size of programs and the amount of data that can be processed, is usually expressed in kilobytes, or k. This stands for 1000 bytes (1024 or 2 to the power of 8, to be precise). Thus, a computer with 64k of main memory is a computer capable of holding approximately 64,000 characters worth of program instructions and data in its CPU.

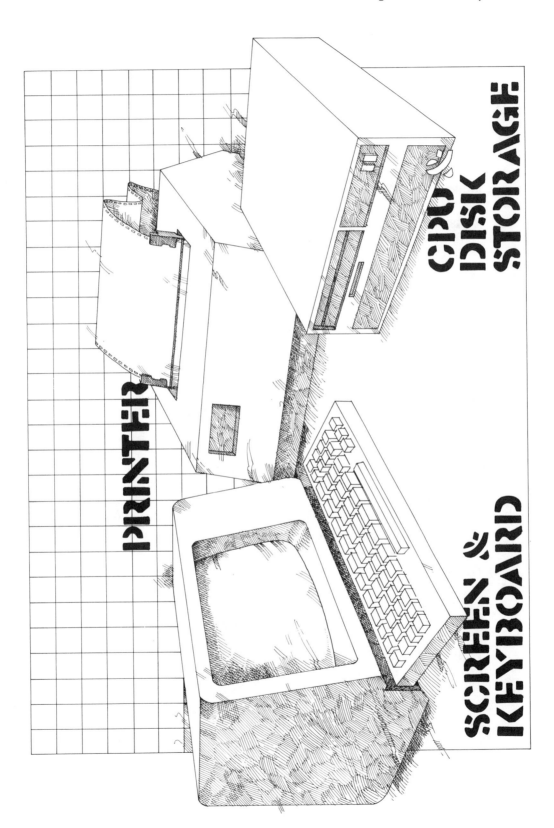

Many small computers use an 8-bit or a 16-bit central processor. This means that the computer is able to address and process either 8 or 16 bits at a single time. As a general rule, 16-bit systems can handle larger programs and more data than their smaller cousins. However, true operating efficiency is also a function of the software, or programs. A 16-bit CPU alone is no guarantee.

Peripheral Devices

Several devices are attached to the CPU to complete your computer system: a terminal, one or more disk drives and a printer. The computer terminal consists of a screen (also called a video display or CRT, for cathode ray tube) and a keyboard. This is the basic workstation.

Disk Drives

Most computers use either floppy diskettes, hard disks or some combination of the two for information storage. Floppy diskettes look like little phonograph records in paper sleeves. They range in diameter from about three inches to eight inches. Hard disks, which have a much greater capacity, use a very precise technology that compacts stored information very densely. As a result, hard disks are extremely sensitive to dust and humidity, and are usually permanently sealed inside the computer.

Floppy diskettes, regardless of their diameter, typically hold about 300,000 characters of information, or about 300k, although this figure varies considerably from manufacturer to manufacturer. Given an industry standard of 2000 characters per page, 300k is enough storage for about 150 pages. Hard disks store anywhere from about five to 80 megabytes (Mb), or million characters of information. Eighty Mb is enough storage to handle 40,000 pages of text.

Printers

Printers come in a variety of models. For word processing, a letter quality printer, which operates at a speed of about 55 characters per second, is preferred. A letter quality printer uses fully-formed characters on a printwheel to make impressions; as a result, the print quality is very high.

For data processing applications, print quality is generally sacrificed for speed. A high-speed printer composes characters from a dot matrix, usually at the rate of 120 to 200 characters per second. Some dot matrix printers can be slowed to "correspondence mode," which means dots are overprinted to give a more finished appearance. However, the quality is still not as good as true letter quality printing.

For printing graphics, such as charts or schematics, a plotter is often used. A plotter uses a tracing pen to produce drawings according to plot points you define with the help of a computer graphics program. However, if your graphics consist of simple bar charts and line drawings, you may be able to produce them on a letter quality or dot matrix printer.

Software

Operating Systems

The remaining component of your system is software, a term which refers to the programs that tell your computer what to do. The operating system is the heart of it all, the super-program that reads all the other programs, such as word processing or payroll, and tells the machine how to carry out their instructions. Many small computers use standard operating systems, such as CP/M (Control Program for Microcomputers, a trade name of Digital Research), MS-DOS (developed by Microsoft) or a version of UNIX (originally developed by Bell Labs).

There are programs for all types of applications and businesses which run under these various operating systems. The section on using data processing later in this chapter identifies the various program options open to you.

Programs are written in programming languages such as COBOL (COmmon Business-Oriented Language), FORTRAN (FORmula TRANslation), BASIC (Beginners' All-purpose Symbolic Instruction Code) and C. These allow programs to be written in English-like commands, which are then translated into the sequences of on's and off's that the computer's operating system understands. This translation process, which is run on the computer, is called compiling or interpreting a program.

Compilers and Interpreters

It is important to realize that you may have to buy a compiler or interpreter for your computer, even if you do not plan to write any programs yourself. You will need the compiler to translate any programs you purchase into a code that is compatible with your machine's operating system.

That's the end of our brief overview. More information on software programs appears later in this chapter in the section on Using Data Processing. Now let's return to word processing.

USING WORD PROCESSING

No doubt, some of you are wondering why word processing is included in a book on records management. If so, you need to refer back to the first chapter and remember that we said that 68% of all records maintenance costs are for labor. We also noted that even greater costs are incurred before the records ever get to the filing cabinet: while they are being generated and processed.

Properly used, word processing can effect real savings in the cost of creating records. Therefore, it is as much a part of a good records management program as a sound filing system or proper use of micrographics. Further, word processors now perform many of the tasks usually associated with computers.

Administrative Applications

The traditional use for word processing is as part of the secretarial function. If 20% or more of your support staff resources are committed to typing, and if that typing falls into the repetitive or revision categories, word processing can probably be used effectively.

There are a number of different levels of equipment available, from electronic typewriters to video-display word processors to large shared-resource systems. As a general rule, electronic typewriters work best where there is a limited need for storage, usually 15 to 20 pages or so, and where editing is less important than professional-looking documents.

Video-display Word Processors

Video-display machines are recommended for revision typing. The screen allows the typist to see and experiment with text before printing a document, an essential component of efficient editing. Furthermore, these machines permit simultaneous input (typing) and output (printing), which increases their efficiency substantially over electronic typewriters.

Shared-resource Systems

Sometimes, several typists need to draw from large libraries of prerecorded material, such as standard paragraphs in legal documents or contracts. Other times, they may need to divide very large documents among several people, in order to get them out faster. In both of these cases, a shared-resource system is appropriate. This configuration allows several typists, each equipped with a terminal, to work from the same storage media (typically a multimillion character disk). Depending on how the shared system is set up, the typists may also share the same central processor and peripheral devices, such as printers and plotters.

Professional Applications

Many professionals spend a large part of their work day writing. This pertains less to top executives than to lawyers, auditors, administrators, engineers and other staff who produce and revise long documents. Many professionals find that the ability to experiment and revise as part of the writing process is easy to learn and very useful. At least one study at a major aircraft company has shown that significant productivity increases are gained when authors have their own terminals.

Even for professionals whose hunt-and-peck typing limits them to 20 or 30 words a minute, there is still a tremendous advantage: hand-writing slows them down to seven or eight words a minute, and they still have to wait for the typist to keyboard what has been so laboriously drafted. Touch typing, although useful, is not required for effective use of word processing.

Professional input is appropriate during the writing and editing stages of document production. However, some tasks still properly remain within the purview of support staff: final editing for syntax and grammar, proofreading and formatting (including defining page breaks, etc.). Thus, professional keyboarding works best when support staff are likewise equipped with WP terminals to handle the clerical tasks.

Professional word processing terminals can also be taken a step further by turning them into true professional computers. However, this discussion properly belongs to the section on the merger of WP and DP, later in this chapter.

Advanced WP Applications

Many word processing systems offer data base management capabilities, usually referred to in WP circles as records processing. As with any data base, records processing allows you to enter like items of information about a large number of individuals (clients, employees, products). This information can then be retrieved and formatted selectively.

For instance, you can readily identify either the number or the actual individuals who meet a particular set of search criteria (such as all employees who qualify for a specific job opening, fall within the appropriate salary range and would rather work in Philadelphia). Basic mathematical functions can also be performed, such as calculating the average pay of the qualified employees, or their average length of service. When records processing is coupled to the production of correspondence or statistical reports, you have a streamlined information processing system.

For example, in one Western state, all building and industrial trade apprenticeships are coordinated by one agency. At any given time, as many as 10,000 enrollees are involved. In the course of providing services to the enrollees and their unions, as well as in complying with federal reporting requirements, countless references to the apprentices' files are made. Many of these result in the preparation of correspondence, such as notices to appear for progress reviews. Others result in the preparation of extensive statistical reports, such as analyses of the participation of women and minorities in the various trades.

In the manual system, apprentice records were kept in an eight-foot card file. Correspondence was invariably behind, and the entire office shut down for three days at the end of each quarter to compile the requisite federal reports. Now that the system is automated, apprentice records are stored on magnetic media. Records are retrieved by appointment schedule or other parameters upon request. Individual addresses and meeting dates are merged with standard notices for the production of timely correspondence. Best of all, quarterly reports are automatically updated without disrupting the office routine.

THE MERGER OF WP AND DP

As can be seen from the above example, the line between WP and DP is often very fine. Because the merger of WP and DP has such a significant impact on records management, and because it is such a popular concept among automation users, it is very important to understand just how these functions fit together, and how their merger can work for you.

WP and DP: Technology vs. Function

Text is what word processing is all about. It is a narrative medium, with the text meant to be read in its entirety. There is no such thing as reading every 50th word to get a sense of what the document says. Word processing, with its heavy emphasis on format, is quality-oriented. The attention given to the placement and appearance of text on the page relates to its principal function: communication.

Data processing, on the other hand, deals with discrete units of data. Typically, these are meant to be sorted, tabulated or compared. Often, only exception items are of interest. Rarely do you need to look at the whole file. DP is quantity-oriented. Most DP applications simply couldn't be handled manually. If WP is characterized as communication, then DP is characterized as information.

WP/DP Applications

The merger, of course, is quite logical. In many cases, the equipment components are the same. And in many offices, one of the principal forms of activity is retrieving information, manipulating it in some way (comparing or tabulating) and then reformatting it into a narrative report.

For example, a bank leasing corporation handles fleets of vehicles and aircraft, manufacturing plants and other major commercial investments. The lease computations are complex and require sophisticated data processing software. The leases themselves, however, are legal documents that must look professional and be letter-perfect. They are also subject to revisions while the lease is being negotiated. Clearly, word processing is indicated. In this situation, the bank uses a computer for the lease computations. The final results are electronically communicated to word processors and merged into the finished documents that are presented to clients.

Many small companies have similar types of applications, if perhaps on a smaller scale. For instance, monthly reports on all personnel or sales activities must be compiled and presented to management. However, until recently, these companies have not been able to merge their WP/DP applications. No single system could handle both WP and DP successfully, nor could users afford to buy two separate systems and link them together. Even if they were willing to pay the price, the link was not always easy to implement.

To some extent, the above situation still exists. Many word processors are too slow or too limited to handle the kinds of information storage and retrieval applications described above. Many data processing systems offer very limited text processing, typically without any of the sophisticated formatting capabilities found on true word processors. However, advances being made in office automation in general and personal computer technology in particular are rewriting these rules.

THE ROLE OF PERSONAL COMPUTERS

Personal computers started out as hobby machines. Most used a slow technology that made them no more efficient at managing large data files than a typical word processor. Even as these machines began to use larger and faster processors, they still were limited to a single user performing a single function at a time. And their word processing was hardly deserving of the name.

Defining Personal Computers

Today, the situation has changed. One effect of this change has been to make it very difficult to define a personal computer. Aside from obvious differences in capacity, it differs from a traditional mainframe (maxi) or minicomputer in its most basic design: a personal computer is designed to be used by a non-computer person. This does not mean that a DP professional would not choose one. It does mean, however, that you do not have to have a DP background to use one.

Operating Systems

Another way in which personal computers differ from their larger cousins is in their operating systems. CP/M and MS-DOS, for example, are relatively simple to work with. These operating systems are usually stored on a floppy diskette and read into the machine's memory each morning. Thus, personal computers do not need to be left on 24 hours a day, as do most larger machines.

From a programmer's perspective, however, personal computer operating systems are not nearly as powerful as those found on larger-scale computers.

For instance, a system running under CP/M might be able to handle the accounting for a business grossing $500,000 per year. However, it would not be able to handle the range of tasks required to manage the financial affairs of a business grossing $5 million per year.

Business-oriented vs. Hobbyist Computers

At the other end of the scale, there is a difference between a personal computer designed for business use and one intended primarily for the hobbyist. One test of the former is the availability of business programs, such as for accounting, inventory control or word processing. Another test is the quality of the hardware itself.

Typically, business-oriented personal computers use their own video screens rather than hooking up to your television set. Their keyboards are likely to have extra keys that perform special functions, such as deleting or recalling text, at the touch of a button. Most business computers also offer a hard disk storage option, to accommodate the size files that WP and DP applications typically require.

The evolution of personal computers makes it possible to focus on them as the system of choice for a wide range of office information processing requirements. They offer substantial advantages in terms of ease of use, flexibility and, especially, cost.

Because personal computers offer so many advantages, the balance of this chapter will concentrate on office applications (WP and DP) that can be satisfied using these machines. If, instead, you want more information about word processing systems, I suggest my own title, *The Word Processing Handbook: A Step-by-Step Guide to Automating Your Office* (see bibliography).

If your data processing requirements are larger than a personal computer can handle, then I recommend contacting a consultant or other source of data processing expertise. The problem, of course, is defining just where the boundary of "larger than a personal computer can handle" occurs.

The Limits of Personal Computers

The dollar volume of a business is only a partial clue, since a small computer may be perfect for a small problem in a large company. Neither is the volume of data a very reliable indicator. A personal computer can easily store and process 40 megabytes of information, the equivalent of about 20,000 pages of text.

The number of users and the number of programs to be run concurrently is another clue, but again it is not complete. Many personal computers are designed around a central processing unit that can support several terminals, all sharing access to the same disk storage and printers. Often, the CPU allows different users to be working with different programs at the same time. (In computer terms, this mode of operation is referred to as multi-user, multi-tasking.)

The real limit of a personal computer's range is perhaps best defined by the complexity and interdependence of the programs to be run. If you occasionally want to move information from one program to another, a personal computer will work. For instance, you can pull the names of past due accounts from your accounts receivable program and use word processing to send these customers a suitably disgusted letter.

On the other hand, many data processing functions involve a sequence of tasks, such as order entry, inventory control and accounts receivable. Information processed in one module, such as order entry, must flow through several other modules to complete the sales, shipping and accounting processes. Furthermore, this transfer must happen automatically, and often according to a very complex set of rules.

If your data processing requirements fall in the second group, you may well need a more sophisticated computer, as well as the advice of a data processing professional. It is worth stating that there are still many data processing applications that do require a technical background to be set up successfully.

The Evolution of Personal Computers

Several factors have contributed to the rise of personal computers. Understanding these provides a useful orientation to microcomputer technology.

Systems Integration

As noted earlier, personal computers now offer sophisticated word processing linked to a variety of computer programs. Among other things, this means that a single machine can satisfy both WP and DP needs.

Some vendors now offer a special subset of personal computers: professional computers. Professional computers are designed primarily for professional tasks, such as budget preparation, sales analysis or management reporting. Typically, professional machines support the same types of programs as are

run on any business-oriented personal computer. The difference is in the degree of integration.

Almost all personal computers allow you to move information from one function, such as word processing, to another, such as graphics. Using a standard personal computer, you follow a step-by-step process that closes out one function before moving on to the next. This is slow at best, and often very awkward. A professional computer makes the move from function to function appear "seamless."

Professional computers offer high quality video displays. Rather than requiring users to work through menus (lists of functions a computer is ready to perform), the functions are displayed on the screen as file folders, writing tablets and mail boxes. This kind of visual feedback enhances the usefulness of the computer for a non-technical person. You pay more for these features, to be sure, but professional computers are becoming increasingly popular in the office.

Reduced Systems Costs

Miniaturization and improved mass production methods have placed computers within the range of almost every business user. The price of a business-oriented personal computer ranges from roughly $5000 to $15,000 for a typical single-user system, depending upon the software, amount of diskette or disk storage and the quality of printer. This compares very favorably with the cost of a minicomputer, which is more likely to start at $20,000 to $25,000 for the basic system, to which you still must add software and printers.

Today, a small budget no longer precludes your affording a computer. Instead, the determination focuses on the size of your problem and how much computer power you should buy to solve it.

High Level Computer Languages

In the early days of computers, programs were written in assembler or other highly technical and machine-oriented languages. These languages maintained a very close correlation between a line of code (a single program instruction) and a machine operation. Thus, programs written in assembler were very easy for machines to execute, but very time-consuming for people to write. For instance, you might easily require 3000 lines of code to write a program to produce a simple report.

As machines dropped in price, the emphasis shifted to making programmers more efficient. Higher level programming languages such as COBOL and BASIC condense many lines of assembler into a single line of program code. A COBOL or BASIC program still has to be compiled into machine language, of course. However, the same report described above might require a programmer to generate a few hundred lines of written code.

The next level of innovation was query languages. It is important to note that these are not true programming languages. You can't use one to write a program to compute your budget for next year. Instead, query languages are used for filing and retrieving information. They are the languages of data base management systems.

For instance, in the case of the state apprenticeship program described earlier, you would use a query language to enter individual apprentice records and to request a particular report. The statement "I want a report showing the distribution by age, sex and race of participants in the plumbing trades" might be all you type in. You will get the same report it would have taken 3000 lines of assembler or 600 lines of COBOL (and a lot more time) to produce. It is this kind of innovation that makes computers so much easier to use, and that puts them at the service of so many non-computer people.

Availability of Standard Software

Nice as they are, query languages don't satisfy all your data processing needs. Sometimes you do have to analyze your budget or compute your quarterly tax returns. For these kinds of applications, you need a more structured program that takes the data you enter, processes them in some prescribed way and provides the answers you need.

Using structured programs is not particularly difficult for non-computer people to do. The problem is finding the programs in the first place. This is where the standard operating systems play such an important role.

If two different computers use the same operating system, such as CP/M, the same programs will usually run on both machines. Since programs are not restricted to one manufacturer's equipment, there is an incentive for software firms to develop and sell many types of software packages commercially. The quality is certainly mixed, but many good programs are available. As more and more firms enter the competition, your chance of finding a program that meets your needs goes up considerably.

USING DATA PROCESSING

Before analyzing your data processing requirements, you need to understand the types of programs that are available to you. There are two categories of programs: data base management systems, which are generally preferred for managing files of information, and structured programs, which are best for "number-crunching."

Data Base Management Systems

We already know that data bases contain standard items of information about a set of like individuals, be they customers, inventory items or whatever. Data bases typically are constructed in one of two ways. In many applications, the data base is created as the by-product of other computerized transactions. For instance, as purchase orders are keyed into an order entry program, a customer sales history file is created automatically.

Another way to build a data base is to enter information about manual transactions. For instance, your company may not use a computer for purchase orders. Thus, there is no automatic way to capture information about sales in a computerized customer sales history files. However, you still have the option of keying this information into the system from hard copy records, in much the same way that you might have set up a card file.

Manually entered data bases have two potential drawbacks. First of all, you have to enter all that information into the computer. This process can be expensive and must be justified carefully. Don't forget to budget for data verification as well as data input. A simple typographical error in a card system can become a record lost forever in a computer.

The other potential drawback, which really applies to all data bases, is that they are only as good as the query put to them. Typically, this means that they are management-driven. In other words, professional staff are involved in the day-to-day use of the system. Some sophisticated data base packages do allow you to set up automatic production of routine reports. However, data bases are not ideally suited to highly standardized applications. For these, you may require a more traditional structured program.

Structured Programs

A structured program always takes the same basic information, processes it in the same way and produces the same result. As a general rule, flexibility is limited. If you want to change something so minor as the format of a report, a programmer's assistance is required. On the other hand, structured programs function automatically with little requirement for daily management involvement. As long as proper procedures are followed, clerical employees can handle most systems operations.

There are basically two types of structured programs: applications and generic. Each of these has its special niche.

Applications Programs

An applications program is written for a specific application, or business function. Examples include general ledger, accounts payable, accounts receivable, order entry and inventory management. Some applications programs, such as accounting packages, are quite general. They can be adapted to almost any business. Others are specific to certain industries, such as programs for dental practice management or rental property management. There is even a program available for automating records center operations.

Generic Programs

This is software that can be used in almost any business and for almost any application. Perhaps the best example is VisiCalc, the electronic spreadsheet software made famous by VisiCorp (and vice versa).

VisiCalc (and a host of variations on the same theme) allows you to specify row and column titles, as well as the relationships between them, on a computerized spreadsheet. For instance, the categories in your budget might be listed in the rows across the top of your spreadsheet. The columns might be used to represent the four quarters of the year, with a fifth column for the annual total in each budget category. You can then tell the system that it should add rows A and B (perhaps professional salaries and wages for hourly employees), multiply this figure by 60% (for overhead) in row C, and so forth until you have your total budget.

The beauty of electronic spreadsheets is that you now can start asking "what if" questions. In other words, how will your total budget be affected if the union negotiates a 10% salary increase in the third quarter? What if the social security rate goes up at the same time? Once you have defined the row and column titles and their mathematical relationships, you can change the actual numbers on the spreadsheet as often as you wish.

Some electronic spreadsheet programs are linked to graphics packages. For example, once the budget has been finalized, you can display the relative dollar values of the various items in your budget as a bar or pie chart. You can even slide out one section of the pie for emphasis. And all of this can be done without having to reenter the numbers.

Electronic spreadsheets and graphics are only some of the generic programs available. There are forecasting programs, project scheduling and management programs, and statistical programs, to name a few of the more popular ones. In a sense, all of these programs have one thing in common: they offer the non-computer person the ability to perform number-crunching operations with the same flexibility and freedom from programmers traditionally available only with data base management systems and query languages.

The above is just a sampling of the types of programs available for personal computers. If you believe that one or more of these categories is right for you, the next step is to perform a needs analysis and develop a systems specification.

ANALYZING YOUR NEEDS

Procedure for Collecting Information

Performing a needs analysis can be summed up in three simple words: quantify, quantify, quantify! No matter what your application, you need to follow the same basic procedure:

- List the functions you are planning to perform, for example, accounting, job costing, management of circulation in a library. Break each function down into its unit components. For instance, accounting can be broken down into general ledger, payroll, accounts payable, etc.

- For each function, list the files you need to keep and how each is structured. For example, for the general ledger, you need to identify the structure of the chart of accounts, including the coding system and the number of accounts and sub-accounts. You should also specify whether line item entries or journal summaries will be carried in the general ledger. Likewise, you should indicate whether you want the system to track month-to-date and year-to-date expenditures for each account and sub-account. Finally, you should indicate whether you want to keep track of prior-year monthly and yearly expenditure summaries by account for comparison purposes. All of this information is required to ensure that your program offers the capabilities you need, and that your computer has sufficient storage for all your files, including any growth.

- For each function, describe what you want the computer to do. For instance, you may want to use the general ledger to produce financial statements and tax returns, as well as to monitor actual and budgeted expenditures in each account. Be sure to note any unusual requirements or special features that are important to you.

- For each function, you should also describe the processing cycle. This identifies how often the files will be used. For example, you might specify that an order entry program be online during the full work day, with an average of 60 and a maximum of 100 orders posted per day. Be sure to identify all possible concurrent operations, as this has a major impact on the capacity and efficiency of the computer you will need.

Preparing a Flowchart

When you have collected the above information, prepare an overview of your system in a flowchart. This identifies how information gets into the system, how it is processed through the various modules and what reports and other output documents are produced. The flowchart is also very useful for checking the logic of your system. If you're having trouble creating a flowchart for your system, maybe your design isn't quite right.

If you are considering word processing, identify any special features you need, such as generating outlines or tables of contents, or producing extra-wide financial documents. In order to determine the number of machines your workload requires, you should estimate your daily workload in lines per day. If at all possible, define the workload mix in terms of original, repetitive and revision typing.

A full-time typist can produce about 750 lines of typing per day using a standard electric typewriter, and about 1000 lines using an electronic typewriter. With video display equipment, and presuming a fairly equal mix of original, repetitive and revision typing, the same typist can produce about 2000 lines of output typing (about 50 pages). You can divide your total lines or pages by these numbers to determine how many machines you require. Don't forget to adjust the figures downward if your typists also have non-typing duties.

WRITING A SYSTEMS SPECIFICATION

The next step is to present the above information in a systems specification. The purpose is to enable you (or a software firm, programmer or consultant) to compare your requirements to the capabilities of a particular program and decide whether or not the program is suitable.

Aside from the information above, you need to provide some additional information about the size of the system you require. Otherwise, you may find software that does everything you need, but runs on a $100,000 computer. Your specification should cover three major requirements: the amount of main memory, the amount of disk storage, and the number and features of terminals and printers.

Memory

If you don't know the amount of main memory you need, then be sure to describe as fully as you can how your system will be used. It is imperative to identify *peak loading*. This is the heaviest concurrent use to which the computer will be put, including the simultaneous use of programs, terminals and printers. With this information, your computer supplier can help you select a system that will not degrade (slow down unacceptably) under peak loading conditions.

Disk Storage

The amount of disk storage required is a function of your file size (current and projected), and is expressed in bytes. One of the reasons it is so important to quantify your files is to make sure you have all the storage you need.

For example, if you have a data base of 1000 customer records, with 1000 characters of information about each customer, your basic file size is 1 million characters or one Mb. However, your disk must also have room to store your operating system, the programs you are using and any other data or word processing files.

If you can't figure out your file size requirements by yourself, either get help from someone who can or be very sure that you provide complete descriptions of your files to your computer supplier. Whatever you do, don't cut your storage capacity too close. Disk costs have come down dramatically in the past few years. My advice is simple: buy as much storage as you reasonably can. I've yet to meet a computer owner who complained of having too much storage.

Terminals and Printers

The number of terminals you need depends on how many people you want to equip. The number of printers depends upon whether you need draft and/or letter quality output, as well as where your terminals are going to be.

If you are doing word processing, you will want at least one letter quality printer at every typing location. Experience has shown that it simply isn't practical to ask secretaries to use remote printers. However, if you have two or even three word processing terminals at a single location, they can share one printer.

If you are doing data processing, you probably can make do with fewer printers. In this case, it becomes a question of how many pages you need to run and how long you are willing to wait for them to print. Obviously, two printers can double your output, as well as allow two users to print at the same time. My advice is to start with the minimum number of printers that you think you will need, and to add more only as it becomes apparent that your system is inadequate.

When developing terminal and printer specifications, be sure to request any special features that are important. For instance, a movable screen and separate keyboard are important for operator comfort. For your printers, you need to specify the speed, the quality (letter or draft) and any extras such as the need for proportional spacing (which assigns more space to an "m" than an "i") for top quality word processing.

SOLICITING AND EVALUATING PROPOSALS

Use your specification as a request for proposals. Submit it to retail computer outlets, manufacturers and distributors of computers and software. Ask them to submit an item-by-item response to each hardware and software requirement you have listed. Be sure to specify a due date, usually about three weeks from the day you mail your request for proposals.

Although there are many commercial software packages available, locating potential suppliers who should receive your proposal request is not always easy. Good places to start are computer hardware vendors, professional associations and other companies in your same line of business. Consultants can also be helpful, particularly if they are familiar with your industry. In addition, many of the computer magazines listed in the bibliography advertise and review software. If you don't subscribe to any of them, you may find copies in your local retail computer store or public library.

Evaluating Software Sources

Evaluate vendors' responses to your request for proposals very carefully. Since software is harder to obtain than hardware, focus your analysis on this area first. Make sure the programs incorporate all the information essential to your operation. Ask to see copies of sample reports, and look at the training manuals to see how the programs work. If you find a program that looks good, ask for a demonstration. If at all possible, take a few minutes to work with the program yourself, as well as having a salesman show it to you.

If you can't find programs that do everything you need, ask about the possibility of having standard programs customized to your needs. Before entering into such an agreement, make sure you understand what it will cost. You should also ask about documentation and training support. In other words, you should receive a copy of all the program modifications that were made, and you should be trained in how the modifications work.

Evaluating Hardware

Once you have narrowed your choice to one or two software sources, it is time to look at the hardware each runs on. In evaluating hardware, there are two primary issues to consider.

State of the Art Technology

It is much more important to find a system (software and hardware) that meets your specification than it is to worry about whether you are getting the latest hardware technology. However, you must be very precise about defining your needs, if you don't want to leave your computer behind. For instance, if you expect to have two or more people running different programs at the same time, you are going to require a more powerful machine than if your system will be limited to a single user. It is for this reason that it is so important to describe processing cycles and concurrent uses in your specification.

Growth Path

This is also much more important than the level of technology per se. Most companies stay with a computer for at least three years and usually five or more. After that, both your needs and the technology may have changed enough to warrant a reassessment. However, even then, you may still want to stay with the same basic system.

Look for computers with expansion room: the ability to add more main memory; the ability to add larger disks and multiple disk drives; the ability to use tape drives or removable disk cartridges for file backup once your disk storage exceeds 20Mb or so (up to that point floppy diskettes are usually acceptable); the ability to add as many terminals, printers and communications links as you are likely to need; and the ability to link two or more computers together in a network. Ask your supplier if you can upgrade your computer to a larger model without having to reprogram your applications.

If you are working with a programmer or computer company, look for one that will grow with you. Your next-door neighbor's sister-in-law may be a terrific computer hot-shot, but will she always be around when you need her?

PAYING FOR YOUR COMPUTER

This issue has two facets: 1) Should you wait until technology gets cheaper, better, etc? 2) How do you do a cost-benefit analysis?

When to Buy

The answer to the first question is actually fairly simple: What will it cost you to wait? If buying a computer makes sense today, then waiting does not make sense. You will be continuing an inefficient operation when help is available. Further, at the end of the waiting period, the same question will apply. If you wait one more year, won't there again be something even better? At some point, you just have to jump in. The only time it really makes sense to wait is if your business plans are unsettled or your current need is marginal.

Conducting a Cost-Benefit Analysis

The answer to the second question is more difficult. Traditionally, cost-benefit determinations are resolved through a return-on-investment analysis (ROI). In this process, you compute all your costs for the next five years for both your current and your proposed system. In theory, as a result of labor savings and increased productivity, somewhere in the third year you reach the crossover point: your system has paid for itself.

The problem with ROIs is that they are often based on faulty projections of labor savings. People tend to doctor the figures (with varying degrees of subtlety) to make the equations come out. However, even if the figures don't look right on the first pass, there may still be a sound justification for equipment acquisition. The problem arises from the difficulty of incorporating intangible benefits into a bottom-line equation.

Unless you are in a very structured industry, it is often difficult to assign a real dollar value to such benefits of automation as expanded access to information, faster response to customer requests or better control over operations. However, this is where the real benefits of your new system probably lie.

To oversimplify a bit, there are two ways to look at technology: you can do the same work you are doing today, but with fewer people; or, you can do more work, and perhaps more kinds of work, with the same number of people. It is the latter case that usually applies. You may have trouble demonstrating this approach in an ROI, but if you can use automation in this way, your system is likely to pay for itself long before it becomes obsolete.

USING YOUR COMPUTER

Depending upon the type of computer you buy, you may or may not receive training and implementation assistance from your computer supplier. Chances are that you won't. If training is available, it is strongly recommended, even if you have to pay extra for it.

In either case, when your computer first arrives, you need to do two things. First, allow some time to familiarize yourself (or whoever will be involved) with the system *before* you load real data onto it. Second, make use of that time. This requires a certain amount of self-discipline. There is a real temptation to rush the conversion or else to let the machines sit idle because you are "not quite ready." Don't fall into either of these traps.

Maintaining Your Computer

Once your system is up and running, you have two other issues to deal with. The first is deciding whether to put your system on a maintenance contract. There are several contract options to choose from. One way to save money is to take your computer in to the shop. However, if you depend on your system for day-to-day operations, you probably will want in-office service.

Even so, you are not necessarily tied to your hardware supplier. Third party maintenance companies are appearing on the scene in ever greater numbers. The reliable ones are factory-authorized, and often undercut sales organizations' maintenance prices.

Ask maintenance suppliers about their monthly contract fees and what they cover. You should also ask how time and materials are charged if you do not sign a contract. Find out if you will receive the same service priority if you are not on a regular maintenance contract. If so, you may decide that you can afford to self-insure, especially since you should have a 90-day warranty period to test out your new machine.

Maintaining Your Computer Files

The second issue concerns the application of records management principles to your new computer system. The first question to resolve is how much information to retain on magnetic media. The answer usually lies in your need to maintain complete files of incoming and outgoing documentation, in order, and in one place. Therefore, most companies store their WP and DP records as hard-copy printouts, along with other records to which they pertain.

Hard-copy storage is especially important for long-term records. Magnetic media have a limited shelflife, which may range from one to several years depending upon storage conditions. Another problem is that your disks and tapes become unreadable when you change your word processing or computer system. While it is possible to convert media from one manufacturer's computer to another, this step is often overlooked for older storage media.

Computer files, once damaged, are often expensive to recreate. In some cases, reconstruction may be impossible. To protect against accidental loss, you should establish a regular procedure for copying your computer files and storing them in fireproof cabinets or off the premises. How often you copy your files depends upon how your computer is used, but daily or weekly backup is usually recommended. Then, in the event of an accidental loss, your files can be recovered to within a few days of the date of the loss.

This leads to a final point, one already made in earlier chapters. Your word and data processing records are subject to the same classification and retention requirements as other records. You should provide for these records in your classification system. It is also very important that your machine-readable records be properly scheduled for final disposition.

10

Disaster: Planning For Recovery

by Julia Niebuhr Eulenberg

Almost daily, someone opens the door of an office, central files or records storage area, and discovers water on the floor, on records containers and on the records themselves—with water still dripping from a broken pipe in the ceiling. This is only one possible scenario for disaster. Others include fire, smoke and subsequent water damage from firefighting procedures, or the mud and debris of retreating flood waters.

Faced with any of these disasters, would you know what to do first? Would you know which records were the most important, or the most vulnerable to damage from heat, dirt and water? Would you know where those records were located? Would your microfilm and data processing vendors or service bureaus be able to help you in the event of such a disaster?

A written disaster plan is the most effective insurance you can have against a disaster involving your organization's records. But, like all insurance policies, your disaster plan must be in place before a disaster occurs.

The best justification for a written disaster plan is the importance of the records it covers. The effort required to write a disaster plan for your organization's records is both cost and time effective. Most people think that disasters can't happen to them. But disasters can and do happen. You have good reason to worry about the safety of your records.

This chapter addresses the basics of disaster recovery. Its goal is to convince you that disaster planning for records is justifiable, to provide you with guidelines for developing a disaster recovery plan for your company's records and to help you determine which recovery efforts you and your disaster team can handle, as well as those which will require professional help. The bibliography suggests additional resources for readers who want more detailed information on disaster planning and recovery techniques.

TYPES OF DISASTERS

Fire Damage

A fire generally inflicts more than one type of damage on records. The intense heat generated by a fire may damage records which otherwise seem to be all right. This is particularly true with magnetic media and photographic materials. Moreover, even after a fire has been extinguished, enough heat may remain in enclosed areas to cause secondary fires. Delayed ignition of paper records can occur in file cabinets as late as three days after the initial fire has been extinguished.

Fire also produces smoke damage. The impact of such damage varies from negligible to severe, again depending on the vulnerability of the media. Discoloration of most paper records does not affect their value, and gritty smoke particles can be brushed off or otherwise removed from paper with relatively little difficulty. However, the effect of smoke damage on magnetic media and photographic materials can be much more significant. In the case of magnetic media, the particles and their greasy residue may damage data processing or word processing equipment, as well as the media themselves. In such cases, professional advice from vendors or consultants in media retrieval is always advisable.

Water is another component of fire disasters. In some cases, water may be used to extinguish fires without inflicting any water damage on paper records. A firefighting technique known as fogging uses only enough water, in mist form, to extinguish the fire. Often the heat of the fire dries off the disaster area and its contents, leaving no visible water damage. Paper records rarely suffer from fogging; however, photographic materials and magnetic media subjected to fogging techniques will be water damaged, and appropriate recovery actions must be instituted.

Fire damage may create safety hazards that necessitate relocating the damaged materials. Once the immediate danger of the fire is over, recovery team members can remove records from the disaster area, using caution in dealing with filing cabinets or other record containers that retain heat. As in all disasters, recovery depends on staying organized and following your established disaster plan (see below).

Water Disasters

Water can also inflict multiple forms of damage to records. Water alone is damaging to all records media; the addition of dirt and other contaminants requires a combination of salvage efforts, and may require professional help from conservators, restorers or service bureaus. Clean water can become contaminated as it flows through unused crawl spaces, acoustical tile ceilings and record containers full of water-soluble ink and paper. Flood waters may bring additional debris to the disaster site.

Water damage also presents its own safety hazards: the potential of electric shock is always present, broken glass and other hazards may be hidden in the water covering the disaster area and the weight of water-soaked paper records may make lifting record containers and opening the drawers of file cabinets dangerous.

Irradiated records are a possible consequence of fire or water disasters for some organizations. If radiation contamination is a possibility in your case, you should check the records at the disaster site with radiation monitors before moving them to drying facilities. Irradiated records should be dried only in facilities that can be decontaminated following the drying process.

THE PROBABILITY OF A DISASTER

What is the likelihood of a disaster befalling your organization's records? Is it really necessary to invest any time and effort in recovery planning before a disaster? Several factors suggest that the danger is great and advance planning essential.

- Many companies today are located in modern office buildings whose windows do not open and whose climate control and support systems are maintained year-round by complicated networks of water-filled pipes running between the floors and walls of the building.

- Water is the most effective and most frequently used firefighting tool.

- Inactive records are often stored in the basements of buildings and are thus extremely vulnerable to minor flooding that may go unnoticed for several days or even months.

- Depending on the temperature and humidity levels in the disaster area, most major recovery decisions must be made and carried out in less than 72 hours.

- Few service bureaus would be able to handle the disaster recovery requirements for all of their clients in the event of an area-wide disaster like that caused by flooding or a hurricane.

- Much is still unknown about the effects of smoke, heat and water damage on data processing media, or about the best way to resolve such damage.

- Mold can develop in water-damaged records that have been returned to the storage area without adequate salvage action.

If the records you keep are of any value to your organization, they are important enough to protect. If your organization is concerned about unnecessary expenditures of money, it should *require* a written disaster plan that specifies which records are worth saving and which can be cost-effectively and legally discarded. It should also require that the plan specify the appropriate salvage action to be taken in the event of various kinds of disasters.

DEVELOPING A DISASTER PLAN

The first step in writing a disaster plan is to review your organization's records carefully. The kinds of records your company creates and uses will partly determine how you handle the disaster. Some records are more important than others, and some storage media are more easily damaged than others.

Whoever is in charge of your organization's records management is the most logical person to write a disaster plan. As a result of a records inventory, he already knows which records are the most important for the company's day-to-day operation and may already have established a vital records protection program to protect them. The records manager also knows what kinds of records media (paper, micrographics and magnetic media) your organization uses.

Vital Records Program

A vital records program assures preservation of your company's most important records, elsewhere, in a usable format. In the event of a disaster, a vital records program allows you to move quickly to the recovery of less vital, but still important records. A vital records program allows your company to stay in business, despite a disaster. Vital records protection must be an ongoing process. It cannot be something that you suddenly do when you are faced with a disaster. Your vital records program must be in place and tended regularly, if it is to have any meaning.

Identifying Vital Records

Vital records are the records that your company must have in order to continue its regular, day-to-day operations. These records include perhaps 5% of all the records that your organization creates and uses. The following questions may help you determine which records should be considered vital.

- Will these records assure the company of collecting the income due it? (For example, accounts receivable records, contracts.)

- Will these records protect the company against possible fraud or overpayment of claims against it? (For example, accounts payable records, contracts, stockholders' records, pension benefits.)

- Do these records provide adequate information about company assets? (For example, equipment and product inventories, securities listings, real estate deeds and/or maps; even your disaster plan.)

- Are these *essential* records—must the organization have them to stay in business? Or, are they only *important* records—would the organization function more easily if it had them, as well as the essential records? (For example, general ledgers and even journal entries could be reconstructed from accounts payable and receivable files, if necessary.)

The difference between vital and important records is sometimes difficult to sort out. However, you can resolve this issue by giving both protection. You are less likely to have trouble differentiating between these higher levels of record value and the one below which includes useful and nonessential records. The latter require no special protection, and should not be included in the vital records protection program.

Vital records protect your organization's financial and legal status; they preserve the rights of your organization, its employees, clients or customers, and its stockholders. Some vital records may be inactive; their pattern of daily use does not detract from their value. These are still essential records, required over the long run, if your organization is to stay in business.

Protecting Vital Records

One of the most common methods of vital records protection is duplication. Obviously, not every record that your organization creates can or should be backed up or duplicated. Such a requirement is not only expensive, it is bound to fail, because no one can keep up. You must determine what should be saved and establish a regular routine for duplicating such materials and storing them off site. Duplication of records may include a variety of formats: micrographics, paper copies or duplicates of data processing media.

Dispersal or storage at one or more different locations is the second step in vital records protection. In fact, some vital records are routinely duplicated and dispersed to different offices or locations as part of regular business operations, and need not be duplicated again. A vital records survey will indicate which records should be included in a special effort.

In today's automated office, many vital records are created in machine-readable formats (for example, micrographics and data processing media). In some ways, this makes the updating required for many vital records easier for you to assure. In other ways, it complicates your vital records protection program. You must be sure, if you are dealing with duplicates in machine-readable form, that you back up both the records and the equipment required to read them. This is why many people still suggest maintaining the vital records copy in a paper format. You may choose to provide both machine-readable and paper format (for example, the data processing disk or tape and the paper printout of an accounting record); this is not an unreasonable choice if both are regularly produced for active records use.

Storing Vital Records

Ideally, vital records storage should be off site. For vital records which cannot be duplicated (because the duplicate would not be accepted as a legal document) or which cannot be stored off site for various reasons, you should consider storage in fire-resistant vaults, cabinets or safes. (If the vital record is on either photographic or data processing media, you should use caution in choosing fire-resistant storage equipment; be certain that it is guaranteed for these types of media.)

The off-site storage area should not be so far away from the regular business site that it is inaccessible, nor so close that it is vulnerable to the same disaster.

The most economical and effective method of records protection depends both on the records value and on the probable severity and extent of a disaster. Boxes of duplicated records stored on a few feet of shelf in a commercial records center may be perfectly adequate. On the other hand, if your company has a significant amount of machine-readable vital records, you may need to provide a fairly extensive off-site vital records center, complete with equipment and adequate working space for staff.

Records and updates of vital records should be transferred to the vital records storage area on a regular basis (usually weekly or monthly). Old versions should be destroyed regularly, as they are updated. You may wish to use a special form to indicate information about your company's vital records (see Figure 10.1). You may also choose to develop a vital records master listing, to help you maintain continuing control over your vital records program. Such a listing would cover vital records by department or work group and should include both retention periods and regular update periods.

Figure 10.1: Vital Records Information Listing

Records Title (Records Series as Files Title)	Originating Department	Back-up Information			Comments
		Location	Format	Generation	

Other Records Priorities

The disaster plan that you write should include specific information about your company's records. Initial recovery efforts should concentrate on the most important and the most vulnerable records, in terms of records media and records title (either records series or specific file title).

Recovery Priority by Records Media

Figure 10.2 gives recovery priorities for various types of records media. In addition, initial and follow-up salvage techniques are listed for each records medium along with other pertinent comments. The most vulnerable records media are magnetic media, most photographic materials and coated papers. These must be dealt with immediately, in order to prevent further damage. Other types of papers can be dealt with within 48 hours (depending on the extent of damage), and diazo and vesicular films can be left until last.

Recovery Priority by Records Title

Some records will also have a recovery priority based on their records title. Such records may not be considered vital records, but are still necessary to the long-term operation of the company. Figure 10.3 lets you list the recovery priority of your company's records by records title. Each of the areas to be filled in is explained below:

- *Records title* may be limited to specific records within a records series, or it may include the entire records series.

- *Originating department* should be specified since, if the record consists of multiple copies, and the damaged records are neither originals nor of priority to the work group or office involved in the disaster, they do not have recovery priority. Moreover, if a copy is available elsewhere, it may be an acceptable substitute for the damaged copy. Each time a damaged record can be eliminated from recovery actions, your company saves time and money.

- *Records media* information, both about the original and back-up media, is extremely important. For example, if original microfilm records are damaged, but back-up diazo copies are available, the copies can be used initially and may later satisfy legal requirements for the damaged materials, if properly documented.

Figure 10.2: Recovery Priority by Type of Records Media

Media	Recovery Priority	Salvage Techniques				Comments
		Initial		Follow-up		
		Action	Purpose	Action	Purpose	
Magnetic Media Mag tapes Disc packs Floppy diskettes and disks Flexible disks Audio and video tape cassettes	Immediately	Contact vendor	To obtain professional advice	May include freeze or vacuum drying, special cleaning techniques or professional assistance in retrieving data.	To remove all moisture and other contaminants from the media; to access data in case of damaged media	Such advice should be sought well in advance of a disaster. Contingency plans for data and word processing groups may be advisable. Heat and water damage to media may result in subsequent damage to hardware or to irretrievability of data. Proper back-up and salvage procedures are essential. It is worth noting that such records are among the easiest to duplicate and store off site.
Photographic Materials Color films and photographs	Immediately	Once wet, keep wet	To avoid further damage and image loss			Color dyes are inherently unstable and should be handled immediately to prevent loss of color and other damage.

Figure 10.2: Recovery Priority by Type of Records Media (cont.)

Media	Recovery Priority	Initial		Salvage Techniques			Comments
		Action	Purpose	Follow-up			
				Action	Purpose		
Color films and photographs (cont.)	Within 48 hrs.	Obtain professional advice and/or assistance with cleaning, drying and restoring.		Freeze if professional help must be delayed longer than 48 hrs.	To stabilize color dyes		
Silver or emulsion films and photographs	Immediately	Immerse totally in water	To avoid further damage	Seek professional advice and help with cleaning and drying. Freeze only if necessary.	To restore film to original state Freezing may lead to image damage, but less damage is likely to be caused by freezing than by delayed treatment.		
	Within 48 hrs.	Formaldehyde, to a 1% solution, may be added to cool, clean water. One teaspoon of salt may be added to hard water	To avoid softening or frilling of gelatin or emulsion layer. If materials are allowed to dry out, they tend to stick to adjacent surfaces, with image loss and other damage.				

Figure 10.2: Recovery Priority by Type of Records Media (cont.)

Media	Recovery Priority	Salvage Techniques				Comments
		Initial		Follow-up		
		Action	Purpose	Action	Purpose	
Diazo or vesicular (duplicate) films	Last	If time and staff are available, rinse off and lay out flat to dry; otherwise, leave until last.	To prevent water spotting and curling of films or fiche	Wash with liquid detergent and rinse and lay out on absorbent paper to dry.	To remove water spots and other contaminants and to restore film	Diazo and vesicular films are nearly impervious to water damage and should clean up easily. Diazo films sometimes fade with age. Fading or other damage discovered after the disaster can be related to poor quality control rather than to the disaster.
Paper Bond, rag, duplicating, other	Within 48 hrs. (depending on temperature and humidity levels at disaster site and on extent of damage) In fires, paper is least vulnerable media.	Air dry in well-ventilated area: If volume of wet records is large, consider freeze or vacuum drying.	To prevent further deterioration of paper materials and eruption of mold or fungus	May include freeze or vacuum drying. If mold erupts, treat with fungicides.	To remove moisture from materials and to reduce humidity levels in damaged materials; to eradicate mold.	In high-humidity levels, deterioration of wet paper records can begin within 2-3 hours.
Coated or clay papers	Immediately	Freeze	To hold damaged materials until freeze or vacuum drying can be arranged	Freeze or vacuum drying	To remove all moisture from paper, without damaging or removing coated surface	Freeze or vacuum drying is the only successful recovery technique for this medium.

Figure 10.3: Recovery Priority by Records Title Listing

Records Title	Originating Department	Records Media	Back-up Information			Comments
			Location	Format	Generation	

- *Other back-up information*, such as location, format and generation (e.g., original or first copy), will enable affected work groups to update their back-up records while they continue working.

- *Comments* lets you list any other information that will help determine the recovery priority of the listed records.

Management Support

An effective disaster recovery operation requires management support. The person in charge of the operation may need to supervise staff members from other work groups during the recovery operation. He may need to acquire additional supplies and equipment without delay, or be in work areas after authorized working hours. He will undoubtedly need to make some decisions on the spot, rather than wait for approval from management levels that may not yet be affected by the disaster. A statement of purpose for the plan and signed approval by management of the final plan are guarantees of such support.

Figure 10.4 suggests a way to begin. The "Statement of Purpose" is a written justification to management for the time and effort that have been put into developing a written disaster plan. The rest of the disaster plan must be specific to your company's needs and records; that is, it should acknowledge the specific requirements of the company's records media, records priorities and an ongoing vital records protection program. In addition to such organization-specific information, the disaster plan should include copies of the lists of disaster team members, emergency phone numbers and disaster box contents (see below).

Figure 10.5 is a disaster plan approval sheet, which should be signed by the appropriate level of management and attached to each copy of the written disaster plan. This approval sheet provides authorization for action in the face of an emergency.

You now have a beginning and an ending for your disaster plan. The middle must include the details of how to handle an actual disaster. This portion of the plan should be very specific. Sections of it may even resemble procedures manuals. The goal of a written disaster plan is to impose order on the chaos at the disaster site.

Figure 10.4: Disaster Plan for the Records Management Program of (Company Name)

Statement of Purpose

The disaster plan outlined below should be followed in the event of an emergency or disaster involving the business records of _____(Company Name)_____ to safeguard, salvage and/or preserve such records.

The disaster team named within this plan is to be considered a working team. In the event of a disaster, members of the disaster team should be prepared to follow instructions and to carry out appropriate salvage and recovery procedures for water or otherwise damaged business records.

The disaster team leader(s) should be prepared to train and to supervise individual team members in carrying out appropriate salvage and recovery techniques. Disaster team leader(s) should also be trained to recognize situations that require professional assistance, and to work with the professionals should they need to be involved in the salvage operations.

One member of the disaster team should be designated to contact other members of the disaster team. Another member of the disaster team should be designated to notify management, supervisory and other appropriate staff on the emergency contact list.

(OTHER COMMENTS RELEVANT TO YOUR
ORGANIZATION SHOULD FOLLOW)

Figure 10.5: Disaster Plan Approval Sheet

The following salvage priorities have been established for the business records of (Company Name) in the event of a disaster.

These priorities are based on the value of the records to the company, on the secondary availability of the records elsewhere in the company or through other sources outside the company, and on the salvage priorities for the specific records media. This disaster plan should be followed as it is written. Modifications or changes in the plan should be approved in writing, by (Records Manager) and/or (Appropriate Management Level)*.

Approval for changes in recovery priorities should be made in writing, even for those changes made during actual salvage actions, although such approval may be obtained after the fact, if necessary.

Date of Disaster Plan: _____

Approved by: (Records Manager)

_____
(Appropriate Management Level)
_____

*The appropriate management level may vary from organization to organization, but should be high enough to assure cooperation during salvage procedures from staff at all levels.

HANDLING A DISASTER

Following the Plan

The disaster plan for your company's records was written after a careful, thoughtful review of your records. But such calm, collected reasoning rarely prevails at disaster sites. The disaster recovery period is not the time to rewrite a plan that was prepared before the disaster occurred. The best advice now is to follow the plan.

If for any reason you cannot follow parts of the disaster plan or if unexpected situations arise, you should document the changes you make or authorize. You will need this information later, when you review the overall recovery effort, and you may need it as legal backup for auditors or insurance claims adjusters.

Notifying Team Members

After you have appraised the extent of the damage at the disaster site, you are ready to begin implementing your disaster plan. The first step is to notify the members of the disaster team (see below) and emergency contacts (see Figure 10.6). Supervisors and department heads must be alerted to the disaster and its extent, so that the safety of the disaster team staff and the company's physical assets can be protected. Normal work operations may need to be halted for the length of time required to clean up the area or to move to temporary office space. These are decisions that only management can make.

Figure 10.6: Emergency Phone List

Name	Organization Title	Department	Phone Work/Emergency

(The following functional titles should be included on this list: emergency director for the organization or site; facilities, maintenance or custodial staff for affected site(s); managers or department heads; data and/or word processing managers; librarian; and the records manager, if the last is not already included as a leader or member of the disaster team. Nonstaff members should include such professionals as water disaster recovery experts, fumigators, emergency water removal firms.)

As soon as possible, find out when the disaster team will be allowed on the site to begin salvage operations. The timing for this step may be crucial to a successful recovery. Safety should be the only reason to keep the disaster team away from the site.

Role of the Leader

At the disaster site, the person in charge of the recovery effort should be involved in as little hands-on work as possible. He must make sure that the initial disaster has been dealt with and that clean-up crews have begun both to clean up the area and to resolve any new or potential problems, such as electric shock hazards or secondary fires. He must make sure that additional supplies and necessary equipment are on the way. He should be in contact with other managers and appropriate staff members. He should also be in contact with any outside members of the disaster team, such as service bureau and data processing and word processing service representatives.

Throughout the disaster, the leader must be available to the disaster team and to the overall recovery operation, to answer specific questions, to initiate subsequent phases of the recovery operation and to determine other remedial steps. He cannot afford to become involved in the flurry of activity going on around him or to leave the disaster area to hunt for supplies.

The Disaster Box

Having a well-stocked disaster box is like carrying an umbrella. An umbrella may not keep you completely dry, but it will keep you from getting soaked. In the same way, a disaster box won't see you completely through a disaster, but it will allow the work to get started while additional supplies are gathered.

The disaster box should contain enough supplies to allow the disaster team to begin work immediately. The disaster box should be stored away from the primary records holding area, above ground level. If your company is large, you may want to stock more than one disaster box and to store them in separate locations. A word of caution: some of the contents have a limited shelf life and should be checked periodically; some recovery supplies are flammable and should not be stored in records storage areas. Figure 10.7 suggests a format for listing the contents of a disaster box, along with information about the location and availability of additional supplies.

A well-stocked disaster box should contain:

- Absorbent paper: 5-20 reams; optimum size, 9×12 inches. *Do not use newsprint for archival or permanent records series.*

- Bone folders or plastic letter openers: 2.

- Sharp knives: 2-3.

- Roll of plastic sheeting (clear or black) or one dozen 9×12-foot plastic drop cloths.

Figure 10.7: Disaster Box Supplies Listing

Item	Storage Location	Purpose	Immediate Supply on Hand	Local Supplier
				(List by firm name, address, phone number— include emergency phone number, if available.)

- Mylar sheets: 2-3 dozen.

- Small crowbar or large screwdriver: 1.

- Multicell flashlight with extra batteries: 1. *Replace batteries every six months.*

- Clothesline or nylon fishing line: 200 feet.

- Colored chalk: 1 box.

- Paper tags with string or wire holders: 25.

- Small, hand-held fire extinguisher, water-based: 1.

- Manila file folders: 1 box.

- Large, strong plastic garbage bags: 10.

- Fungus and mold inhibiting chemicals: initial supply.

- Rubber gloves: 4 pair.

- Protective face masks: 8.

- AM/FM transistor radio: 1. *Check batteries every six months, if necessary.*

- Absorbent toweling: 50 feet (ten 2×5-foot towels).

- Scissors: 2.

- *A copy of the disaster plan and the emergency phone list—wrapped in a waterproof packet.*

- Disaster recovery guidelines (see bibliography), wrapped in a waterproof packet.

The Disaster Team

The disaster team is a working team; it has no honorary members. The team's leader (in most cases, the records manager) should select individuals who can work together, under his supervision.

Members from Within the Company

The leader should establish a good working relationship with the company's facilities or maintenance staff, and may wish to include a member of this staff on the disaster team. The person should be familiar with your location's electrical, plumbing and heating systems, able to assist in supervising repair and clean-up operations or to handle them himself.

Other individuals who make good disaster team members include files clerks, specialized media clerks or technicians, and secretaries. (No more than one from each work group should be selected, to limit disruption of normal work routines as much as possible.) Such people are familiar with the records themselves and will in some cases already be aware of the vulnerability of certain types of records.

Outside Representatives

If your firm's records include microfilm, data processing or word processing media, some outsiders may also belong on the disaster team. These include the service representatives from your microfilm service bureau and your data processing or word processing vendors. These people may not work with you throughout the entire recovery operation, but their help early in the operation may be crucial to a successful recovery of the specialized media they service.

The disaster team should receive some training in disaster recovery techniques before a disaster occurs. In addition to hands-on training, a practice recovery operation should be staged once the disaster plan is in place. All members of the disaster team should attend this session. Although the sights, sounds and smells of a disaster are impossible to simulate, the experience of at least one emergency drill will give the team a better idea of what to expect. This will enable them to work faster and more efficiently in the event of a real disaster.

Figure 10.8 provides a sample format for listing disaster team members. Both work and emergency (home) phone numbers should be included on the list—disasters do not respect regular work schedules. For the same reason, the team leader should keep a copy of the listing at home.

Figure 10.8: Disaster Team for the Records Management Program of (Company Name)

	Name	Organization Title	Phone Work/Emergency
Leader(s):			

Telephone Committee:
    Contact Team Members:
    Notify Emergency List:			

Members:			

A telephone committee of one or two individuals will free other team members to begin work immediately while the remainder of the team is assembled. The telephone committee may have no other recovery responsibility, so that this task could be assigned to the receptionist or to some other individual elsewhere in the company.

The Recovery Operation

The first step is to review your disaster plan, with special regard to all of the recovery priorities established for your company's records. Locate those records with the highest priority, remove them from the disaster site to the recovery area first and begin appropriate recovery activities immediately.

Paper Records

Paper records may be air dried if only a small volume is involved or if water damage of the individual records is not extensive. Look around for drying space; large expanses of file cabinets may provide many linear feet of drying space, for example. Cover the cabinets with plastic sheeting, to protect the contents and the surfaces of the cabinets from water damage.

Paper records that have suffered more extensive water damage may be interleaved with absorbent paper. To interleave, place a dry sheet of clean, absorbent paper between the wet sheets. Use no more than a ratio of one dry sheet to five wet sheets for bound records, to prevent breakage or severe warping of the bindings. Unbound records can be interleaved one for one, if water damage is extensive, although a ratio of one dry sheet to from five to 20 wet sheets is usually adequate.

Film and Other Photographic Records

Film and other photographic materials that have sustained water damage should be kept wet until they can be professionally cleaned and dried. If film or other photographic materials have sustained even slight water damage, completely flood them with cool, clean water and keep them wet, to ensure a successful recovery. Allowing water-damaged photographic materials to dry out before treatment may lead to severe damage and loss of film images. The addition of salt to hard water (one teaspoon per gallon of clean, cool water) or a 1% solution of formaldehyde added to ten gallons of water, may help prevent softening of the gelatin or emulsion layer. (Recovery priorities for film and photographic materials were listed in Figure 10.2.)

Diazo and vesicular films can be left until late in the recovery process. Some fading may occur in older diazo films, but generally such films are able to withstand significant levels of water damage, without being ruined.

All film and photographic materials should be reviewed for residual damage after the disaster recovery efforts have been completed. Apparent damage should be checked against control copies, to be certain that the problem is really related to the disaster, and not to a poor quality control program.

Magnetic Media

Magnetic media should be professionally cleaned and dried before they are used again. Even then, recovery of water-damaged magnetic media is a risky business, with no guarantees. The ideal situation is for important data to be backed up, so that recovery can take place at the keyboard or at other input devices. If this is not possible, you should contact your vendor or service bureau; they may be able to help you themselves, or to put you in touch with the few experts in this field who can solve such problems. The lack of general knowledge regarding the recovery of water-damaged magnetic media is the best reason for consulting your vendor in advance of a disaster, and for backing up important magnetic media.

Freeze and Vacuum Drying

As noted above, small volumes of water-damaged records can often be air dried or interleaved and dried in facilities located at or near the disaster site. Large volumes of records, extensive water damage or certain types of records may indicate the use of freeze or vacuum drying techniques. Vacuum drying is the only effective technique for the recovery of water-damaged coated papers (see Figure 10.2).

The freeze and vacuum drying process is expensive and will also require an investment of time and effort on the part of your staff. However, it does buy you time. While records are frozen, you can deal with more immediate problems and you can determine how necessary the recovery of the frozen records actually is. It may be possible, for example, simply to keep them frozen until they reach the end of their retention period, and then to destroy them without ever having to perform any further salvage actions.

Remember that freezing does not dry records, nor does it permanently inhibit mold or fungus formation. Subsequent drying and sterilization processes will still be required for many records. Furthermore, records which have been water-damaged are more susceptible to mold and fungus growth, whether or not they have been frozen. Once thawed, the records are once again wet records, but now at an advanced stage of water damage.

Vacuum drying has been used successfully with all types of records media. However, because the process involves the use of a certain amount of heat, you should consult your vendor or service representative before using it to dry magnetic media or photographic materials.

Two major problems remain with the vacuum drying process. First, vacuum dryers or similar equipment are generally located only in large urban areas. Even when one is located near you, it may not be accessible to the general public. Second, because vacuum drying is expensive, you must determine whether or not the value of the records involved justifies it before you begin. Your disaster plan should address this question, and you should attempt to make some sort of contact with the vacuum drying facility during the planning stages.

Whatever drying technique or combination of techniques you use, you should use the drying period to make some assessments of the records and the salvage operation. The records themselves should be reviewed and appraised as to their actual value. If back-up records can be located, you should make no further effort to salvage damaged records. Any extensive salvage efforts must be based on some established cost-benefit ratio or proof of need.

If you decide to discard records because you have determined that they have no value, are backed up elsewhere in the company, can be less expensively replaced or cannot be reclaimed at all, you should document your decision. If there is ever any need for the missing records, you will be able to show that their destruction was carried out for legitimate reasons. Your documentation may also be required for insurance purposes.

REVIEWING THE DISASTER PLAN

How did the salvage operation go? How well did your disaster plan meet the needs of an actual disaster? Should the plan be updated or revised? If another disaster occurred, what would you do differently? What were your successes? Were you able to get the supplies and equipment that you needed, when you needed them? Did you need things that were not on your list or that were not readily available? What were they? Did your disaster team work well together? Is more staff training needed?

You will be able to answer such questions much better immediately after the disaster than if you wait several months. You will also be more likely to revise the disaster plan or to make other changes related to carrying out future disaster recovery actions if you make them soon after the disaster.

Once you have completed the major recovery activities and made the necessary changes in your disaster plan, you can begin to breathe more easily. However, you still need to remember that damaged records remain more vulnerable than other records. Even after the records have been returned to their storage areas, they should be checked periodically during the first year, and annually thereafter, for signs of mold, fungus or other deterioration.

You have now reached the end of the disaster recovery process. You should feel very confident. You've taken your disaster plan through its most rigorous test—and succeeded. With luck, you will never have to get this far. But a written plan still makes good business sense: it is your best insurance in the event of a disaster.

11

Records Centers

by Terence Murphy

A separate storage area for inactive records is called a records center. This chapter will tell you if you really need one and, if you do, how to decide between setting up an in-house records center or using a commercial facility. It also explains how to set up your own in-house center and keep it running smoothly.

DO YOU NEED A RECORDS CENTER?

In most cases, 95% of references to business records occur in the first two years. Yet many records must be kept longer than that for legal or other reasons. These are considered inactive records. No one wants to deal with them; they are hardly ever looked at; they don't produce any revenue; and they are usually stored in a dark, dingy area. However, they still contain information that is valuable to your company.

If you are looking into inactive records storage, it's probably because one or more of three situations exists in your organization: 1) the files in your office are bulging, with no room left for the new ones; 2) your present inactive storage space is in the same crowded condition; 3) your inactive records are so hopelessly disorganized that it takes hours of searching to find anything.

Advantages of a Records Center

There are three advantages to putting your inactive records in a records center—economy, security and retrievability. All of these advantages are supported by two underlying principles. The first is that removing inactive records from your active files is essential to maintaining current files in workable condition. The second is that inactive records can and should be handled differently from active files.

Economy

Cost-justification has long been the primary reason for establishing a records center. Low-cost warehouse-type storage space can save you a great deal of money over higher priced office space. In today's markets, typical office space runs about four to eight times as much per square foot as warehouse-type space suitable for records storage.

Cheaper space isn't the only advantage: you can also use lower-cost storage equipment. Although the traditional four- or five-drawer file cabinet is an effective means to organize and retrieve active files, it is an expensive way to store inactive records. In an inactive storage area, you can substitute boxes and low-cost, high-density shelving.

Table 11.1 shows what it costs in a typical office to store records in a four-drawer file cabinet. If you compare your own in-house filing to a records center, you will probably find you can save 90% or more for every cubic foot of records stored.

Security

A well-planned and maintained records center offers security for your firm's valuable business records. Records that are simply stuffed into some out-of-the-way storage area risk being lost through water or fire damage, or neglect. Confidentiality can also be compromised through the threat of intrusion.

Table 11.1: Annual Cost of Maintaining One Four-drawer File Cabinet in Office Space

Space[1] (8 sq. ft. @ $15.00)	$120.00
Cabinet[2] ($300 prorated over 10 years)	30.00
Supplies[3] ($30 per drawer prorated over 10 years)	12.00
Labor[4] ($14,000 divided by 30 cabinets)	467.00
Benefits (25%)	117.00
Overhead (15% of above items except space)	94.00
	$840.00

[1]Space-One letter-size file cabinet requires 8 sq. ft. of floor space including the space for the drawer to pull out and a 2 foot aisle in front of the cabinet.
[2]Cabinet - New, full-suspension, office file cabinets range from $300-$650 per cabinet.
[3]Supplies - Each drawer outfitted with a hanging file system with 50 hanging folders.
[4]Labor - The average cost of a file clerk is divided by the average number of file cabinets that one file clerk can maintain.

Retrievability

A well-planned and maintained records center also allows you to retrieve files when you need them. Taking time to organize your records before you store them is the key. This practice may mean the difference between winning and losing a lawsuit years after the records were stored. It also makes it practical to go after more marginal information. For instance, your claims department might be settling smaller claims for too much money because it's hard to locate the substantiating paperwork. A records center can reverse this situation.

IN-HOUSE VS. COMMERCIAL STORAGE

If you've decided to establish a records center, you have two alternatives: set up your own in-house center or use the services of a commercial facility. There is also an interim option that, if appropriate to your situation, can save you time and money over the first two—creating a semi-active files area.

Semi-active Files Area

This is an area within your office but apart from the regular active files area. The only distinction between a semi-active files area and a records center is that the semi-active files area is located within your regular office space. Otherwise, records are handled as they would be in an off-site, warehouse-type center.

Advantages

A semi-active storage area has two advantages over an off-site location:

1.) Depending upon the availability of space in your office, you may be able to avoid or defer the cost of obtaining an off-site records storage area.

2.) If your company has never used a records center, it may be easier to convince people to use an office location, rather than an off-site center.

There are always some people who feel they must have their records close at hand. The semi-active area keeps their records close enough for comfort, while establishing the principle of handling active and inactive files differently. Later, when people have become used to the set-up, you can ship the original semi-active records off-site and pull a new set of records into the semi-active area.

Disadvantages

Setting up a semi-active files area is not an ideal situation. You are still using expensive office space when inexpensive warehouse-type space would do. You should consider this option only when you have some office space that would otherwise go unused, or when you are faced with strong resistance to sending records off-site.

In-house Records Center

An in-house records center can be set up in basement storage or warehouse-type space in your building. You can also use an off-site location, as long as the cost and quality of the facility meet your needs and are within an acceptable distance. (This would still be considered an in-house center, because it is set up and managed by your staff for your firm's records only.)

Advantages

The principal advantage of an in-house center is control. You decide how your records will be stored and how fast you can retrieve them. If something is not functioning correctly, you can make the necessary changes. Control is particularly important to firms that produce paper as the primary result of their work, such as law and accounting firms. It's often a struggle to convince these professionals that their records will be as well maintained in a commercial facility as they would be in the office. With an in-house records center, this issue is avoided.

Disadvantages

The principal disadvantage of an in-house center is the cost, in terms of both space and staff. Unless you have the use of "free" space (space that cannot be used for any other purpose but still must be kept and paid for), an in-house facility will almost always be more expensive than using a commercial facility. Even if you have "free" space, as your business grows you may be asked to move your records storage to a new area. Moves are expensive, time consuming and a logistical headache.

With regard to staffing, the problem is one of priorities. Your time as a manager can be more productively spent elsewhere. Thus, the task of managing the center either drops to a low priority or is delegated at too low a level. As a result, after a year or two of inactive management, most inactive storage areas return to their original state of disorganization.

Commercial Records Centers

Generally, commercial records centers are professional full-service companies offering a wide variety of records management services. You pay for only the services you use, while having available all the resources you may need.

Advantages

There are several advantages to using a commercial records center, especially for a small- to medium-sized business. The cost is almost always less than for in-house records storage, owing to economies of scale in space and equipment. Further, a commercial center can afford to maintain a trained, professional staff by spreading the cost among a large number of users.

A commercial records center can also employ staff members with different specialties, such as records classification or computer-indexing of inactive records. You may require these skills only rarely. Being able to draw on them—and pay for them—as needed can substantially improve the quality of your records program at a very reasonable cost.

Another advantage of using a commercial center is that much of the work of handling inactive records can be done off your premises. This eliminates disruption of your office routine, and eliminates the need to hire extra or short-term workers.

A commercial records center provides more flexible space arrangements. Additional storage space is available as your needs demand, without your having to pay for future—and now empty—expansion space. Further, you avoid the possibility of having to relocate inactive records when someone finds another need for your in-house space.

Finally, sending inactive records to a commercial records center imposes a certain discipline on your office in relation to those records. Often, after a company-wide records clean-up, the effort is not maintained, and the in-house records soon return to their disorganized state. Moving your inactive records to a commercial center ensures that the initial clean-up effort is not lost. Your records at the center will be maintained in a well-ordered condition, and your in-house records will have a better chance of remaining organized.

Disadvantages

The primary disadvantage of using a commercial records center is psychological; the records are thought to be "out of hand," not under your direct physical control. However, the real test is not geographic distance, as most people think, but time. Your files are as close as the *time* it takes to deliver them to your desk. Thus, your files in a commercial records center may actually be closer to you than they are in the back room, in terms of the time it takes for you to get them.

Most commercial centers will return records to you, either by the box or even by the folder or paper. You may be able to get "immediate" delivery, although 24-hour turnaround time is usually standard. However, for most requirements, this is adequate. The key is that return of the records is assured, and with minimal retrieval effort and cost.

This does, however, lead to the second potential disadvantage of commercial records centers: misuse of services. Storing records that should have been destroyed, or storing them long after their retention date has been reached, can run up your bill. Likewise, if you store records that are still somewhat active, you may end up paying excessive fees for returns. Deciding to use a commercial records center doesn't mean you can forget about the records. You also need to monitor your usage of storage and other services on an ongoing basis to make sure you are getting your money's worth. Don't let "out-of-sight" become "out-of-mind."

Making the Choice

Your own requirements and the proximity of a good commercial records center will, of course, play a major role in determining which way to go. Cost is the major factor to consider, but not the sole criterion. Efficient retrieval, security and long-term expansion plans must also be taken into account. So must the quality and level of service offered by local commercial facilities. For instance, some moving and storage companies will also store records. However, they may not be set up to provide specialized services, such as indexing and retrieving your records. Environmental and security controls may be marginal. Thus, in checking their costs, you must also look closely at what you are getting for your money.

Budgeting the Alternatives

Because cost is so important, you should project a three-year budget for both the in-house and commercial operation before making a final decision. The material in the last sections of this chapter will help you cost out the in-house alternative. Your local commercial centers can help you develop three-year costs for their services.Don't forget to add in fees for all the services you are likely to use, such as records retrieval. Storage costs alone do not tell the whole story. For in-house centers, don't forget to factor in the "hidden" costs of management and training time.

Cost Factors to Consider

In determining the costs of records center alternatives, you will need to know the following about your files: How many cubic feet will you start with? (See Chapter 3 for an explanation of how to compute cubic feet of records.) How many cubic feet will you destroy and add over the next three years? What is your projected level of reference activity? And what services will you require?

With regard to reference activity, you need to project both the number of requests and the number of trips per month, since it may be possible to economize by batching some reference requests. With regard to services, the following section includes a checklist of services offered by commercial records centers. The list should help you determine which to budget for, and can also help you select a commercial records center with the right mix of services.

SELECTING A COMMERCIAL RECORDS CENTER

As indicated above, not all commercial records centers are equal. Some are just warehouses that make little concession to the special handling records require. Others specialize in records, often providing consulting services as well. And some are highly specialized, offering remote underground storage for extremely valuable records that require the maximum protection available.

Services

Obviously, no commercial facility offers all of the following services. The key is to identify those services that are important to your company, and to find the center that is the closest fit with your overall requirements. Possible items to include in your budget and checklist include:

- Guaranteed availability of adequate storage upon demand.

- Pick up and delivery of records.

- Indexing of files within a box—simple listing or computerized index.

- Retrieval of boxes or specific folders and papers within a box.

- Refiling of retrieved records when no longer required.

- Handling of retrieval and reference requests by phone.

- Records destruction of various kinds: recycling, shredding, microform chopper.

- Specialists' services: sorting prior to storage, research, purging, etc.

- Records management consultation for active records.

- Archival consultation for historical records, including preservation and restoration.

- Microfilming services.

- Photocopying.

- Facsimile transmission for handling retrieval requests.

- Boxes provided, and at a competitive price (see below for tips on good boxes).

- Other office supplies and equipment sold, and at competitive prices.

- Reports provided on yearly activity levels and costs.

- Automatic notification when records are eligible for destruction.

- Temperature and humidity controlled storage for microfilm, computer tapes, archival records.

- A safe and secure facility including the following:
  1) concrete or masonry construction;
  2) above ground level to avoid flooding;
  3) fire supression system (sprinklers) hooked into a 24-hour monitored alarm system;
  4) intrusion alarm system, also monitored;
  5) a maximum protection underground storage vault.*

---

*Such vaults (there are only a handful in the U.S.) are off-site locations, often deep within caves or mines, which afford maximum security for records. Only a few types of organizations would need such protection.

Other Selection Criteria

Once you have narrowed your choice to one or two prospects, obtain references from them of long-term and new clients. Ask clients about the company's quality of service. You should also visit the records center. Don't expect to see plush office space in an elegant neighborhood or staff in high fashion clothes. But do expect to see *security* and *order*. While there, you should ask some important questions:

- Is the center a member of, and does it adhere to the standards of, the Association of Commercial Records Centers (ACRC)?

- How is storage charged, by the cubic foot or box? From the day of deposit, or from the first day of the month? Are storage charges paid by the year, quarter, month? Are payments made in advance? Is there a minimum charge?

- What services are included in the storage charge?

- Is storage credit given when material is destroyed (assuming you have paid in advance)?

- How are special services charged, by the hour or by the activity?

- What is the charge for "extra" activities not covered in the published rate schedule?

- What is the normal delivery turnaround time? Guaranteed delivery time? Rush delivery time?

- Are the employees bonded?

SETTING UP AN IN-HOUSE RECORDS CENTER

If you've decided to set up an in-house records center, this section tells you how to do it. Whether your records center is small (one hundred boxes) or large (several thousand boxes), the principles are the same.

PERSONNEL

The first and most important ingredient for a successful records center is the person in charge of it. As in most work situations, the actual people working in the records center can make it or break it.

Skills Required

An average amount of physical strength is required—enough to move and heft boxes weighing up to 40 pounds. Employees must be attentive to detail.

In a records center, accuracy is much more important than speed. The repetitive nature of records center work does not provide much variety. Someone who values predictability, neatness and order will do well. Someone who seeks glamour, variety and speed will not.

Records center personnel should also be service-oriented and fairly personable. Users' willingness to send records to the center depends in part on their confidence in the center staff. Someone who is abrasive or unresponsive does a disservice to your program.

Part-time vs. Full-time

If you have a small center, a member of your office staff need spend only part-time at the center. Records center duties will be secondary to some other primary assignments. As your records center grows, you may need to think about dedicating a full-time position to the center. In that case, the center staff person may still be assigned some additional duties, but the center will be the primary assignment.

The difference between the two above situations is very important. If non-records center responsibilities are someone's "main job," the records center work will suffer in priority and quality. If, on the other hand, the "main job" is managing the records center, it's the records center that will get first priority and attention.

The frequency of records transfers, the type and level of reference and research services offered, and the volume of records dictate the number of part- or full-time staff that is needed. The ability to maintain appropriate standards for quality and thoroughness dictates the point at which records center tasks should be assigned as primary or secondary duties.

Limited Access

You should consider limiting access to your records center to two people: the primary records center staff member and one backup person (in case of sickness, vacation, etc.). Otherwise, if you allow unlimited and uncontrolled access by all users, the organizational integrity of your center will deteriorate. If you do allow users to service their own records, at a minimum the center staff should approve all transfers, and control all retrievals and records destruction.

STORAGE BOXES

One of the primary ways in which inactive records storage differs from active storage is that records are usually kept in boxes rather than in cabinets or on open shelves. However, not all boxes are suitable. The main types are described below; sizes refer to the inside dimensions of the box.

Types of Boxes

Letter/Legal Box

The standard records storage box is the letter/legal box. It is made of 200 pound test corrugated cardboard, as are most records storage boxes. It measures 12 inches wide × 15 inches long × 10 inches high, and has a lid and cut-out handholds on the ends. Letter-size files fit one way in the box, legal-size files fit along the other. Computer printouts fit flat lying down. Typically, 90% of a firm's inactive records will fit into this box.

Check Box

This box is of similar construction to the letter/legal box and measures 8½ inches wide × 24 inches long × 4 inches high, also with a lid. It is designed for check-sized records, deposit slips and microfilm reels.

Except for some odd-sized documents, these two boxes should be able to accommodate all of your records sizes. The odd-sized records may fit better in one of the following boxes.

Rolled Drawings Box

Sizes vary greatly, but all are designed to hold rolled drawings varying in length from 24 inches to 48 inches. A size that holds most drawings, and also makes very efficient use of the standard 30 × 42-inch records storage shelf, measures 5 inches square by 40 inches long.

X-ray/Ledger Box

This box is usually made of heavier cardboard, 275 pound test, to handle the heavy weight of X-rays. It measures 7 inches wide × 15½ inches long × 18½ inches high. Large accounting ledgers and other outsized items can be stored in this box.

Good Box Design

There is a great variety of box designs, with many bad designs on the market. Here are some features to look for.

Box Bottom

The design of the bottom of the box should not allow paper to slip through, or the bottom to come apart when loaded with files. With the box made up, put your fist inside the box and press on the bottom. Does the box bottom have a tendency to come undone?

Box Sides

Look at the sides of the box. Corrugated cardboard is made by sandwiching a corrugated or fluted piece of cardboard between two outer layers of flat cardboard. This inner corrugated layer should be running vertically to support the weight of other boxes stacked on top of it. If the corrugation is horizontal, the sides will simply crease and buckle when any weight is put on the box.

Lid

Put the lid on the box. The lid should be deep enough to hold the sides of an overstuffed box. If the lid is too shallow, it will not close an overfull box well enough for it to be transported. If it is too deep, it will force the handholds too low for a comfortable grip.

Handholds

The letter/legal box should have handholds conveniently located on the ends for lifting the box. The holds should not be hidden by the cover, nor should they be too far down the ends of the box. The sides of the box where the handholds are cut in should be doubled-sided to prevent the handholds from tearing out. The cut cardboard from the handhold space should be hinged and pushed in and up to form a comfortable grip.

Assembly

The procedure for setting the box up should be relatively simple and foolproof. If the box is designed so that it can be folded together wrong and still look right, you can be sure someone will do it. The problem will become apparent the first time you try to move the box: it will fall apart, spilling its contents on the floor.

Box Designs To Stay Away From

There are many styles and brands of boxes on the market that are designed to hold a complete file drawer of records. These boxes are large and heavy. They are unwieldy for retrieving files. Their only attraction is for the person filling the box up. Conceptually it is easy; transfer each file drawer into one box and label it as the file drawer was labeled. But if the file drawer was only half full, the storage box is only half full, wasting space in the records center. The materials in the file drawer may not even belong in the same box in the records center (see the section on Boxing Records, later in this chapter). For anyone who has to lift and transport these boxes, they have no attraction at all. They also cost two to three times as much per cubic foot of records as the letter/legal box. Don't buy them.

The other type of records storage box to avoid looks like an active file drawer. It is made of cardboard, with pieces of steel along the sides to permit stacking and clipping together, to form a bank of boxes similar to file cabinets.

Again, the concept of transferring the contents of a file drawer directly to this cardboard file is often appealing. However, as these boxes have none of the drawer suspension equipment of steel file drawers, file retrieval is tricky at best. The drawers tend to break down over time, and the interlocking setup deteriorates badly if it is taken apart and moved. The cost of this type of container is usually five to seven times as much per cubic foot of records as the standard letter/legal box. Again, don't buy them.

RECORDS CENTER SHELVING

The key efficiency of a records center is its use of "air space"—how well the *cubic* volume of the storage space is used. Shelving can help you achieve a greater efficiency and lower your overall storage costs.

Records center managers use a certain ratio to indicate the efficiency of space usage. To calculate this ratio, determine the total capacity, in cubic feet of records, of your storage area and the total square feet of floor space including aisles, offices, dock space, etc. The ratio is then stated, for example, as 2:1 or 2 cubic feet of records per square foot of floor space.

Do not make the mistake of considering six cubic foot boxes stacked on a square foot of floor space as yielding a space usage ratio of 6:1. This leaves out the space needed for aisles, offices, etc., and does not account for the fact that the standard 1 cubic-foot records storage box actually has a "footprint" of about 1½ cubic feet. Therefore stacking boxes on the floor six high in this manner actually yields a space usage ratio of 2:1. The only way to calculate your space needs properly is to draw up a rough layout of your intended space and count up the maximum number of boxes that will fit into it.

Stacking Boxes on the Floor vs. Shelving

For determining the maximum number of boxes your center will hold, you have two choices: stack your boxes on the floor or use shelving.

Actually, boxes are not stacked directly "on the floor"—all records storage boxes should be kept a few inches up from the floor at all times. This is to prevent water damage in the case of water spilling across the floor. Wooden pallets are very inexpensive (about 5% of the cost of the equivalent steel shelving) and easy to use.

On-the-floor Storage

A typical floor plan for stacking boxes on the floor (on pallets) puts two rows of pallets back to back. From each aisle, the boxes are arranged two stacks deep. You can stack the boxes however high you wish; usually six high is the practical maximum.

The *advantage* of on-the-floor storage is that the system involves a very low capital expenditure, i.e., no shelving. The *disadvantage* is that it takes more time to retrieve files: a layout of six high, two deep will require moving as many as 11 boxes to reach the back bottom box. A layout with only one stack deep yields faster access time but less efficient use of space.

Using Shelving

Floor stacking also means that you may not be making good use of the air-space in your storage area. With shelving 9 feet high, for example, you can achieve a ratio of 3:1—a 50% increase in efficiency or a one-third decrease in the amount of square feet needed to house the same number of boxes.

The other major advantage you gain with shelving is faster access time. Two variables affect access time: the number of boxes *deep* you put on each shelf and the number of boxes *high* you stack on each shelf. With one box deep, you gain faster access time but again lower your space usage ratio. With one box high per shelf, you also gain faster access time but increase the need for shelves. It's a trade-off—faster access time versus a lower space usage ratio or higher shelving costs. The standard configuration that has evolved over the years for inactive records storage is two boxes high, two boxes deep. It represents the best compromise between access time and space usage.

When you are deciding which setup to use, on-the-floor or on-the-shelf, consider what is important in your particular situation: saving up-front capital expense or long-term space and labor costs. Also consider how active your records will be: the more active the records, the more important will be the ease and quickness of retrieval.

Types of Shelving

First, a word about wood shelving. It is often tempting to build shelving out of two-by-fours and plywood, because of the low cost of lumber versus steel shelving. Don't do it. The wood framing takes away a significant amount of space from records storage and, equally important, it won't readily disassemble when you're forced to move to a new storage area. In the long run, it's more expensive than steel shelving.

There are many brands of shelving on the market today but really only two basic types: all-steel bolt and clip shelving, and a combination of steel framing and wood pressboard shelves.

Bolt and Clip Shelving

This is the traditional shelving used for decades by records centers. The steel uprights and angle bracing are bolted together and the shelves are placed in clips hung on this frame. The most commonly used shelf is 18 gauge (which denotes the thickness of the steel shelf), 42 inches wide × 30 inches deep. The shelf holds three boxes wide and two boxes deep (with a few inches of box overhanging in front).

The cost of steel framing and shelving is directly related to its weight; it's almost as if you pay by the pound. Among the major competitive brands, prices vary only slightly. This type of shelving is time-tested and will last for decades.

Pressboard Shelving

As with the all-steel shelving, pressboard shelving manufacturers each have a slightly different design. However, they all basically work the same way. The frame is made of steel and there are no bolts holding it together. The frame is held in place by horizontal bars which are designed to interlock with the uprights. The wood shelves simply rest on top of these horizontals.

The main advantage of this type of shelving is that it is less expensive than the all-steel type. First, the wood shelves are less expensive than steel shelves. Second, the steel used in the framing is slightly thinner than that used for the all-steel shelving. It is also significantly faster and simpler to erect and disassemble pressboard shelving. A rubber mallet is all you need.

There are several disadvantages to pressboard shelves, however. The frame members, being slightly thinner, are also less durable. The pressboard shelves, being wood, are *much less* durable. Pressboard shelves are supported by their edges on the framing. Unfortunately, it is the edges that tend to wear out over time, especially when moved around. Worn shelves with chipped edges have to be replaced from time to time.

The wood shelves also introduce an additional fire hazard to your records center. However, the increase in risk is not great considering that you already have a room full of cardboard boxes full of paper. Fire-resistant treated pressboard is available at additional cost, to reduce this extra risk.

Pressboard type shelving is limited in its height. Seven to 9 feet high is a safe installation height for this type of shelving. The manufacturers do not recommend building it over 15 feet high. All-steel shelving installations, on the other hand, are often 8 to 16 feet high, with several installations built to a height of 24 feet.

Design and Assembly

Rely on your vendor to help you find the most efficient shelving layout for your space. Using a floor plan of your space, try drawing out a few different configurations. If you are in an area subject to earthquakes, you should also check local earthquake codes before determining how high you want to build your shelves.

It is very important to assemble shelving properly, with special attention to adequate bracing. This cannot be stressed enough. In one installation of 20,000 boxes, the shelving fell together like a domino fold (fortunately while no one was about). Inadequate bracing was the cause.

ORGANIZATION OF BOXES

There are two systems for organizing boxes in a storage area: 1) a functional or date order system, or 2) a location system. If you have established a semi-active area, the functional or date order system is recommended. Otherwise, the location system is strongly recommended.

Functional or Date Order System

The functional or date order system is similar to an active file system. The storage area is divided into different areas or shelves for each department. Within a department's area, each records series is shelved together and put into alphabetical, numeric or date order, whichever makes sense for each particular record series.

The advantage of this system is that it is "common sense" organization, easily understood. The disadvantage is that you eventually fill a certain area and still need to add more records. You then have two alternatives, neither of which is satisfactory: you can start a second area for the overfull section, thus degrading your original order; or you can shift large amounts of records around to recapture some under-utilized shelf space area where you need it.

In a semi-active area, user-departments typically do their own filing. Further, files stay a relatively short time (perhaps a year), before being transferred to the records center. With these arrangements, the advantage of "common sense" organization far outweighs any disadvantages. In a records center, on the other hand, where records may stay an average of seven years and access is infrequent, the use of a location system is much more efficient.

Location System

In this method of arrangement, each individual *space* for a box is given a location number, or address. Space is assigned on a "next available" basis. A cross-index is used to identify holdings by department and records series.

When a new box comes in, it is assigned the next available location number. When a box is destroyed, its location number becomes immediately available for reuse. Boxes from any one department are not necessarily located together in the same area. However, they can still be located very quickly by using the storage index.

The advantage of this system is that you can make use of all the space in the records center without ever having to shift any boxes around. The disadvantage is that you must use an index to find any box. A department's boxes will not be all neatly lined up in one certain area of the center. Conceivably, one department's 100 boxes could be in 100 different areas of the records center.

There are as many different number and addressing location systems as there are records centers. Make one up that makes sense to you, but keep it simple.

If your center is relatively small, say up to 1000 cubic feet, simply give each vertical stack a consecutive number and each box space within the stack a number. With a larger center, you may want to give each aisle a letter. The "location number" for a box then becomes that unique combination of aisle, stack and box space letters and numbers that pinpoint that location in the records center.

CHOOSING SPACE FOR YOUR RECORDS CENTER

In setting up a records center, a major consideration is obviously the actual physical space in which it will be housed. Perhaps you don't have a choice—you've been told to use this space, period.

This is particularly true if you are using space in your office building or in an off-site unimproved warehouse or building that your company already owns or rents. But if you do have a choice of off-site locations, you should inspect the space carefully, keeping in mind the following criteria. (You can also use some of this information to evaluate space that has been assigned to you.)

Type of Construction

Choose concrete or masonry construction. Wood frame buildings are simply too much of a fire risk. With a concrete or masonry building, if a fire starts in the building only the contents can burn—the building frame will not contribute fuel to the fire. Tightly packed records actually burn less quickly than you might expect.

Floor Load

When looking at space as a potential records center site, find out the weight-carrying capacity of the building's floor construction. This is called the floor load capacity and is readily obtainable from the building's owner, manager or architect.

Next you will need to calculate the floor load capacity that you will require for your records. To do this, use the rough layout of your center drawn to plan the shelving, and then compute the volume of records your center will hold when it is full. To calculate the total weight of these records, multiply your total cubic feet by 35 pounds/cubic foot (the rule of thumb measure for most records). Divide the total weight by the square feet the records will occupy. This will give you a number like 100 pounds per square foot, or the average weight of records for each square foot of floor space.

Don't cheat on this figure. The floor load capacity of the space you use *must* be rated high enough to carry the weight of your records. This is one of the reasons records storage areas often end up in basements on the concrete slab directly on the ground.

Security Systems

Check into the security systems present and/or the cost of installing security systems to cover the three primary concerns.

Fire

The center should have a sprinkler system or a smoke detector system. There are other, more expensive systems such as a halon system. However their cost is hard to justify for normal business records storage.

No smoking should be allowed in the records center. No other flammable materials should be stored near or with your records.

You should install a water-flow detection system to alert the authorities when fire trips open a sprinkler head. All your fire detection systems should be hooked up to a 24-hour monitoring service. Since many centers are in low-traffic locations, the ringing of an outside building alarm alone may not bring help soon enough, especially at night or on weekends.

Water

Water can come from many directions: from leaky plumbing, sprinklers or roofs; from flooding or leaky basements if below ground level; from a sprinkler head or fire hose while putting out a fire. The only real protection against water on the ground is to keep everything *off the floor*.

There is no real protection from water from above. When there is an obvious problem you can use plastic sheeting while you correct it. Plastic is such a nuisance, though, that it is not practical for extended periods of time. Besides getting in the way, plastic tends to sweat, dampening the protected boxes.

Of all the threats, while fire seems the most likely, water damage is by far the most common. It can also result in large-scale destruction and very high costs. Chapter 10 describes disaster recovery procedures, particularly for water damage.

Intrusion

The building should have an intrusion alarm system. This should protect all openings and glass areas. Again, the alarm should be hooked up to a 24-hour monitoring station. Your best protection, of course, is to choose a site in an area with a low incidence of break-ins.

Location

When evaluating sites, think in terms of the *time* it takes to service your primary clients. This involves both physical distance and ease of access to the building. Since it is unlikely your center will be staffed full-time, you should also consider how comfortable you or one of your employees will feel going into the building alone.

Environmental Control

Temperature and humidity levels are not critical for most records. However, if there is a sprinkler system, care must be taken to ensure that it does not freeze and burst. A minimum temperature of 40° F is required. Some storage areas are heated to 60° F for employee comfort. Adequate lighting is needed for files retrieval and box movement. Humidity should be kept below the level at which the records become damp, so that they do not grow any mold.

ORGANIZING THE SPACE IN YOUR RECORDS CENTER

No matter how large or small your records center is, it will contain several spaces for different purposes.

Storage Area

Most of the space in a records center will be occupied by the storage area, which serves its main function. You need enough storage space to handle present storage needs plus space for future expansion.

Generally speaking, you should be able to handle five years' projected expansion in your original setup. If you plan for longer than five years, you end up paying for unused expansion space for too long a period of time. If you plan for less, you have to move your records center too often or end up with records scattered in several different locations. A rule of thumb is that most businesses generate approximately 10%-15% net new records (percent new records minus the percent old or inactive records) each year. Your records center will likely expand at about the same rate. If you find it difficult to determine your company's real growth rate, you can probably rely on the standard rule.

Receiving Dock Space

The receiving space should be at standard dock height if you plan to use large trucks. Otherwise, ground level is best for unloading or loading a van. Since you will be working with the incoming boxes in the receiving area much of the time, it is nice to have this space enclosed and heated. The receiving areas should be located next to the entry to the records center so that unnecessary hand-trucking is avoided.

Reference Work Space

This space is used for special projects such as rearranging files within boxes, arranging files pulled for requests and purging outdated files. The reference area should be enclosed, heated and well-lit. You will need a few tables and chairs to enable workers to spread their papers out.

Destruction Space

Boxes pulled for destruction are accumulated in this area. If you use a commercial service to destroy old files, it will pick up the boxes here. If you are shredding documents in-house, your destruction area will become messy with paper dust and scraps. Make sure it is well-enclosed. In any case, the destruction area should be physically removed from the incoming area in the records center, so that there is no chance for the boxes to become confused with one another.

Office Space

Some general office space is needed: space for tables, chairs, desks, file cabinets, shelving, photocopy machine and, if space permits, a coffee area.

When you are planning your records center, spend some time planning the relationship of these spaces, considering the logical flow of the work. New boxes come into the center, locations are put on the boxes, boxes are put into the storage area, files are retrieved from boxes and refiled. Boxes are eventually pulled off the shelves and destroyed. The control of all these functions is centered in the office.

SPECIALIZED EQUIPMENT

Following are some pieces of equipment useful in a records center. Depending on the size of your center, you may be interested in some types, but probably not all.

Ladders

If your shelving is higher than 6 feet, you will need some means of reaching these shelves, usually a ladder. The pulpit ladder is a step-ladder on casters that enable it to roll along the floor. When a person steps on the ladder, the casters retract and the ladder locks into position. There is handrailing along the side. At the top is a platform with a railing that resembles a pulpit.

The taller the pulpit ladder, the broader the base. When designing your center, make sure your aisles are wide enough to accommodate the ladder you will use. You should also incorporate safety procedures. Although the pulpit model is the safest ladder, it is still possible to have accidents.

Mezzanine

A good alternative to ladders for installations higher than 12 feet is a mezzanine. This is a steel grating built into the shelving system at, say, the 8-foot level. A stairway leads from the floor to the mezzanine. A mezzanine eliminates the need for a ladder. It enables you always to work with your feet on the "floor," which is safer than working on a ladder. In some large records centers, shelving goes up 24 feet and two mezzanines are used over the ground floor level.

Hand Trucks

These are essential for moving boxes around, and up and down the aisles.

Pallets

Pallets are indispensible for keeping your boxes off the floor. They are also very convenient for moving numbers of boxes around the records center, especially if you use a pallet jack.

Pallet Jack

A hand-operated hydraulic-type pallet jack is very useful for moving records around a records center, and is considerably less expensive than a powered fork lift. If you have a mezzanine, you may want a pallet jack that is capable of lifting pallets up to the mezzanine level.

GETTING RECORDS TO THE CENTER

Whether you use a semi-active files area, an in-house records center or an outside facility, certain questions and procedures are dealt with in the same way.

When to Send Records

How do you know when to establish an inactive storage area? As long as you have enough room in your office to keep your records close at hand and well-organized, there is no problem. It may be time to establish an inactive storage area 1) when there is not enough space in the office; 2) when you are contemplating buying more equipment to house inactive records; or 3) when older records are beginning to slow down access to more active records.

Deciding when to send specific files to the inactive storage area is a function of your records retention schedules. However, when developing and implementing those schedules, a good rule of thumb is to keep the current year plus one in your office. Other records should be moved off-site and disposed of according to schedule.

Another rule of thumb is that any records series from which you retrieve documents once a month (or more) is considered active. If your retrievals are less frequent but still fairly regular, the series is considered inactive. However, it may not yet be ready to send off-site. Ideally, you should only send to your center records for which retrieval is the exception rather than the rule.

Boxing Records

Once you are ready to send records to a center, the first step in the office is to put them in boxes. The rule to follow here is to limit the contents of any one box to a single records series. If this is truly impractical, because of the very low volume of some series, you should still limit the contents of a single box to series having the same retention period.

The guiding principle here is that labor costs are always higher than space costs. Mixing series in a single box means that it takes more staff time to list and index box contents. Mixing retention periods is even worse. The only way to manage destruction is to purge folder by folder. Since this is very labor-intensive, most people simply let the entire box sit until all records are eligible for destruction. It is far more economical to waste a little box space than to require additional handling of records.

Boxes should be packed fairly tight, but with some work space left. Otherwise retrievals are difficult to manage. If the box is overfull, this tends to push the lid up which makes the box difficult to shelve.

Keeping Track of Stored Records

This problem is of prime importance to any records center. Indeed, as far as users are concerned, it is the *only* question that matters. Put another way, the heart of the question is: "How do I find a file once it is sent to storage?"

Transmittal Slip

The transmittal slip (see Figure 11.1) is the tool to answer this concern. Basic information to be listed on the transmittal slip includes: name of office or department from which the records originate; contact person in that department or office; date of slip preparation; records series title and description (e.g., cancelled checks, correspondence); inclusive dates; destruction date and instructions; and the records center location number. You may also want to provide for a "box number." This is usually a consecutive number assigned by the originating office.

The transmittal slip is usually a three-part (or photocopied) form. One transmittal slip is filled out for *each* box, by the same person who fills the box. The first copy stays with the originating office. It is the office's primary source of information for requesting retrievals from the center. (This is why it is important to describe the box contents carefully on the form.) The second and third copies go with the box to the center.

Some commercial records centers will fill the boxes and list the contents for you. This can be very helpful, especially if a computer is used to sort the lists by records series, originating department, destruction dates, etc. It doesn't really matter where the transmittal slip is completed, as long as both the originating office and the center wind up with complete copies. In this case, the center will not return the original of the transmittal slip to you until the records center storage location has been entered on it.

Index file

This is the principal finding aid in the records center. It is compiled from the second copy of the transmittal slip, usually filed in a three-ring binder. Within the binder, organize transmittal slips by originating department. Within departments, you should further organize them according to records series, date, alpha or numeric span, or whatever else makes sense for the records in question. When users want to refer to their stored records, the index file is your key to pulling the right box.

Destruction index file

This is composed of the third copy of the transmittal slip, organized by destruction date. Within destruction dates, usually grouped by month, quarter or year, the slips should be organized by department. When you pull the batch of slips currently eligible for destruction, you should review them with departments prior to actually destroying the records.

RECEIVING RECORDS IN YOUR CENTER

If you set up an in-house records center, these procedures will help you keep it running smoothly. If you use a commercial facility, the professional staff should take over from here on.

Receiving the Box

The first step when you receive any box is to verify its contents against the transmittal slip. Errors do occur; if you don't catch them here, chances are you never will. The next step is to assign a location for the box, writing it on the box and on all copies of the transmittal slip. The transmittal copies can then be filed in their appropriate binders.

To keep track of all the locations in the records center, and the availability of any particular space, you should keep a location assignment book. Typically, this is a three-ring binder with a list of every location in the records center. A

Figure 11.1: A Typical Transmittal Slip

RECORDS TRANSFER AND DESTRUCTION NOTICE		See Instructions on Back of Goldenrod Copy

TRANSFER NOTICE   Date _____

ORGANIZATION/DIVISION/DEPARTMENT	BUILDING/ROOM	TEL. EXT.

The records listed below are transferred to the Records Center per Records Retention Schedule No. _____.
We have assigned "Box Numbers" as indicated below.

Schedule Item No.	Record Date	Records Title	Range (Alpha/Numeric)	Dept. Box No.	Records Center Location

Department Approval		Records Center - Transfer Completed		
Transfer Notice — Signature	Date	Transfer Completed — Signature	Date	Page ___ of ___

This transmittal slip can be used to list several boxes on one sheet. For this company, the "Schedule Item No." column is used to determine the destruction date. Courtesy Weyerhaeuser Co.

space next to each location identifies whether it is full or not. You must be careful to update the list when you pull boxes for relocation or destruction.

When assigning locations, you can make things easier by assigning boxes with high activity to front positions on low shelves and those with low activity to the back and on higher shelves.

Handling Retrieval Requests

The procedures for handling requests are designed to keep track of where the file is and to provide a history of all requests.

Request Slip

When a file request is initiated, a request slip is filled out. The key elements of a request slip include: date, who requests the file, who should receive the file, the department, the description of the file requested and the box location, if known. A three-part form is recommended, as described below.

If the request slip identifies the box location, you can go straight to the box. Otherwise, you will need to refer to the index file first. Check the files both in front of and behind the requested file to be sure you get the whole file. Pull the requested material, insert an out-card in its place and write the box location for the folder(s) on the outside. This greatly simplifies refiling.

Out-card

When a file is pulled from a box, an out-card should always be left in its place. Otherwise, it is impossible to track down the file later. The easiest way to handle charge-outs is with a tag board that has a window pocket. You insert one copy of the request slip in the window. The out-card should have a tab that sticks up above the files, showing its location in the box. Remove all out-cards from boxes when files are returned.

Tickler File for Out-files

The second copy of the request slip should be filed in a tickler file (a system for reminding users when to return materials). There are different ways to organize this file, depending on what is important to you. If you want to contact all requestors when they retain a file longer than 30 days, organize this file by request date. If you want to keep track of requests by department, organize the out-file by department. In either case, make sure you follow up on files that remain out too long.

Chronological Request File

A third copy of the request slip is filed by department, in chronological order. This provides a historical file of all requests by each department. This information is useful for monitoring the reference rate of a particular records series. Retention schedules can then be adjusted accordingly. The chronological file also comes in handy when you are searching for missing materials. Finally, requests can be summarized on a regular basis, to provide usage statistics to user departments.

Refiling

When folders are returned for refiling, look on the folder for the box location. When you put the file back, double check the folder information against the out-card to be sure that the correct file is going back into the right place. Pull the out-card and match it up with the corresponding request slip in the tickler out-file. The out-file box should contain only slips for files that are still out to requestors.

Interfiles

Sometimes a file belongs in a box already sent to the records center, but it has never been included. When this situation occurs, it is called an interfile. Unless the user tells you what box the file belongs in, you may have to do some careful research in your index file to determine the right location. When interfiling, examine the surrounding folders carefully to make sure of placement.

Interfiles should be sent using a transmittal slip. Interfile transmittal slips should be filed separately. The primary use of this file is for problem-solving. The fact that the file was not sent as part of the original shipment indicates that it is a likely candidate for further difficulties later on.

DESTROYING RECORDS

Good records management principles dictate that all records being sent to storage should have a retention period assigned to them. In many cases, however, you may not be able to obtain users' agreements before they store their records. In this case, you should at least determine a review date for each box.

Obtaining Authorization

Whether or not the records have an assigned destruction date, it is always wise to notify the appropriate department about records you intend to destroy. For non-scheduled records, you should obtain written authorization *before* destruction begins, or else assign a new review date. For scheduled records, you can rely on a notification process, giving the department 60 days in which to cancel the destruction order. Copies of transmittal slips can be used to notify and to obtain authorizations. Make sure that descriptions adequately tell the originating department what you are planning to destroy.

After obtaining authorization, pull boxes off the shelf into a separate area from incoming boxes. As a cross-check, have a second person review the boxes against the original list of materials authorized for destruction.

Methods of Destruction

The most tempting choice is to throw your records out in the garbage. This is a bad choice, destroying all the security and the confidence in that security that you have so carefully built up.

A second alternative is to use a commercial recycler. This kind of service picks up your paper, and prepares it for recycling at a paper mill. Some recyclers simply bale the material, which provides reasonable security for most material. Other recyclers use a "hogger," which chops paper into palm-sized pieces, mixes it up in a blower system and then automatically bales it. This system is the preferred destruction method for 99% of your material.

Shredding is time consuming, and is recommended only for highly confidential material. There are numerous shredders on the market that cut paper into one-sixteenth to one-quarter inch strips. There are also machines that chop microforms into material so small that it cannot be read. This is a very time-consuming process and more expensive than shredding. It can only be justified for highly confidential microforms.

After destruction is complete, don't forget to update the location assignment book. This space is now available for new boxes.

USING AUTOMATION

The foregoing discussion has focused on manual ways of handling records center operations. However, all the paper-based systems described lend themselves extremely well to automation. Any microcomputer or even the new generation of word processors can handle most records center automation requirements. There are a few specialized software programs available for records center management, or you can set up your own program.

Advantages of automation are accuracy and speed: you gain better control over information with no likelihood of lost file cards or misplaced indexes. The computer is also considerably faster. One of the principal benefits of automating is flexibility. The information input from transmittal, request and destruction slips can be sorted in a variety of ways to monitor activity, costs and expansion needs.

KEEP YOUR RECORDS CENTER PROGRAM RUNNING SMOOTHLY

Monitor the quality and level of service. A records center is supposed to allow you to retreive inactive files when you need them. Establish a schedule for retrieval, so that all users know what to expect in terms of delivery time. Monitor how well you are meeting this schedule, and whether it is meeting users' needs. You should also monitor your costs, to make sure your services are delivered efficiently.

A sign that your system is not working is an accumulation of inactive files in active files areas, or a sudden drop in transmittals to the center. Either situation warrants immediate attention.

SELL YOUR RECORDS CENTER PROGRAM

This is important whether you use an in-house or a commercial center. Records management—and, in particular, records center management—is a low visibility activity in any organization. To keep management support high for the records operation, you need to continue to remind management of the value of your service. Regular activity reports, as described below, are very effective. It is also helpful if upper management hears of how the records center was able to provide timely information that saved the company money. Unless the records management program remains visible, it is likely to be cut next time the budget is considered. *Do not be taken for granted.*

With regard to activity reports, make a schedule to report on various aspects of your service: records volumes and services delivered, quarterly activity reports, yearly charts and budgets. Include dollars saved over previous methods, continuing cost-avoidance figures and a reasonable estimate of the number of company-wide staff hours saved through information provided by your center. The total figure may surprise you, and will provide a convincing case when budget time comes around.

12

The Corporate Archives

by Julia Niebuhr Eulenberg

What is a corporate archives? Should your organization have one? Why? How does a corporate archives differ from a records management program? How are the two related? What is the "hidden" value of a corporate archives? To whom? How do you go about setting up a corporate archives for your organization? This chapter will help you answer these questions.

DEFINING ARCHIVAL TERMS

The historical records of business and industry have various names: corporate archives, business archives, company archives and, simply, historical records. In this chapter, the term "corporate archives" will be used to designate the collection of materials that you have determined has permanent historical value to your organization.

A corporate archives includes two kinds of records: the archival materials, which are the *raison d'être* of the archives, and the record-keeping materials and finding aids that enable the archives to carry out its purpose of preserving and making accessible historically relevant information. Some of the terms used to describe the adminstrative records will be familiar to you and other management personnel. Others are more specific to the archival profession and, where necessary, will be defined within the text. Archival terms are included in the glossary of this book. A listing of additional reference materials is included in the bibliography.

PURPOSE OF THE ARCHIVES

The first corporate archives in the United States was established only in 1943, by Harvey S. Firestone Jr. Even then, it took a national emergency to spur creation of the archives. Firestone realized that the wartime production records of business and industry could provide important primary sources for future historians writing about the war effort in the United States. His initial goal was to serve history; however, Firestone was also a good businessman. The corporate archives he founded 40 years ago has not only served historians; it has been a valuable corporate asset as well. The archives of the Firestone Tire and Rubber Co. has supplied background materials for public relations efforts and for a 50th anniversary history of the company. It has also yielded information and data used in the day-to-day operation of the company and in developing forecasts for the company's future.

Your organization can reap similar benefits from the records it creates, but it can do so only if those records are properly collected, arranged, described and preserved, according to professional archival standards. A corporate archives should preserve significant information, in its most accessible and comprehensive form.

Only about 2% to 5% of the records your organization creates have long-term or archival value. You will need to limit the volume of records that you save, so that you and others who use the archives can find the information you need promptly and easily.

ESTABLISHING A CORPORATE ARCHIVES

Justifying the Archives

Your organization expects some kind of return on each of its investments. The corporate archives is an investment in this sense. What is its real corporate value?

The corporate archives is a resource that can and should be used by management to develop—and review—corporate strategies and policies. Patent and trademark records, correspondence files, production runs, sales records, personnel and pension benefit files, as well as annual reports to stockholders and the public, are significant business assets. They can be as important as your organization's accounts receivable records if used properly.

What specific uses can your organization make of the records of its past? A corporate archives can be an invaluable resource for developing production forecasts, verifying or locating patent and trademark information, and creating public relations materials and marketing promotion packages. The history of an organization and the reasons it has for doing things its way make interesting reading for new employees and can be very helpful to those responsible for developing staff orientation materials. But new employees are not the only ones who need to know why your organization functions as it does; the corporate archives can supply important information for management development programs and corporate policy reviews.

Establishing a Collecting Policy

Ideally, the archives and records management programs should come into being at the same time and should be considered a cohesive unit with responsibility for managing all of the organization's records. But it rarely works that way. Corporate archives are usually established by an organization as an afterthought.

Your organization is likely to give serious thought to such an undertaking when it reaches a significant anniversary date, when its founding officers begin to retire or when the records manager chances upon some of the organization's original documents during a records survey. Lucky finds can be exciting. The only problem with them is that you find yourself wondering what else may have been thrown out by mistake.

Deciding What Records to Include

When your organization does decide to establish a corporate archives, you must decide which records to include in the collection. The corporate archivist (often the same person as the records manager) will need to work with other managers in your organization to determine the scope.

Your goal should be to document all of your organization's history. The materials you collect should include stories of individuals, work groups, projects, products, mergers and even company failures. You may choose to collect written documents, photographs and even physical items. You may also find yourself collecting magnetic media. Table 12.1 gives a fairly complete listing of the kinds of materials and media that are generally included in a corporate archives.

Archival vs. Vital Records

A corporate archives may appear at first glance to have much in common with your organization's vital records program. Both are concerned with the preservation of your organization's important documents, and many of these documents are in fact the same (see Table 12.2). But there are significant differences between the two programs.

Table 12.1: The Materials and Media of a Corporate Archives

Archival Materials	Paper	Media Magnetic Media	Film[1]	Other[2]
Correspondence	X	X	X	X
Minutes of significant meetings (board of directors, upper management, stockholders, organization-wide, etc.)	X	X	X	
Financial records (such as sales records, price catalogs and lists, production runs, general ledgers, journals, etc.)	X	X	X	
Stockholder records and stock certificates	X	X	X	
Legal records (including records of significant litigation, mergers, acquisitions, bankruptcy proceedings, etc.)	X	X	X	
Organization charts (especially those showing changes over time)	X	X	X	
Publications (including annual reports, organizational newsletters, histories, etc.)	X	X	X	
Personnel files	X	X	X	
Sample products (both the actual samples and other documentation)	X	X	X	X
Patent files, trademark materials, and letterhead collections (to indicate development of the organization over time, mergers, retirements, origin and legal ownership, etc.)	X	X	X	X
Blueprints, maps and architectural drawings	X	X	X	X
Scrapbooks (newsclippings, ephemera, photographs, etc.)	X	X	X	X

Table 12.1: The Materials and Media of a Corporate Archives (cont.)

| | | Media | | |
Archival Materials	Paper	Magnetic Media	Film[1]	Other[2]
Miscellaneous collections (including photographs, recorded and/or videotaped interviews, etc.)	X	X	X	X
Biographical records (including records and/or interviews related to founders of the organization, former company presidents, policy-making officers; may include personal papers, occasional family records, photographs and recorded and/or videotaped interviews, etc.)	X	X	X	X
Administrative data (including information about major changes and improvements, mergers, dissolutions, management information systems, etc.)	X	X	X	

[1]May include microfilm in its various forms and formats, motion picture film and other photographic materials.
[2]May include bulky items such as product samples, antiques, etc.

Table 12.2: Comparison of Some of the Documents Included in a Vital Records Program and a Corporate Archives

Documents	Vital Records	Archival Materials
Minutes of significant meetings	X	X
Accounts receivable	X	
Journals	X	X[1]
General ledgers	X	X[1]
Stock certificates	X	X[1]
Sales and production records	X[2]	X[1]
Legal records	X[3]	X[3]
Organization charts	X[2]	X
Publications		X
Patent files	X	X
Blueprints and engineering drawings	X	X
Scrapbooks		X

[1]Often sample runs will satisfy archival collecting patterns.
[2]Current materials that could be used to reconstruct business operations, rather than historical records.
[3]Appropriate records for each category might not be the same, and might not include all legal records, for example.

A vital records program is intended to safeguard the company's assets in case of an emergency, by enabling the company to maintain its operation and reestablish its legal or business position. Such information is dynamic and subject to revision, but the total volume and scope of the program rarely expands much beyond that originally established. Records maintenance is important, but rarely involves more than regularly updating materials, periodically verifying the continued value of records included in the program and occasionally adding new records.

A corporate archives preserves materials that can be used to reconstruct your organization's history, policies and ways of doing business. The archival materials that make up this collection include records that were created early in the organization's history; they also include current records. Not only must these materials be collected over many years, they must also be maintained in usable condition over time. You must see to it that such records can be used. This means identifying their contents, arranging them in a useful manner and promoting their use. Professional archival standards and guidelines exist for each of these steps. (See bibliography.)

Statement of Purpose

A written statement of purpose outlines the policies and procedures of your organization's corporate archives. The statement of purpose should explain what will be collected, how and by whom it will be used, and who will be responsible for the collection, both organizationally and functionally. The collecting policy that you develop will determine the kind of information and materials to be included in the corporate archives. You will also need to establish policies governing the acquisition and appropriate use of the materials.

Access to Records

The corporate archivist must have access to all company records. Occasionally, such materials may include business-sensitive records. To acquire such records will require management approval and may impose special restriction on their use. Restricted access to records is generally discouraged by the archival profession, but it may be the only way that some records can be acquired by the corporate archives.

Restriction policies may include a range of limitations. For example, they may prohibit any access to the organization's records for a specified period of years. Or, they may limit access only to individuals within the organization with a defined need to use the materials or the information contained in the records. Or, they may restrict only certain records, and then only for a specified period of time. Restrictions should be imposed only for legitimate reasons: in general, the less restrictions there are, the better.

MANAGING THE CORPORATE ARCHIVES

Archival materials are documented and arranged so that they can be located and used easily. Records are arranged according to the two basic principles of archival management: the principle of provenance and the principle of original order. Finding aids describe the archival materials and direct the user to the information being sought.

Arrangement of Materials

Principle of Provenance

The principle of provenance governs the compiling of records. Records are filed according to the individual or office that created them. This means that you should not combine all of the correspondence files that you collect into one large set of correspondence records. Instead, you must develop a system of arrangement that clearly indicates organizational relationships. For example, the correspondence of the board of directors should be filed with the minutes of its meetings and other related records, whereas the correspondence of the research and development department would be filed with laboratory books, patent files and related materials. The principle of provenance assures continuity and completeness of information about individual segments of the organization.

Principle of Original Order

The second principle of arrangement, original order, governs the filing order of materials within records series. Materials should be filed in the archives as they were filed by the originator. However, some archivists have begun to question the validity of this rule in all cases. The reasons for doubt are fairly simple, and you should be aware of them in order to decide for yourself where and when it is appropriate to follow this principle in arranging your company's archival materials.

If your organization has an established filing order or system, you should continue to use that system in organizing the archival collection. If you are dealing with the records of an individual who clearly established the arrangement of his or her own files, you should also follow the original order in arranging the archival files. In such cases, the principle of original order makes good sense. However, in many organizations, the original filing order is often devised by secretaries or files clerks who do not always understand the organizational relationships or the broader relationships of the organization itself. Here, the principle of original order may detract from the arrangement of the archives rather than contribute to an understanding of the information contained in the records.

One of your responsibilities in your role as corporate archivist will be to recognize the importance of the principle of original order, as well as its purpose. You may need to revise the filing order that you find, in terms of what you know about your organization and the originators of the materials you have collected. Again, your goal is to assure completeness, continuity and ease of access.

Description of Materials

The most successful archives are those which are used. You can assure the success of your organization's archives by describing the materials it contains clearly and simply, and by developing finding aid systems that make it easy for your users to locate the information they need.

If your organization's corporate archives contains a variety of media, you may need to develop more than one type of finding aid system. You may choose to prepare separate catalogs for publications, sample product collections, photograph and film or video tape collections, sound recordings and other specialized collections. But you must link all of these catalogs together in one centralized finding aid system, either a catalog or a simplified index. The user needs to be able to come into the archives and be led easily to the information that is needed.

The simpler the archives is to use, the more likely sales managers, personnel administrators, middle management and public relations staff are to use it. Each time such people do use your company's archives, they prove the value of the archives to the organization, and they make the archives' continued existence more certain.

Conservation

Good archival management also includes the conservation and preservation of the collection. You should be prepared to preserve microfilm, photographs, motion picture film; magnetic media, including sound recordings, video tapes and data processing media; engineering drawings, maps, blueprints; and paper records. You may even find yourself responsible for artifacts and/or a corporate museum.

Controlling Temperature and Humidity

Particular techniques are required for different archival materials, but the basic environmental needs are just about the same for all media. The archives should be maintained in a clean, constant environment, one that is controlled for temperature and humidity.

A minimum temperature of 50° Fahrenheit, and a maximum of 70° Fahrenheit, are recommended for archival records. However, fluctuation over such a wide range can actually be as damaging to records as steady temperatures above or below the recommended range. The same is true of fluctuations in relative humidity between the minimum of 40% and the maximum of 60%. The better policy, especially if your archives is housed in an office building that supports other functions and work areas, is to determine the standard range of temperature and humidity for your location, and to see to it that the temperature and relative humidity in the archives area do not fluctuate more than 10° and 10%, respectively, within that given range.

Other Preservation Issues

Temperature and humidity fluctuation is not the only cause of deterioration in archival materials. Careless users, water damage, mold, insects, animals, ultraviolet light, containers constructed of acidic paper and records constructed of poor quality materials are all harmful.

Archival containers, such as boxes, folders and envelopes, should be constructed of acid-free materials. Such supplies are available through archival suppliers. They are not inexpensive, but they are generally thought to prolong the life of archival materials.

You may be able to correct some problems before they reach the archives, by encouraging the use of better quality materials to create the records used by your organization. For example, washable inks really have no place in an organization's records, and you can certainly not be expected to guarantee their archival stability. Nor can you assure the archival stability of highly acidic papers, so common among today's records.

Magnetic media present unique archival problems. One area of concern is the incompatibility of different hardware and software systems. As computer systems are expanded or replaced, tapes and disks created on the original system may no longer be usable. Your organization must be alerted to this problem. It is important to have communication among everyone involved in the creation and maintenance of records: the archivist, the records manager (if another individual) and data processing personnel.

Whatever the format of archival records, you must be aware of the requirements for archival stability and long-term accessibility. You must be able to ensure the availability of such materials for many years. You need not be a conservator to do so, but you must know what is required, both to ensure that you do no harm, and in order that you know whom to call upon if and when you do need expert advice.

COMMITMENT

A corporate archives requires a long-term, professional commitment. The establishment of a corporate archives is only the first, most basic step in creating a useful—and usable—collection. Long-term financial support is crucial to the program's success. Archival materials are extremely vulnerable. You cannot neglect them in bad economic times and tend them in good without limiting the value of the collection, because much of the value of a good archival collection lies in its completeness and continuity. A hit-or-miss collecting pattern and incomplete documentation will make the entire collection less valuable.

The corporate archives is a business management resource made up of records created in the past. Such historical records can serve many functions within the organization. The establishment of a well-thought-out collecting policy, the development of clear and easy-to-use finding aids and the active conservation of such materials will make it possible for the archives to fulfill those functions.

13

The Library

by Jane Cargill

Records management is actually one aspect of an organization's overall information management effort. For many firms, information management includes the use of an in-house, or "special," library. The special library is one designed to meet the information needs of a specific firm or organization. There is a great deal of overlap between the functions performed by the librarian and those performed by the records manager. Both exist to expedite the flow of information through the organization. Both handle material generated internally and externally. Either may have to deal with word processing, electronic mail, micrographics and automated indexes or data bases.

This chapter will help you determine whether or not you need an in-house library and, if you do, how to establish one.

ROLE OF THE SPECIAL LIBRARY

Many firms have a facility called the "library," but not all of these would be regarded as such by professionals in the field. To the information professional, a special library is one that gathers and selectively disseminates information. It draws on materials generated in-house, by other firms and organizations, and by commercial sources. The space in which these materials are housed is important, but the facility only becomes a library when the elements of organization and control are added. The library realizes its full potential when all the information resources available to the firm are employed.

Levels of Service

Housekeeping

In many companies, complete library services are not necessary. A central storage area that houses such materials as promotional literature, internal reports, journals and newspapers is enough. This facility may be supervised by a clerk or receptionist with no library training or experience, whose only function is to shelve materials in some semblance of order. Such facilities are not true libraries. The level of service they offer can best be referred to as "housekeeping," since no research or reference service is offered. If your primary need is for current information in a few very specific subject areas, you should consider this option.

Reference

The next level is a facility staffed by a library technician who can perform reference work and handle selective dissemination of information, or SDI (routing information or records of interest to users). A library technician usually holds a two-year degree from a community college and is trained in basic classification and cataloging, acquisition of materials, the use of elementary reference tools such as atlases and directories, and the routine housekeeping functions of the library. A library technician can perform satisfactorily if your information needs are neither large nor complex, and if standard library systems can be used. If you do not require extensive research services, you should consider this option.

Research

The highest level of service is provided by a "special" library managed by someone with professional training in the organization and retrieval of information. Typically, this person holds a master's degree in library science, although some librarians successfully substitute experience for formal training. (Qualifications of a special librarian are described below.)

Depending on your specific requirements, your special librarian can do quick reference work or in-depth research, maintain awareness of new technologies and resources, design indexes and other information control systems, and evaluate and use commercial information sources. These may include microform publications and computerized data bases in such diverse areas as education, law, science, medicine, the humanities or even the daily news. In some firms, the librarian is also expected to translate, serve as a technical writer and abstract articles and reports.

If there are many professionals in your firm who spend a significant percentage of their working hours gathering and evaluating information, you should seriously consider investing in a special library with a professional staff. Such a facility will free your key personnel to concentrate on the income-generating functions that only they can perform, while ensuring that their decisions are based on timely, accurate and complete information.

QUALIFICATIONS OF THE SPECIAL LIBRARIAN

Most special librarians have at least one college degree in a subject specialty before entering library school. They usually prefer to work in firms where their technical expertise complements their library skills. This technical knowledge is an asset to any industry with its own unique jargon and body of knowledge.

Unlike the average researcher, the librarian draws on a broad range of resources and technologies, including computerized data bases, interlibrary loan, microforms and resource sharing with other libraries. All of these require knowledge of the resources available, and skill in their use. A strong ability to index, classify and catalog is also an important asset. Those librarians who have a thorough knowledge of indexing and cataloging rules and techniques, and who enjoy the work, can ensure the production of consistent, standardized indexes—an essential prerequisite to successful information retrieval.

The person responsible for your library's operation must be resourceful and flexible. When we think of a "library," we tend to think of a collection of books, newspapers and magazines. A more experienced user might include slides, films, maps, graphs and microforms in the collection. Any of these may be found in a special library.

However, the library's scope is not limited to such materials. For example, if your firm manufactures clothing, a trademark for each garment may appear on it in the form of stitching, or the kind of fastener used. Your library collection may include a sample of each garment manufactured. If so, your librarian will find it difficult to organize and control this collection using standard techniques, and innovation will be essential.

Like any other manager in your firm, the librarian must be a competent administrator. During normal working hours, the librarian's attention is drawn to serving the library's patrons. However, administrative tasks such as planning, budgeting, personnel evaluation and report writing still must be done. Technical skills alone are not enough. Without sound administrative skills, your librarian will flounder.

ANALYZING YOUR NEEDS

The first step in determining an appropriate level of service for your firm is an analysis of your needs. The process begins with the definition of the types of information your firm needs. Ask yourself (and other potential library users) whether the information most frequently needed is internally or externally generated. Determine whether that information is available within the firm, or whether it must be obtained from other sources. Find out what sort of information is most often requested, by whom and for what purpose:

- Management/technical reports;

- Studies done for clients;

- Maps/blueprints/charts/drawings;

- Ephemeral material, such as pamphlets;

- Legal documents;

- Reference and research materials
  Scientific and technical
  Business
  Humanities/social sciences
  Government.

From this complete picture of your firm's information needs, you can determine which level of service is best for your firm. If your information-gathering process was thorough, you should also be able to identify the specific services your library should provide: automated research, selective dissemination of information, etc. Decide whether you want to include any recreational reading matter in your library. Also, evaluate the importance to your firm of confidentiality, efficiency and economy, the timeliness of information and its technical accuracy.

In conjunction with your analysis of your firm's current information needs, you should consider the potential growth of the firm, as well as any changes in its functions that may have an impact on support services. If possible, project your planning for at least 10 years. Your long-term goals for the library also must be defined. Do you want your library to:

- Attract good personnel to the firm?

- Improve your product or services?

- Provide the flexibility to meet changing economic/service demands?

- Provide multipurpose space for various uses?

- Impress clients and/or your industry?

CHOOSING THE BEST ALTERNATIVE

Perhaps you have decided that your firm needs a high level of library service. Next, you must ascertain the most cost-effective way to obtain such service. What options do you have?

The In-house Library

Most obvious is the in-house library. This is a very expensive option, but usually offers the highest level of service to its users. The collection can be tailored to the needs of your firm. Your professionals will have access to the facility whenever they wish. The amount of working space and type of library seating provided can be geared to their needs. You can even design the library so that it can be used for other purposes, such as meetings.

The in-house library staff can maintain close contact with users, which allows the staff to define and fill user needs efficiently. Staff can offer extra services such as translation and technical writing if these are important to the firm's activities. Confidentiality can be ensured, because only the firm's employees and guests have access to the facility.

The private library's drawback is its cost. When anlayzing this factor, you must consider both the obvious costs, such as salaries, and the hidden ones. These include the initial capital costs, the cost of acquiring the collection and the continuing costs of collection maintenance, space and so on. Expenses vary with the type of library furniture and equipment used, the materials' format and the type of industry in which your firm is involved.

For example, architectural drawings may be kept in their original form, which requires a great deal of space, or in micrographic format. If your firm's work is scientific or technical, its professionals will need current, accurate information. In this case, a large part of the library collection will be serials (journals, newspapers and other materials published on a regular basis). The cost of these subscriptions may increase as much as 50% with each renewal.

The Shared Library

Perhaps you find an in-house library attractive, but your firm is unwilling or unable to finance it. One alternative that is gaining in popularity is the shared library. These are typically found in large office buildings or complexes that house several firms engaged in the same or related businesses. These firms pool their resources to develop a common library that all may use. A library administrator and staff are hired, a collection useful to all participants is developed and the desired level of service is delineated by common agreement.

Shared libraries offer their patrons the advantage of convenient location. To some extent, the library staff can recognize and meet the needs of individual patrons. The cost to each contributor is much less than that of a private library. Further, if there are several participants, the shared library may have a stronger financial base than could a private one. Because of this, the shared library may be able to afford new technologies to a greater extent than the private one.

There are some disadvantages to a shared library. For instance, the staff is less able to provide personal service to clients, because it serves so many, and with some diversity of purpose. The shared library may not be able to provide as much seating as the private one, and its patrons are unlikely to have access to it after business hours. Because there are more users per title, the patrons may have to wait longer for a specific item. However, if you are among those who find the cost of a private library prohibitive, the shared library presents a viable alternative.

The Building Library

A "building library" is one kind of shared library. The building library is distinguished from other shared libraries by the fact that it is owned and administered by the building management, rather than by contributing firms. The library design is incorporated into the building plans, and the librarian reports directly to a representative of the management company.

Building libraries serve the tenants of the building or complex, each of whom pays a service fee. Because more users are served, there is usually more financial support for a building library than for other shared libraries, even though the individual service fee is apt to be smaller. The larger budget of the building library provides a larger collection and more research capability. However, such services as routing of journals or translating are not likely to be provided.

The Public Library

If you are in a heavily populated area, your public library may be a good information source. Its collection may not include specialized technical works, but it probably will have strong business and reference collections. If the area's economy is heavily influenced by one industry or corporation, the public library may have an extensive collection related to it.

Public library holdings are augmented by participation in regional and national interlibrary loan systems. Many use modern technologies, such as micrographic card catalogs and computerized data bases. Most issue library cards to firms, if an officer of the company will sign the application and act as guarantor. Also, most offer telephone reference service, and some provide research services. Your state library is another rich resource, offering telephone reference service and interlibrary loan.

Other Institutions

Complementary library services may be available from local educational institutions, government information centers or private institutions. A college may not be able to lend you materials, since it must keep them available for student use, but you will be able to use them in the library. Federal information centers offer telephone reference service. Some government libraries have extensive holdings that are available to the public. For example, the Seattle district of the U.S. Army Corps of Engineers maintains a collection of technical and engineering information, government regulations and government contract law materials. An automated inter-library loan network links this collection with more than 2000 other libraries across the nation.

Information Brokers

If your firm relies on external information sources like those described above, but occasionally needs intensive research services, you may want to use a fee-based information service, or information broker. These firms provide various information-handling services for a fee. They may be involved in consulting, research or library planning. Most subscribe to, and are good at using, commercial data bases. Their "products" include analytical reports, bibliographies, catalogs, indexes or actual documents. Fee-based information services emphasize efficient, cost-effective information delivery. If your in-depth research needs are limited, the information broker can be a useful alternative to the library.

RESOURCE SHARING AMONG LIBRARIES

Just as individual firms often expand their library services by establishing shared facilities, libraries share resources to meet their users' research needs in the most cost-effective manner.

Interlibrary Loan

One of the most frequent means of resource sharing among libraries is interlibrary loan: the process by which one library lends materials to another. Until recently, interlibrary loan required that a borrower locate materials in other collections by using a "union list" (a record of the holdings of each library participating in the system). A printed loan request had to be sent to the lending library, and the materials shipped to the borrower. This time-consuming process is often no longer necessary. Libraries are becoming more involved in electronic interlibrary loan; searches and requests are made online, which facilitates the timely delivery of information.

Why can't a patron borrow materials directly from another library, rather than through interinstitutional loan? Some regional library systems permit this, but in general a library will lend materials directly only to its own patrons or to another library. If a library loaned directly to other patrons, and the materials were not returned, the library would have no jurisdiction or recourse. This is not true of interlibrary loans, which are governed by formal written codes that delineate borrowing procedures and conditions.

Further, a library can locate materials outside its collection more rapidly than could the patron. The library staff's finding aids are much more efficient than the hit-and-miss search likely to be conducted by the patron.

Interlibrary loan is used by public, educational and institutional libraries more often than by special libraries, which view the protection of their employer's interests as their first priority. The special librarian always maintains confidentiality, and keeps all materials available for the employer's use. Other special libraries within the employer's industry are often regarded as competitors. One advantage of shared libraries over private libraries is that they are better able to participate in resource sharing.

Cooperative Acquisitions

Although special libraries are less likely than others to share resources, some cooperative arrangements do exist. For example, depending on their proximity and degree of competitiveness, it may not be necessary for all the special libraries in a given industry to duplicate each other's holdings. One option that may be tried is planned collection development, or "cooperative acquisitions." Any number of libraries with similar interests may participate in a cooperative acquisitions system. Each undertakes to avoid purchasing duplicates of titles held by others, unless demand necessitates their doing so. Each contracts to devote funds to develop a collection focused on a specific subject, and to make its holdings available to the other participating libraries through interlibrary loan.

The value of cooperative acquisitions has been proven repeatedly. Because cataloging and resources are shared, each participant has access to an increased number of materials without a corresponding increase in cost. To the librarian, and to the firm that supports a special library, this is of incomparable value. Much of the librarian's life is spent in recording descriptions of the library's materials. These descriptions are transferred to catalog cards, microform or display terminals for patron use. Cataloging and classification are essential to successful information retrieval, but they are expensive—and often unnecessarily so in special libraries.

Given the duplication of titles in an industry's libraries, there is much duplication of cataloging effort. Shared cataloging can eliminate unnecessary duplication. Some of the commercial data bases which offer online research services also make shared cataloging services available. Alternatively, you may wish to automate your cataloging, using your librarian's unique indexing skills to control the acquisition and circulation of materials while reducing cataloging costs.

SETTING UP AN IN-HOUSE LIBRARY

If you have decided that you need a private, in-house library, the next question is: How do you start? First, consolidate the information collected in your needs analysis. Presumably, through consultation with potential users, you have defined the level of service your library should provide. Through discussions with other managers in the firm, you should determine what priority the library will have, and what its place will be in the firm's organizational structure. You will also consider your firm's future, and how the library can best grow with and support your business.

Next, if possible, identify comparable facilities in your area and visit them. Consider the level of service each offers and ask about the cost of both start-up and continuing operations. This will help you see what is possible for your own firm. At this point, you also need to focus on who your library patrons will be and what tasks they are likely to perform in the library:

- Manual or automated research;

- Reference work;

- Group study or conference;

- Light or recreational reading;

- Photocopying;

- Writing or dictation;

- Use of non-book materials (slides, microforms, films, recordings).

You must decide where your library should be located to be near the maximum number of users. Take into account how much your space needs are apt to fluctuate during the next 10 years. Determine whether you want to reserve the space for library use, or whether it is to be multipurpose. Finally, keeping other office priorities in mind, decide how much space and money you are willing to allocate for your library operation. Is the library to support activities carried on elsewhere? These support services may have a substantial effect on library space. For example, if your employees use portable microform readers, they may be stored in the library and checked out to patrons for occasional use.

Using a Professional Library Consultant

How much planning can you do without advice from a library professional and still achieve satisfactory results? There is no easy answer. Remember that in order to plan an effective facility, you must understand its functions, and place efficiency above beauty on your priority list. Usually, private libraries are designed by an architect or interior designer without consulting a library professional. Neither understands the library's daily operational requirements. Some of the tasks performed by a library staff are highly visible and easily understood—for example, reference work, research and circulation control. Other functions are equally essential, but almost invisible to the layman. Often, these are neglected by non-librarians, with the result that the library cannot realize its full service potential.

Designing the Facility

Acquisitions and cataloging procedures take place behind the scenes. They are essential components of collection development and organization. These functions require a large, quiet work area, where material can be gathered and processed without disturbing the library's patrons. Here, materials are packed, unpacked and prepared for the bindery. Supplies are stored nearby, where they can be retrieved easily and quickly.

To design adequate work space for library staff, the functions performed in each work area must be delineated, the necessary furniture and equipment defined, and a feasibility study done. Floor plans and flow charts must be prepared, along with scale models of the basic library elements such as stacks, chairs and tables, desks, carrels and other furniture used by staff and patrons. All the elements affecting space design and use within the library must be measured and quantified:

- The total library floor space and its configuration;

- Projected growth patterns and traffic patterns;

- The total linear footage of the shelving, its size and the square footage of the stacks;

- The distances and relationships between areas of the library which serve various functions.

You will be saved many hours of research and costly mistakes if an experienced professional helps you plan the facility you need to provide the desired services. This person may be either an outside consultant or your own librarian, if you have already hired one. Tell your advisor what you have determined about user needs, and ask for recommendations about the most cost-effective way to accomplish your purpose.

Long-range Planning

Your advisor should be able to recommend efficient methods of acquisition, maintenance, delivery and service. A consultant can also provide long-range planning that takes into account the projected growth rate of the collection, program changes that may require space modification and new uses of technology. This sort of long-range planning will allow future expansion of your library, if necessary, without excessive expense and disruption.

Obviously, final decisions about library costs and space allotments must be made at the management level. However, if you make the mistake of finalizing library plans based on inadequate information, it will be very costly and time-consuming to modify them. Once you have fixed the size, shape and location of the library, it is almost impossible to change them. (Further discussion of collection and facilities planning appears later in this chapter.) Your consultant's greatest value to you will be in allowing you to make informed decisions about the library. A consultant, or librarian with experience in library design, can identify the factors that most affect the library's functions and size. The tasks performed by the library staff will be defined for you, and you will be shown how they work together to provide the services you require.

Hiring Your Librarian

If you plan to have a librarian, initiate the hiring process as early as possible. The search process and the length of time required to find your librarian will vary with the level of service you want. If you plan to hire a library technician, contact the nearest community college with a library technician training program. Choosing this option will necessitate hiring a consultant as well: the library technician, particularly if inexperienced, is unlikely to be able to design efficient information control systems, or an adequate physical facility.

Qualifications Necessary

In contrast, a professional librarian may enable you to bypass the consultant. When you hire a librarian, what qualifications should you require, and what guidelines can be used in evaluating a librarian's skills? First, it is important to hire someone with a degree in library science. Personnel who lack the library degree also lack the librarian's intensive training in administration, reference and research techniques, and effective methods of information control and management. Further, since most special libraries have only one librarian, non-degreed personnel who have come from that background are unlikely to have received on-the-job training from a qualified professional.

Second, look for a person whose subject specialty and complementary training are in areas useful to you. The librarian may be trained in science, technology, business administration, computer science, the social sciences or the humanities. Some are also trained in records management, a natural adjunct to library science. If it is important that your librarian be fluent in a particular language, this should be specified.

Where to Find Staff

You may hire an inexperienced librarian by contacting the placement service at the nearest library school. Finding an experienced special librarian is more difficult. In addition to advertising the position, you might enlist the help of the Special Libraries Association. Many prospective employers attend this organization's annual conference to interview and hire. Alternatively, ask a special librarian in another firm to put you in touch with the local chapter of this association, which probably maintains its own placement service. You may find a highly qualified employee in the immediate area. You may even find a part-time employee, or a consultant who can devote a few hours each week to your library's administrative duties, leaving routine chores to be done by less costly personnel working under the professional's supervision.

DEVELOPING COST PROJECTIONS

Like long-range planning, cost projections fall under management jurisdiction. Some fixed expenses can be easily forecast:

- Wages and salaries;
- Utilities;
- Maintenance of the physical plant;
- Office equipment;
- Cost of the space.

Cost Factors to Evaluate

Other library costs vary greatly. Because complex cost-benefit studies are essential to accurate financial planning, the advice of a consultant or experienced librarian is critical at this stage. Among the factors evaluated will be:

- The library's possible functions and services
    Dictation or recording
    Viewing of slides or films
    Typing or photocopying
    Writing, translating or editing
    Information dissemination
    Telephone or ready reference service
    Manual or automated research
    Group study or conferences
    Microfilming, binding or mending

- Work areas within the library
    Conference or study rooms
    Quiet research areas
    Reference areas
    Listening/recording/telephone booths
    Micrographics or computer rooms
    Photocopy or typing room
    Librarian's office
    Work space for library staff

- Specialized equipment or furniture
    Study/index/reference tables and carrels with or without specialized lighting and wiring
    Newspaper, periodical and paperback racks
    Binding, mending and processing equipment
    Book returns and trucks
    Special cabinets for ephemeral or oversized materials

- The space required for each area
    How many users will there be? Will this figure fluctuate? If so, how much?
    What furniture or equipment will this area house? How big is it? Does servicing require extra space?
    Does this area require special attention to climate and noise control, wiring, lighting or traffic patterns?

Would other equipment such as a telephone or calculator be useful in this area?

Should this area be near library staff, or a particular part of the collection?

In what format will material be acquired: hard copy, microforms, audiovisual or electronic?

How long must each title be kept, and in what format?

How wide must the aisles between stacks be, to allow convenient passage for users and book trucks?

What type of shelving is most desirable for the specific applications in your library?

- Specialized services and supplies for library staff
  Commercial or automated in-house cataloging
  Electronic interlibrary loan
  Catalog card reproduction facilities
  Mending, binding or microfilming supplies and equipment

COLLECTION AND FACILITIES PLANNING

Paper vs. Microform

The materials in your collection, and their formats, will have a greater influence on the size of your facility than any other single factor. Thus, you and your professional advisor must plan not just what the library will contain, but in what format. For example, your library may need a complete run of a particular scientific or technical journal. In the journal's paper version, the issues to date may fill 36 linear feet of shelving, 10 inches deep and 10 inches high. If you acquire and keep this journal for another 10 years, 50 linear feet of shelving may be needed for this one title. To protect your investment, you may bind each volume as it is completed—at a cost of as much as $30 per volume.

Back issues of this title may be available in micrographic format for half the cost of the paper version, or less. The fiche or film may last for years under normal conditions. The entire run of the journal can be housed in a space the size of a shoebox.

Before deciding that you will buy the microforms, you must weigh the costs outlined above against the cost of microform equipment. To use your fiche or film, you will need a reader and/or a reader/printer. You may want several portable readers, so that the materials may be used in an office or at home. The type and number of readers and reader/printers you purchase must be evaluated carefully, considering:

- Size and space requirements;

- Noise, and the need for noise control;

- Electrical outlets, and the ability to dim lights in the area housing the equipment;

- Proximity to related materials;

- Construction, maintenance and servicing requirements.

You will also want to choose the equipment which best serves your needs. This requires that the purchaser ask:

- Is this machine adaptable?

- Will it handle film as well as fiche?

- Can lenses be interchanged to accommodate material published in various reduction ratios?

- Will it handle materials published in both positive and negative modes?

Remember that if you buy a less costly and less adaptable machine, you may have to buy additional equipment when new material in a different format is added to the collection.

Alternatives to Purchasing Materials

Aside from paper or microforms, there is a third alternative: don't keep the journal at all. There may be a library in your area that keeps this title permanently and is willing to lend it. Also, some data bases include scientific and technical journals in a full-text version. If you plan to have a commercial data base service, many of the journals you want may be available online. In this case, you must weigh the cost of connect time, as your online computer time is called, against the cost of acquiring and housing the journals. Various data bases offer various services. The advantages of each must be evaluated carefully. For computers, unlike microforms, you must analyze the software, the hardware specifications and the communications formats.

User Needs

When doing your cost-benefit analyses, don't lose sight of user needs. Ask yourself whether significant numbers of users will need to have the latest information simultaneously, whether the paper version can be obtained more quickly than the microforms and whether the titles you want are available in more than one format. You may decide to satisfy heavy demand for current materials by subscribing to the journal, and reduce storage and maintenance costs by using microforms and data bases to retrieve less heavily used, older materials. In any case, your facilities planning will not be complete until you have taken into account the equipment requirements of your collection formats.

Space Design

Security

The single most important architectural feature of the library is control. To decrease losses and safeguard confidentiality, minimize the number of entrances to the facility, and place them in full view of the library staff. Control and maintenance functions are best served by a square or rectangular shape. This configuration offers other advantages as well: efficient use of space, internal flexibility, expansion capability and adaptability to multi-purpose use. In general, other physical characteristics of a good library include:

- Its restriction to one level, near the elevators, to enhance the collection's accessibility;

- A location near the heaviest users;

- Adequate lighting;

- Adequate noise and climate control features;

- Enough telephone jacks and electrical outlets to allow flexibility.

If you are tempted to increase the collection's availability by creating satellite libraries, be careful. Satellites present control and maintenance problems, and you may have to increase the library staff to service them properly.

Noise Control

Noise control requires a multi-dimensional approach. Acoustically treated walls and ceilings are helpful, as are carpeted floors. In some areas of your library, there may be multiple sources of noise—especially if your facility contains photocopying machines, telephones, micrographic reader/printers, computer terminals or conference areas. These areas should be isolated from research and study areas. Again, don't try to design the library's interior without professional input. Library furniture and equipment designs have evolved from many years' experience, and the input of many users. As with collection formats, the librarian's experience is invaluable in choosing a satisfactory mix for your specific needs.

Evaluating the Design

When you think you and your librarian have arrived at a good design, test your conclusions by reconsidering the provisions you have made for control, comfort, flexibility and utility. Ask yourself whether this facility is visually attractive and convenient to work in. Decide whether you would like to work there and envision the problems you might encounter in doing so. As a final check, review your plans to use space-saving technologies and techniques: micrographics, computers, shared cataloging, interlibrary loan and cooperative acquisitions. Be sure that in saving space, you haven't planned to house books in reception areas, hallways, conference rooms or offices, where they will be less accessible than they should be.

Above all, make sure that your decisions have been based on sound information. If you've done your research and cost-benefit studies, visited other libraries, solicited input from knowledgeable sources and planned carefully, the information services you have chosen will be a resounding success.

Afterword

by Katherine Aschner

Records management has never been quite the same since the introduction of technology. Some of technology's effects are now so commonplace as to be taken for granted. The telephone, for instance, has replaced many forms of written communications. Other changes, of course, are more noticeable. Computers, magnetic media and micrographics have had a major impact on the format and retrieval of most types of office records.

Until recently, technology has been used to improve records systems and related procedures. Our concept of what constituted a record remained essentially unchanged. Today, however, our basic assumptions about records management are being challenged. The focus of technology has shifted from streamlining paperwork to restructuring the operation of the office itself. The tasks we perform, the resources we draw on, the products we deliver—all are undergoing change. As technology permits us to redesign the place and even the hours of work, our relationships with employers, supervisors and co-workers will be significantly altered as well.

TECHNOLOGY AND RECORDS MANAGEMENT

What are the implications of this change for records management? Or, to put the question more directly, how quickly will technology render this book obsolete? While the timetable is difficult to predict, certain things are clear. For the present, the techniques developed in this book most definitely apply. Records management programs implemented today will earn back their costs many times before full-scale office automation is able to provide better solutions.

Nevertheless, automation will continue to gain ground. This will be especially true for large organizations that can afford the initial equipment and start-up costs associated with implementing new technologies. Once innovations become established, they will begin to filter down to smaller businesses as well.

Much of our increasing use of office automation will be attributable to three interrelated factors: reduced costs; simplified procedures for nontechnical users; and faster turnaround time, especially with regard to electronic rather than hard-copy communications. However, an equally significant advantage of automation lies in a different area: the removal of artificial barriers from records and information systems. This benefit will be realized through the increased integration of software, the linking of different makes and types of hardware, and the merging of information formats in high-density, low-cost storage media.

SOFTWARE INTEGRATION

Professional computers are already eliminating one of the principal barriers in office systems: the line between different types of programs. In the early days, a machine was either a word processor or a computer. Even as a computer it could only do one thing at a time: process a financial statement or compose a graph. Needless to say, office workers don't operate in such exclusive environments. When preparing budgets and reports, users need to compose text, tabulate numbers and draw graphs as part of one continuous, flexible process. The technology to achieve this is here, although it is still evolving. The challenge now is to reduce its cost and to help office workers take advantage of their new tools.

INTEGRATION OF DIFFERENT MANUFACTURERS' HARDWARE

Another of the major barriers faced by (and created by) office systems is incompatibility: word processor A uses different codes for formatting instructions than word processor B. Transferring text between the two results in unintelligible gibberish at the other end.

The incompatibility problem has existed for as long as companies have had two computers to choose from. Therefore, some solutions to the problem are already in place. Optical scanners can translate printed output from one word processor or computer to another. However, scanners are not always reliable. Cleanup of misread characters and format errors is usually required. The technology is also slow.

Another solution is "black boxes." These are specially programmed computers that translate the code of one manufacturer's machine to another's. Black boxes work well in organizations that have standard translation requirements. However, if you need to link large numbers of distant users together, some of whom are only occasional communicators, you begin to exceed the practical limits of the technology.

Enter packet switching networks and the X.25 communications standard. Packet switching networks allow large numbers of subscribers to share access to expensive data communications lines. You get the transmission quality you need, while only paying for what you use.

Packet switching networks have long been used in data communications to link compatible computers. Now, however, they can also be used as a bridge between incompatible systems. The introduction of the X.25 communications standard allows users to exchange "print images" of text and data files. The effect is a facsimile transmission of a machine-readable file, with all of the vendor-specific formatting codes and program instructions removed.

If you need to edit a document sent via a packet switching network, you have two choices: use compatible systems or reenter instruction codes (such as "underline" or "multiply") at the receiving end. However, if your primary need is electronic mail or sharing access to a common data base, you can display or print the file without further ado.

The next advance will be the merger of black box and packet switching technologies. The translation tables for virtually all systems will be built into one or more public communications networks. Programs and files will be fully exchangeable across the hall or across the country. One way or another, the barrier between incompatible systems will be broken down.

INTEGRATION OF DIFFERENT TYPES OF EQUIPMENT

Many offices employ a wide variety of office machines: computers, word processors, photocomposers, copiers, telecommunications devices, high speed printers, mass storage devices, graphics plotters and the like. Again, we have long been able to link some systems together: several word processing terminals sharing a disk drive or laser printer, or several remote data entry terminals linked to a host computer. However, there are some barriers that make the exchange of information more difficult: different floors, different working hours, terminals linked to different host computers. These are barriers that local area networks are just beginning to cross.

Local area networks are user-owned high-speed communications links. They are internal, typically limited to a distance of 10 miles or less. Most use some form of coaxial cable, although other types are available.

Local area networks offer two important bridges for office information exchanges: extremely high speed and exceptional flexibility. Their high speed brings the advantage of packet switching to the office: the ability to service many users simultaneously. This makes it practical to set up large networks. Their flexibility derives from the way local area networks are implemented. In most cases, a facility is precabled; systems are tapped on and off the network as needed. Virtually any communicating device can be tapped on (although compatibility may be required). Devices can be added or deleted with ease. Furthermore, because the network is internal, there are no ongoing tariffs to pay once the cable is in place.

Like the technologies discussed above, local area networks are already commercially available. Their development is still in the early stages, however, and many technical questions remain. Nevertheless, at some point these networks are likely to replace both the telephone and the mail cart as the primary means of office communication and information exchange.

MERGER OF INFORMATION FORMATS

Another of the principal attributes of local area networks is their ability to transmit text, data, graphics, voice and full-motion video. However, without a convenient, cost-effective way to store all these formats on a single storage medium, some of the effect is lost. This barrier is one that optical disk technology will erode, especially when coupled with local area networks. Optical disks are most often cited for their potentially low-cost storage of machine-readable information. However, equally significant is their ability to store almost any form of information, be it digital, graphic, analog or moving pictures, that man has been able to devise.

WHAT HAPPENS TO RECORDS MANAGEMENT?

Will automation render the records manager obsolete? Not a chance. The title may change, but companies will still have the same needs: to establish cost controls; to ensure the quality and currentness of information; and to make sure that the information management needs get into the system. Furthermore, whether manual or automated, the same set of records system objectives must be met: communicating information up and down the line; ensuring that company policies and transactions are recorded; and preserving the order of recorded information.

The very fact that technology eliminates so many barriers introduces new problems. The chronological office file may not be easy to work with, but it does make it easy to maintain a case history. An online data base that is regularly updated is more appealing, to be sure, but it is also much more volatile. Establishing and implementing retention schedules in this environment will be tricky indeed.

As more professionals begin to solve their problems with VisiCalc-like tools, the danger of undocumented decisions is also introduced. For instance, a manager may initiate action based on cost projections that cannot be substantiated at a later date. If methods and assumptions go undocumented, remedial action may be very difficult to establish when the time comes.

Technology itself is neutral. Its characterization as good or bad will depend upon how it is implemented. For example, electronic mail can increase the exchange of ideas in an organization (good), or it can dehumanize the office by reducing face-to-face contacts (bad). Professional records management can play a pivotal role in establishing successfully automated office systems. It has a bearing on the timing of automation, the choice of technologies and, most important, the documentation of systems. Far from eliminating the need for records management skills, technology is likely to render them more critical than ever.

Appendix 1: Instructions for the Files Inventory Form

The following instructions explain how to complete the files inventory form shown on page 20. When you distribute the form to members of your inventory team, provide them with a copy of the instructions as well.

In some cases, explanatory material supplements the instructions. This material is given parenthetically. It is not intended to be handed out as part of the instructions for the form.

LOCATION

Self-explanatory. (The purpose of this section is to identify the location of the records and the principal contact who can answer questions about them. After the manual is developed, this information is very helpful in planning the conversion of existing files to your new system.)

IDENTIFICATION

Describe types of records and how they are used. (This is the information you need to define records series and to determine their hierarchical relationships with each other.)

WORKING RECORDS SERIES TITLE

The title should be brief, and should clearly reflect the function of the records. Typically, the title on the file is the one to use.

CONTENTS/CASE FILES

List the types of records filed in this records series. Describe any case files, and how they are organized. Continue on the back of the form, if necessary. Be sure to check the appropriate block if you do. Do not list out the names of specific case files.

An example of a correct entry here: "Official personnel folders containing original employment agreements, notices of promotions and awards, training records, information on benefits and seniority, and union participation documents. There is one official personnel folder for each current employee and for each employee terminated within the last five years."

USE/RETRIEVAL TERMS

Describe what the files are used for. List all common terms of reference to the files. Continue on the back, if necessary. Be sure to check the continuation block if you do.

An example of a correct entry here: "Official personnel files are used to document each employee's career in the company, and to administer benefits, if any, after a person has left employment. These files may be required long after termination for verifying employment or survivor's benefit claims. Other terms: career file, employee master file."

(It is very important to note all the terms by which people refer to a particular records series, even though only one will be used in the classification scheme. The other terms will be listed in an alphabetical cross-index to the classifications, and will help people make the transition to the new filing system.)

DESCRIPTION

Check all answers that apply in each section; fill in all the blanks completely.

(The information in this section helps in determining appropriate files arrangements. It also highlights how long various records series remain active, how long users want their records to be kept in active and inactive storage, and whether there are any situations that might warrant microfilming or automation. For example, a very large file that has a very long retention period should be evaluated for microfilming—see Chapters 7 and 8. An elaborate cross-reference card file might indicate the need for a computerized index—see Chapter 9. To simplify the task, this section has been arranged as much as possible for filling in the blanks.)

Arrangement. Indicate the principal arrangement of the file. (For example, official personnel folders are arranged in "alpha" order. Correspondence files are typically arranged by "subject" and in "alpha" order.)

Format. Self-explanatory.

Storage. Self-explanatory. If more than one type is used, such as when boxed files are stored on shelves, check all that apply.

Finding Aids. List the type and arrangement of any cross-indexes or other finding aids used as a reference to this records series.

(In many cases, the finding aid may be rather simple: a name index to legal case files that are arranged in numeric order. However, there is often a need for greater indexing than is practical in a manual system. For instance, this might include the name of the responsible attorney, the type of law involved and annual dates when certain kinds of documents should be filed for this client. Whenever you see a cross-reference index to a file, you should evaluate the potential for expanded indexing using a word processor or computer—see Chapter 9.)

Volume. List the total cubic feet of this records series at this location. Also list the expected annual accumulation rate in cubic feet.

(If the same series occurs elsewhere, such as in inactive storage, fill out a new form for that location. Otherwise, the conversion and purging process becomes more difficult to manage. The annual accumulation rate is a valuable indicator of problem files. If the rate is high, running into cabinets' worth of cubic feet, microfilming or computerization may be in order.)

Dates. List the earliest and most recent dates for records in this series at this location. If the file is still being accumulated here, check "to present." (This information will help you to purge obsolete files before any actual files conversion begins.)

Activity. Indicate how often the active part of this records series is referred to at this location.

(Due to inadequate purging, only the recent part of the file at a given location may be referred to on a regular basis.)

User Reference. Indicate how long the records referred to above remain that active. (In other words, if the file is referred to daily, is that for this year's records only, for several years' records or until the current file is superseded. For example, a contract file may remain active as long as the contract is in force, regardless of how many years old it is. If it does, the "current" box applies.)

User Retention. Indicate how long the user maintains this records series in the office. If the user also transfers these records to inactive storage, indicate how long they are held in inactive storage prior to destruction.

STATUS

Check all boxes that apply. (The purpose of this section is to segregate official records from supporting files and reference materials. Typically, only official orginals of records need to be retained for the full retention period. It is important to identify where the official copies are, and to make sure that duplicates are weeded out before records are sent for long term storage. This section also begins to get at records requiring special attention, such as vital or archival records.)

Legal Status. Check one only.

Official files are originals, including official copies of outgoing correspondence, which document policy, operations, property, financial transactions and legal obligations.

Supporting files include duplicates of official records, possibly filed separately from the official file for convenience of reference. Working papers and other records not covered in the definition of official files also come under the classification of supporting files.

Reference files are technical manuals, catalogs, etc., typically generated outside the organization. (You will want to note the location of important reference files. However, as noted above, it is not necessary to survey these files in depth.)

(This information is used to guide the development of retention schedules. Typically, official records are retained longer than supporting files. These, in turn, have different retention requirements from reference files. It is important to remember that the legal status reported during the survey represents the user's understanding of the records and how they are used. Only approved retention schedules have actual legal standing.)

Restrictions. Check all that apply.

Vital records are those that, if lost, would seriously impair the functioning of the organization.

Archival records are those that document the organization's principal activities and history.

(This is very important data, some of which you may have to verify and evaluate after the inventory is complete. In general, this is the kind of information you will have to gather by talking to the people who work with files.)

(The public disclosure information on this form applies primarily to government organizations, which often must comply with public disclosure and privacy legislation. However, depending on the nature of your business, there may be some applications for your company as well. If not, you can ignore these designations.)

File Integrity. Check all that apply. If this file is a subset of a larger file, or if a subset of this file is located elsewhere, please explain.

(For example: a law firm may have a master file of all its case files. However, the files for exceptionally large and important clients may be stored separately. It is very important to be able to piece together the complete file during files conversion.)

Information Duplicated Elsewhere. If a copy or original of this file exists elsewhere, please describe.

(For example, operating departments may have duplicates of the official personnel records held by the Human Resources Department. This is important to know because duplication is an excellent way to protect vital records. If only one copy of the official personnel folder exists, it may be desirable to microfilm it for security's sake. However, if every personnel folder is duplicated in the employing department, this may provide adequate protection without microfilming. Before you can rely on this duplication, however, you must be sure that the duplicate is an accurate reconstruction of the original.)

Information Summarized Elsewhere. If the information contained in these files is summarized elsewhere, please explain. This may be in paper, micrographic or computerized form.

(This section, too, is related to vital records protection. For example, even though no duplicate of the official personnel folder exists, the important information may be summarized in company computer systems for payroll, benefit administration and personnel registers.)

ANALYSIS

This section is filled out after the entire inventory is completed. (As a practical matter, the classification scheme documents most of this information. It is not always necessary to go back and update the inventory forms.)

You should annotate each inventory form with the official alphanumeric file code assigned to its records series. The code(s) goes in the box in the upper right-hand corner of the form. This simplifies the process of creating an alphabetical cross-index to the files manual. For each files classification code, you can quickly identify the appropriate inventory forms and extract cross-reference information from the "Use/Retrieval Terms."

Official Records Series Title. Enter the uniform title that will be used to designate the records series covered by this form.

Retention Period. Enter the approved retention periods for active and inactive storage.

Microfilm Recommendations. Enter any microfilm requirements identified for this records series.

Automation Recommendations. Enter any automation requirements identified for this records series.

SURVEYOR ID

Please complete the bottom line of the survey form, for all forms you fill out. The information is self-explanatory.

(The section relating to additions, deletions and changes is only used for very large organizations where the inventory is computerized. You may wish to leave this off.)

Appendix 2: Sample Files Manual—
Policy and Procedure Section

The following material establishes sound filing policies and procedures. It is designed to precede the classification scheme, retention schedules and alphabetical cross-index in a comprehensive files manual. You are welcome to adapt as much of it to your own files operation as you wish. You may also find it useful for training new files personnel.

The duties of the records management officer and other personnel are included in this material. You will note that the administrative assistant to the president has been assigned part-time duties as the records management officer. This is only one of many possibilities, including assignment of a full-time position.

I. THE FILES SYSTEM

A. Purpose. This manual establishes standard filing and disposition procedures for all records of the (Company Name). It provides for efficient filing and retrieval. It ensures proper retention for current records and prompt disposition of outdated records. The system also ensures continuity of information, economical use of equipment and supplies, and improved aids to management, auditing and research.

B. Policy. All company records are subject to the provisions of this manual. Records belong to the (Company Name) and not to the individuals who create them. Records must be turned over intact to successors.

All company records are to be maintained in proper filing cabinets or other specially designated equipment. Official files are *not* to be kept in individuals' desk drawers. Desk filing limits access for other personnel, and makes it difficult to apply records management controls. Therefore, filing in desk drawers is restricted to personal working papers.

This manual establishes a policy of central control over the classification and handling of all company records. However, the files themselves will remain decentralized, in order to ensure that the people who work with them have adequate access.

C. Personnel and Responsibilities

1. Records Management Officer. The administrative assistant to the president serves as records management officer, and has responsibility for files operations and records disposition programs. Duties include:

    a. Formulating standards and procedures for the management of all company records.

    b. Overseeing compliance with company files and records policies and procedures. This includes conducting an annual review of all files locations (collections of company files).

    c. Providing records management assistance and coordination to all company personnel and files locations.

    d. Providing for the maintenance and security of vital records.

    e. Authorizing all changes to this files manual.

    f. Evaluating filing equipment and supplies, and coordinating all acquisitions.

    g. Supervising inactive records storage operations.

2. Company Officers. Company managers and supervisors are responsible for compliance with the files manual in their respective organizations. This includes designating files coordinators for each files location under their supervision.

3. Files Coordinators. Files coordinators are the persons with primary responsibility for filing and retrieval at given files locations. Duties include:

    a. Creating, maintaining and disposing of files in accordance with the files manual.

    b. Preparing current files location plans of records held at their files location(s).

    c. Recommending changes in the files manual to the records management officer.

II. COMPONENTS OF THE FILES SYSTEM

A. The Files Classification Outline. The classification system outlined in this manual provides a logical arrangement of files based on records *functions*. The major classifications represent activities of significance to the company, such as facilities or personnel management. They do *not* represent organizational units of the company, such as Purchasing or Accounting.

The classification outline arranges records into primary classifications. These primary classifications are subdivided into secondary and tertiary (third level) classifications.

For example:

FEM	FACILITIES AND EQUIPMENT MANAGEMENT
FEM 9	Equipment Maintenance
FEM 9-1	Maintenance Records

The outline contains all the classifications needed for company records. No additional classifications may be used without approval of the records management officer. However, no individual files location will need all the classifications available. Instead, each station will select only those that are appropriate for its own records.

B. The Alphabetical Cross-Index. The cross-index lists all files classifications in alphabetical order for convenient reference. It also includes some commonly used unofficial names for files, and identifies the official classifications to use for them.

C. Records Retention Schedules. The retention schedules in the manual define how long records must be kept. The schedules indicate when to remove records to inactive storage, and when to destroy them.

The retention schedules are based on legal, operational and historical requirements. They are linked directly to the files classification outline to simplify indentification of records eligible for purging.

III. THE CODING SYSTEM

A. Files Classification Codes. The codes in the files classification outline are used to identify individual records for filing. The codes eliminate writing out long series of words.

Codes are alphanumeric, consisting of combinations of letters and numbers. Primary subjects are specified by three letters (e.g., FEM for Facilities and Equipment Management, FIN for Financial Management). Secondary and tertiary classifications are specified by numbers (e.g., FIN 6, FIN 6-1).

B. Retention and Disposition Codes. Retention periods for each files classification are coded in the last two columns of the outline. The retention codes consist of numbers and/or letters divided by one or more slashes. Time in office space appears before the first slash, with time in storage space noted immediately after it. Records can be destroyed at the end of the inactive storage period.

The numbers denote years. Some letter codes are also used as follows: "C" means retain while current or relevant; "P" means retain permanently; and "A" means after. A specific event is always noted after the "A" code in abbreviated form, such as employee termination (Aterm) or project completion (Acompl). Vital records are identified with "V." These records come under the vital records plan, which is maintained by the records management officer.

Retention codes are read as follows: "1Aclose/5," for example, means retain in office space for one year after the case is closed, followed by five years in storage. "C/P" means retain in office space while current, and permanently thereafter in storage. "1Acompl/C" means retention in office space until one year after project completion, and retention in storage as long as the completed project exists.

IV. TYPES OF FILES

A. Subject and Case Files. The filing system organizes records by their general function, purpose or type. As such, it is primarily subject-oriented. However, it is also possible to establish files for specific persons, organizations, actions or projects. These are called case files.

Case files are not identified by name in the classification outline, because they change so frequently. However, these files may be created whenever papers pertaining to a specific case must be filed or retrieved as a unit.

Case files are filed in alphabetic or numeric order behind the appropriate classification. For example, correspondence about standard maintenance schedules would be kept in a subject file called Equipment Maintenance Records, FEM 9-1. Maintenance files for specific items of equipment would be found in alphabetical order behind this folder.

Files from several different classifications can also be pulled together to form a single, large case file. For example, the complete file for the heating plant might contain design, operations and maintenance files, each from a separate primary in the files manual. However, for convenience of retrieval, they are kept together.

B. Special Files

1. Reading Files. A reading file consists of second copies of outgoing correspondence arranged in chronological order. It is used to limit extra courtesy copies. It is also a handy reference source for hard-to-find records. Reading files should be kept by all offices, retained one year and then destroyed. The classification of the reading file is Administrative Coordination (ACO 14).

2. Transitory Files. Files volume can be greatly limited by using transitory files. Transitory files are listed as the fourth secondary in each primary classification. They are set up to hold all records of short-term or otherwise limited value. These may include meeting and training announcements, hotel and travel reservations, subscription offers, etc. Transitory files should be purged every three months.

3. Working Files. In bulky files, working papers should be filed separately from official documents. Working papers include preliminary drafts, notes and informal documents that are normally purged from a file when it is closed. Having these materials filed separately makes the official file much easier to use. Furthermore, working papers can be destroyed much earlier than the official file.

4. Reference Files. Generally of a technical nature, these materials include reports, periodicals and special studies. They typically originate outside the company. Placing them in correspondence files hinders efficient retrieval, retirement and destruction of records. Reference material should be segregated from correspondence files wherever possible.

V. FILES CUTOFF

Files cutoff is the procedure for discontinuing filing in given folders and establishing new ones. It is one of the most important components of an effective files management program. Unless files cutoff procedures are followed, it is virtually impossible to implement records retention schedules.

A. Subject File Cutoff. Cut off old files and establish new folders once a year on the anniversary of the company's fiscal year. Establish new folders only for subjects that accumulated five or more papers in the previous year. Otherwise, use the next higher level classification in the new year.

B. Case or Project File Cutoff. These files are usually not cut off at the end of a fiscal year. They are more likely to close, for example, at the departure of an employee or at the completion of a project. When closed, the case file labels should be marked with the dates of closing. Inactive case files can then be retired or destroyed in convenient yearly blocks.

Case files that are voluminous or that continue over a long period of time should be cut off periodically. Make a new set of file folders and retire the older folders that are referred to infrequently. This can occur annually, or whenever the folders become too full of inactive materials.

VI. PREPARATION OF FILES LOCATION PLANS

These list all files maintained at a particular files location. The files coordinator submits files location plans to the records management officer once a year. The best time to prepare and submit plans is immediately after the annual cutoff and removal of inactive files from the cabinets.

The same information carried on file folder labels (see below) is listed on the files station plan. Include any missing folders that are marked by charge-out cards. Entries should appear in the same order as the files in the drawer.

After typing a new series of labels for a new drawer or a new year, the labels can be photocopied in sequence before being affixed to the files folders. This method of generating a file plan eliminates much repetitive typing.

VII. ANNUAL PROGRAM REVIEWS

The records management officer will review all files location plans at least once a year. The review will be timed to coincide with the cutoff of files from the previous fiscal year. Actual inspection of the files will be made as necessary. Compliance with the manual will be a major factor in the records management officer's review of requests for additional filing space and equipment.

VIII. FILING PROCEDURES

A. File on a Daily Basis. The records most frequently requested are those most recently received. The best way to keep track of them is in the files.

B. File Only What Is Necessary. Unnecessary filing wastes time, space and equipment. Limiting the creation and filing of records from the outset is the best control.

Some suggestions:

1. Avoid formal communications about routine matters.

2. Limit copies to the exact number required.

3. Do not file routine communications that require no record after action is taken.

4. Limit the filing of reference materials to those of lasting value.

C. Preparation of Records. Ready documents for filing as follows:

1. Remove rubber bands, paper clips, pins and other temporary fasteners. Staples may be left in place.

2. Ensure that the file is complete and that all enclosures are accounted for.

3. Mend or reinforce the records with transparent tape if necessary.

4. Destroy all duplicates except originals and official or annotated file copies.

5. See that parts of another file are not accidentally attached.

6. Remove all copies of mail control forms and routing slips, except those which contain remarks of record value. Also remove envelopes, unless address is needed or date of receipt must be documented.

7. Place the official file copy of an outgoing reply on top of the related incoming letter, add any pertinent attachments and staple.

D. Classification and Coding. The key to classifying records is to decide how they will be called for again. Once you have determined the subject, refer to the files classification outline for the proper file code. Select the appropriate primary subject category first, then the appropriate secondary or tertiary classification, if any. When uncertain, use the Alphabetical Cross-Index.

Write the classification in the upper right-hand corner of the record.

Some helpful hints for the classifier:

1. Consider the function of the record. The purpose for writing it usually suggests the subject under which it should be filed. Look for key words and phrases. The subject line of correspondence may be misleading, so do not choose the file code on this basis alone.

2. Refer to previous records on file to be sure.

3. When the subject of a record is impossible to determine, ask the author or someone familiar with the record for more information.

4. When no tertiary classification appears appropriate, use the secondary classification, which is more general. If none of the secondaries works, set up a general folder for the primary. As an alternative, you may need to ask the records management officer to establish a new files classification. However, this should not be done unless at least five documents per year will be accumulated in the new classification.

E. Sorting Records. After marking the records with the proper file code, arrange them in alphabetical order by primary code. Within each primary code, arrange the records in numerical order according to secondary and tertiary codes. This will place the records in the same order as the files in the cabinets. Filing can now proceed smoothly from the beginning of the files to the end.

F. Placing Records in Files. File records in the appropriate folders. Be careful not to place official copies in folders for supplementary or working copies. Retention periods may be different.

Put the latest record on top. Place the top of the sheet toward the left of the file drawer, so folder contents can be read like a book. Keep records completely within folders to avoid damage and keep labels visible.

Do not fasten records to the folders. Fastening is expensive in time and material. The only possible exception is large files that receive extensive use and have a long life, or files that contain very important materials.

Do not exceed file folder capacities (see below). Allow approximately 4 inches of empty working space in each drawer.

G. Preparing Cross-References. If a record has more than one subject and can be requested in more than one way, a cross-reference may be prepared as a finding aid. It indicates that a record belongs in two or more places. Cross-references are also useful when you place records elsewhere for security reasons or because they are oversize. Prepare them as follows:

1. Select the file code for the additional subject and write it on the document directly below the file code for the main subject. Place an "X" in front of it to indicate a cross-reference.

2. Use a copy machine to make cross-references. If the item cross-referenced is lengthy, reproduce only the first page. The file code notation in the top right corner of the copy will show the location of the original. After reproduction, place a check mark next to the appropriate code on each copy as follows:

PER 7-1
x INF 9-2
x LEG 11

File the original record under the first file code indicated. File the reproduced copies under the code checked on each copy.

Avoid making and filing unnecessary cross-reference copies. They take up valuable space and time, and can be a substitute for careful analysis and classification.

3. Use a cross-reference folder when an entire file is located permanently away from its normal filing place. An example would be a contract file put in a separate drawer because of its size. Place a cross-reference sheet inside the folder.

H. Filing Non-standard Records. Non-standard size files and documents may be filed separately when necessary. If they are not voluminous enough to constitute a separate files location, list them in the files location plan where they would normally occur and note their separate location. This provides documented control for such materials as computer printouts, drawings and card files.

I. Restricted Access Records. If access to certain records is restricted, note this in the files location plan. Secure filing equipment should be used for these records.

J. Retrieval. To locate records in the files, follow this procedure:

1. Obtain enough information to identify the file: subject, names of individuals, dates, etc.

2. Go directly to the file if you know the code.

3. If you do not know the code, first refer to the alphabetical cross-index, and then the files classification outline.

4. If you cannot locate a recent record in the files, search the unfiled records.

K. Charge-out System. Complete a charge-out card for any file or record removed. Place the card where the record was located. Note file or record, date and user. Charge-out cards should be larger than the file folders so they can be seen easily.

When records are returned, remove the charge-out card and draw a line through the entry. The files coordinator should check for overdue records and request their return at least every month.

Keep a supply of charge-out cards at the front of each file drawer for convenience. Refile returned records promptly and carefully. This practice helps eliminate losses and misfiles.

L. Folders and Drawer Maintenance.

1. File Folders. Use full-cut letter or legal size manila folders. Uniform file folders are the easiest to scan in a file drawer and make the most efficient use of filing supplies. Make sure they are strong enough to hold up under the use planned for the records.

Hanging (Pendaflex) folders may be used to hold manila folders. When using hanging folders, the box-bottom type are preferred, because the manila folder labels inside can still be read.

For open shelf filing, folders with side tabs may be easier to use.

2. Capacity. When the contents of a manila folder reaches ¼-inch to ⅜-inch, crease the folder along the second line at the bottom so that the contents will remain level.

When a folder reaches normal capacity of ½-inch to ¾-inch, start a new one for additional records. Place the new folder containing the most recent records in front of the old folder. Number folders to maintain order and to indicate that there is more than one.

Also observe minimum folder capacity. Unless more than five papers per folder are expected annually, file documents under the next broader classification. In other words, if a tertiary file is likely to contain only one or two records, file the contents in the secondary level folder to which they relate.

M. File Labels.

1. File Label Type. For manila folders, use oblong labels which require no moistening. They are available in white and with top stripes in various colors. The size is 9/16 x 3½-inch.

Start a new color for each fiscal year; the records management officer will specify the color.

Do not label hanging folders of the box-bottom type. However, if standard hanging folders are used, the labels on the manila folders inside may not be visible. In this case, label the hanging folders as well. Use plastic tabs with pre-applied adhesive. The inserts should be of the same color and format as those used for standard manila folders.

For case files housed in shelves rather than cabinets, only the case name or number is used. (Chapter 4 explains how to set up alphabetic or numeric case files.)

2. Label Content. Folder labels or inserts should show the following:

   a. Full file code.

   b. Title of the lowest level of the classification used, such as secondary or tertiary heading. Include folder number if there is more than one.

   c. Case file title if appropriate.

   d. Year of coverage and retention code.

3. Labeling Guidelines. Follow these guidelines when labeling folders:

   a. Type all labels; handwritten labels should be avoided.

   b. Begin typing two spaces from the left label edge and one space from the top.

   c. Type primary and secondary codes and titles entirely in capital letters. In all other cases, capitalize only the first letter of each important word.

   d. If the title is too long for the width of the label, indent the carryover on the second line.

   e. Omit punctuation and use abbreviations when necessary in order to include essential information.

   f. Use an additional label when you need still more space. Attach it directly below the first.

   g. For case files, follow the year when the file was opened with a dash and blank space. The date when the file is closed will be noted here.

   h. Attach labels in the left position at exactly the same place on each file. The following procedures will guarantee uniform placement:

      Place folders upright and tightly together on a flat surface. Lay a ruler or stiff card over the top edge of the tabs at the point where the labels will be attached. Mark with a pencil across the top edge of the tabs. Affix the label at the pencil mark on each tab.

   i. Use labels for all records, even when folders are not involved. Index card files and binders containing records are no exception.

N. Guide Cards. Pressboard guide cards support file folders and serve as guideposts to speed filing and retrieval. They should begin every primary, as well as major secondary or tertiary, subject. In general, place them approximately every 10 folders, using from four to six guide cards per file drawer. Each label carries the same information in capital letters as the file behind it.

Guide cards are unnecessary for support when hanging folders are used. Instead, plastic snap-on index tabs (not the smaller standard plastic tabs) should be used.

Guide cards are also very important for open shelf files. Guides with top and side tabs are available.

O. File Drawers.

1. Labels. The file drawer label should show years of coverage and contents. Content is usually shown by listing the first and last classification codes and titles. For drawers filled with case files, add the beginning and ending case file name or number.

   Use folder label format instead of drawer format when a drawer contains only one classification, as in the case of a card index drawer.

2. Arrangement of Folders and Guide Cards. Place folders and guides in the file drawer in the same sequence as they appear in the files classification outline, starting from the front of the drawer. The guides precede the related folders. The sequence of the drawers should be from top to bottom of the cabinet.

IX. RECORDS DISPOSITION

A. Disposition Functions. Disposition of records may occur in three ways:

1. Retirement. Records are retired when they are sent to an inactive storage area (records center).

2. Destruction. Records whose retention period has been fulfilled may be destroyed by throwing them away (for small quantities of nonconfidential records) or selling them in bulk for recycling. In the case of confidential information, supervised shredding, pulping or burning is appropriate. Destruction may also involve the erasure of information. Magnetic media, for instance, can be erased and reused.

3. Media Change. Microfilming paper records is the most common example.

B. Implementation of Retention Schedules. The retention schedules incorporated in the files classification outline identify when records are to be sent to inactive storage and when they are to be destroyed. In addition, special means of destruction, such as shredding, and required media changes may be indicated. The schedules may not be altered or deviated from without consulting the records management officer.

1. Annual Files Review. Once files have been cut off as described above, the files coordinator reviews them for disposition.

   When immediate destruction is indicated, dispose of the records directly. In the case of records designated for retirement to a storage area, estimate the volume involved and obtain the necessary records storage boxes.

The capacity of the standard 10-inch x 12-inch x 15-inch storage container is 1 cubic foot. Full letter size and legal size file drawers hold 2 cubic feet and 1½ cubic feet respectively. Storage boxes hold legal files lengthwise and letter files the other direction. Whenever possible, books and other non-standard materials should also be boxed.

2. Packing Records.

   a. All records in a given box must have the same retention period. Otherwise, the entire box has to be kept until the longest retention period is met, which wastes storage space.

   b. Place records in the box in an upright position.

   c. Arrange records in their original filing order.

   d. Do not pack files too tightly. Leave about 1 inch in the box for working space.

3. Labeling Boxes. After filling the boxes, type a storage label for each and attach it to the center of the box front. The label should note office, first and last classifications, inclusive dates, destruction date and consecutively assigned office box number.

   The size of some bound materials does not permit boxing. In such cases, place labels on the binding spines.

4. Listing Box Contents. Prepare a box list for each box or group of boxes, listing the box label information, the records center storage locator (to be provided by the records management officer) and the file folder label identifiers. The format for the labels is the same as a files location plan, which can be adapted to this purpose. Keep the box list at the files location, and provide a copy to the records management officer.

   Box lists serve as retrieval aids. They should be reviewed periodically for records that are eligible for destruction. Line out boxes when the boxes are disposed of, and note exact destruction dates. Notify the records management officer in each case. Retain all box lists permanently.

D. Retrieval of Inactive Files from Storage. All retrieval of records from storage areas is controlled by the records management officer.

   1. Retrieval of Boxes. Boxes retrieved from storage areas must be so noted on all copies of the box list. Document returned boxes that are kept in offices on the annual files location plan.

   2. Retrieval of Files. When retrieving single folders from boxes, be sure to file charge-out cards in their places. Individual records may not be removed from folders; the entire folder must be retrieved and refiled as a unit.

E. Destruction of Records in Inactive Storage. The records management officer is responsible for scheduled destruction of all records in inactive storage areas. Offices will be notified of pending destruction action one month before the scheduled date. The records management officer will evaluate requests for extended retention. When approving such requests, box lists and labels must be changed to reflect the extension.

X. FILES MANUAL MAINTENANCE AND AUDITING

A. General Procedure. Any employee may propose a change in the files manual, by going through the appropriate files coordinator. All changes are submitted to the records management officer. If approved, changes must be incorporated in all copies and all sections (files classification outline, records retention schedule, alphabetical cross-index) of the manual. Updated pages to the manual will be distributed to the files coordinators, showing the revision date on each page.

B. Files Classification Outline Maintenance. The files classification outline allows for growth in the following ways:

1. Upgrading Existing Subjects. Growth in an existing classification can be accommodated by raising the level of the classification. A tertiary level classification may be raised to a secondary; a secondary may be raised to a primary.

2. Adding Subjects. The number of files classifications may also be enlarged. Before recommending additional classifications, consider using an existing classification rather than an additional one. If new classifications are necessary, place them logically at the proper level. Avoid categories below the tertiary level.

C. Retention Schedule Maintenance. Retention schedules may be revised as follows:

1. New Schedules. As new files classifications are added to the manual, new retention schedules will have to be developed as well.

2. Change in Schedule. Retention periods may need to be changed to reflect evolving operational requirements.

3. Change in Law. New government regulations may also affect records retention requirements.

Consider the following factors in recommending changes:

a. The volume of records. Reducing the retention period for low-volume records may increase costs for disposition labor and supplies without realizing appreciable space-savings.

b. The reference rate. Records referred to regularly should be kept in office space for ready access.

c. The nature of the cutoff. Cutoff can occur at a regular date each year, or it may depend on a certain event such as the completion of a project.

Appendix 3: Files Conversion Procedure

The following procedure is designed for the files coordinators to follow in converting to a new filing system. If at all possible, conversion should be timed to coincide with the change in fiscal years. Conversion of files that have been cut-off should be held to a minimum.

For very large organizations, it is sometimes helpful to run off complete sets of all file folder labels on a word processor or computer. These can be distributed to the files coordinators who will select the labels they need. Although this process is necessarily somewhat wasteful of labels, the savings in labor (for typing) and time (to complete the conversion) often make it worthwhile. Complete sets of folder labels can also be run off at the start of each fiscal year.

I. LIST FOLDER CAPTIONS

Start by listing the folder titles now used at your files location. Be sure to include titles for records that are not currently maintained in folders or which are kept in unlabeled folders.

II. NOTE THE CORRESPONDING CLASSIFICATIONS

After comparing files contents to the classification outline and alphabetical cross-index, write the appropriate files classification code(s) next to each current folder title, arranging the new classifications on the listing in correct alphanumeric order. More than one new code and folder may be required for a single old folder. (Note: if you have received preprinted files labels, simply select those that your listing indicates you will need.)

III. REMOVE RECORDS

Remove records from filing cabinets or shelves in the current filing order. This may be done all at once or one drawer at a time, starting from the first drawer to be used. It is best to work with small units of records that can be processed at one time. Use storage boxes to hold records temporarily while conversion is taking place.

IV. PREPARE AND FILL FOLDERS

Begin with classifications at the beginning of the files location plan and continue on through. Place folders in drawers or on shelves. Do not pack folders too tightly. Allow for expansion and search room.

V. PREPARE AND INSERT GUIDES

When folders for one group of records are complete, go back and prepare guide cards or tabs where necessary.

VI. SUBMIT FILES LOCATION PLAN

Revise your preliminary files location plan to reflect any changes made during the actual conversion process. Submit a copy of the final plan to the records management officer.

Appendix 4: Some Practical Information About Filing Equipment

The space utilization statistics presented below were developed for a 432 square foot files room packed to maximum workable density. Our thanks to ACME Visible Records for computing these figures.

I. EQUIPMENT QUALITY

If you are considering conventional drawer or lateral file cabinets invest in quality. Look for a locking mechanism that allows only one drawer at a time to be opened. Otherwise, you risk tipping the entire contents over on yourself. The cabinet should also be braced inside, with good rollers for easy access.

II. DRAWER UTILIZATION

The standard 26-inch file drawer holds 4000 pieces of paper. It was designed for no more than 250 manila file folders, divided with about 10 guide cards. Do not overstuff the drawers. The savings in equipment will be lost in time and labor spent struggling with file contents.

Suspension frames and hanging folders increase your costs for supplies and equipment (because they take more space), but reduce your costs for labor by making the files easier to see and work with. They are recommended for drawer and lateral files.

III. EQUIPMENT TYPES

You basically have five choices:

A. Standard Drawer Cabinets. These come in letter or legal size, four or five drawers high (for most filing applications). The most cost-effective equipment is five-drawer letter files. A five-drawer cabinet takes no more space than a four-drawer and has 25% more capacity.

Legal files are not recommended. They cost more and use more floor space. Furthermore, these cabinets typically end up storing more letter- than legal-sized papers, which means that the extra cost is not justified. Federal courts have discontinued the use of legal files, and many state courts are following suit. This should eliminate much of the need for these costlier file cabinets in the future.

The principal disadvantage of drawer cabinets in office space is their aisle requirement. A 26-inch drawer requires a 28-inch service aisle so that files personnel can get to folders at the back of the drawer.

For the same reason, drawer cabinets are not particularly well-suited to high density filing applications. In the file room described above, the fact that the drawers must be opened and shut all the time limits the total number of file actions to 280 per person per day.

If the file room were fitted out with four-drawer letter cabinets, the filing statistics would be as follows:

total filing capacity:	6200 linear filing inches (lfi)
storage ratio:	14.4 lfi/square foot
cost per lfi:	$2.40

With five-drawer letter cabinets, the numbers change to:

total filing capacity:	7750 lfi
storage ratio:	17.9 lfi/square foot
cost per lfi:	$2.30

B. Lateral Filing Cabinets. These cabinets open from the side and run lengthwise. This makes it easier to see the entire contents of the drawer at one time, and color coding can be effectively used.

Lateral file cabinets project about six inches into the aisle, as opposed to the 28 inches for most drawers. Their appearance is generally considered more attractive than drawer files. In many offices they serve double duty as space dividers. However, they are more expensive to buy. For this reason, five-tier is again preferred to four-tier arrangements. Look for tiers that roll out, so that files personnel can work the bottom tier without having to sit on the floor to do it.

Lateral files don't do quite as well in the file room described above. However, some of this is because of the particular space configuration. In general, they are more efficient users of floor space. In a five-tier arrangement, the statistics would be as follows:

total filing capacity:	5510 lfi
storage ratio:	12.8 lfi/square foot
cost per lfi:	$2.97

C. Power Files. These are appropriate for high volume filing applications. If one person is handling 300+ filing actions per day in 10 or more drawers, power files may be indicated. They are especially appropriate when space is at a premium.

Filing efficiency is likely to increase from about 280 to about 320 file actions per day. The statistics using 18-carrier files are as follows:

total filing capacity:	10,521 lfi
storage ratio:	24.4 lfi/square foot
cost per lfi:	$5.30

D. Open Shelf Filing. For high volume filing, nothing beats open shelves for efficiency or cost. As many as 400 file actions per person per day are possible. When shelves are stacked eight tiers high, it is still possible to see folder labels on the top and bottom tiers. If you go eight tiers high, remember to check your floor loading first.

Although there are open shelf arrangements with doors for security and appearance, these features eat at the cost-effectiveness of the equipment. If these issues pertain to your office, it is better to relegate the open shelf files to a separate room that can be locked to keep out unauthorized personnel.

The statistics in an eight-tier configuration are:

total filing capacity:	14,468 lfi
storage ratio:	33.51 lfi/square foot
cost per lfi:	$.61

E. Motorized Open Shelf Filing. This equipment basically puts the shelves on tracks, so that one aisle can be opened up while another is closed. Space must be at a premium to justify the cost of this approach.

Safety is a problem with motorized equipment. No, you are not likely to be compressed into a paper-thin wedge accidentally. But floor loading is extremely important, and must be planned very carefully.

The statistics in an eight-tier arrangement:

total filing capacity:	21,552 lfi
storage ratio:	50 lfi/square foot
cost per lfi:	$1.41

Glossary

Absorbent Paper: A disaster recovery tool used to speed up the drying of water-damaged paper. Acidic papers, such as newsprint, should never be used to dry archival or permanent records.

Accession: 1) The act and procedures involved in taking records or papers into a records center or archives. 2) The materials involved in such a transfer.

Accession List: A listing of the holdings of a records center in the order in which they are received.

Active Records: Records referred to more than once a month per file drawer; therefore, records that should be retained in office space.

Administrative Value: The usefulness of records for management or summarizing purposes; usually exceeds their operating value.

Alphabetical Cross-Index: A listing in dictionary style of all terms by which records may reasonably be requested. In a files manual, it supplements the hierarchically arranged files classification scheme.

Alphanumeric: A combination of alphabetical and numerical characters.

Annotation: A note added to an index or listing to evaluate or describe the subject and contents of an item.

ANSI: American National Standards Institute, formerly USASI and ASA. ANSI is composed of representatives from industry, technical societies, consumer organizations and government agencies.

Aperture Card: An electronic data processing card with holes, specifically designed for the mounting of a microform image or images.

Applications Programs: Computer software written for a specific application, such as inventory management.

Appraisal: The process of determining the value and thus the disposition of records based upon their current operating, administrative, fiscal, legal and historical use; their arrangement; and their relationship to other records. Sometimes referred to as selective retention.

Archival Inventory: In archives management, describes the individual or work group initiating the records, as well as the record series, by noting dates, titles, record volume and arrangement, relationships to other record series or work groups or individuals, and relevant subjects and terms contained in the collection.

Archival Quality: The ability of film or a processed print to permanently retain its original characteristics.

Archival Storage Conditions: Conditions suitable for the preservation of records or film having permanent value.

Archives: 1) A body of permanently valuable records. 2) The place in which these records are kept.

Archives Box: A specialized storage box for archival materials, generally made of acid-free cardboard in letter or legal length having a width of 2½ inches or 5 inches. Often referred to as a Hollinger Box.

Archiving: In word and data processing, refers to copying online information offline for storage and for a security backup.

Arrangement: 1) The activities involved in organizing materials according to a particular order. 2) The final result of such activities.

ASCII: American Standard Code for Information Interchange. A code that uses a combination of seven bits (plus one for error checking) to represent characters of information in a computer.

Assembler: A computer language that is based on one line of program code for each machine operation.

Bar Code Symbol: A machine-generated and readable representation of data (usually numeric) in the form of a printed series of parallel bars of various widths, spacings and/or heights.

BASIC: A high level computer language used to write programs. The programs must be compiled or interpreted into machine language before they can be executed.

Baud: In electronic communications, refers to the speed at which information is transmitted. Synonomous with bits per second.

Bit: The smallest representation of information recognized by a computer, an electric pulse that is either on or off. Bits are usually arranged in codes, such as ASCII.

Blow Back: Generic term for a microform image projected on a screen.

Bone Folders: Flat tools made of bone and used by book binders to fold and tear paper. Plastic letter openers may be substituted.

Byte: The smallest number of bits required to represent a complete character in a computer.

C: A high level programming language used on some personal computers.

Camera-Processor: A device that performs the functions of both a camera and a film processor.

CAR: *See* computer-assisted retrieval.

Cartridge: 1) In micrographics, a container enclosing processed microforms, designed to be inserted into readers, reader-printers and retrieval devices. 2) In data processing, a container for tapes or disks that permits easy mounting on the computer and convenient offline storage. Used for removable storage media, and hence for backup or archiving of WP and DP files.

Catalog: A list which describes and indexes the resources of a collection or library.

Cataloging: The process of preparing entries for a catalog.

Case Files: Groupings of records that pertain to a specific person, place, thing, event or process. Distinguished from subject files, which group records by general subjects or functions.

Central Processing Unit: *See* CPU.

Centralized Files: The files of one or more organizational units physically grouped in one location.

Charge-out Card: Card inserted in place of documents removed from a file that identifies the records, the person withdrawing them and the date they were taken.

Chronological Filing: Filing in sequence according to date.

Classification: A records series listed in a files classification scheme. It usually is identified with a code and a title, such as: FIN Financial Affairs.

Closed File: A file folder which is assumed to be complete and to which no papers will be added.

COBOL: A high level computer language used to write business programs. It is both more complex and more powerful than BASIC.

COM: *See* computer-output microfilm.

Commercial Records Center: A records center, operated by a private company, housing the records of many different organizations on a fee basis.

Compiler: The software that translates the source code in which a computer program was written into the object code, or machine language, in which it will run.

Computer-assisted Retrieval (CAR): The capability of identifying and/or locating records, including microforms, by commands input to a computer terminal.

Computer Output Microfilm (COM): Microforms containing data produced from computer-generated signals. Typically used in place of hardcopy printouts.

Configuration: The hardware layout of a particular computer system.

Contact Frame: Device for making same-size reproductions from translucent materials. The items are exposed to light through a glass cover and are normally held in position by vacuum pressure.

Convenience File: A set of records created for convenient reference that duplicates official materials kept at designated files locations.

Correspondence: All formats intended to convey information to or from individuals within or outside an organization.

Correspondence Mode: The operating condition of a dot matrix printer that has been slowed down to improve the print quality. However, the product is still not as good as letter quality printing.

CP/M (Control Program for Microcomputers): A trade name of Digital Research for an operating system used on many microcomputers.

CPU (Central Processing Unit): The central device in a computer that controls and executes all other functions. It is the computer in the computer.

Cross-reference Card: A finding aid indicating that a record is filed elsewhere. It is prepared when a record has more than one subject by which it can be requested. Either a copy of the original or a cross-reference form may be used.

CRT (Cathode Ray Tube): A TV tube incorporated into a computer or word processor and used to display information.

Current Records: Those which provide current or most recent information. May include both active and inactive records.

Cutoff: The procedure for discontinuing filing in given folders and immediately establishing new ones, which simplifies retrieval and disposition. Cutoff usually occurs once a year, at the end of the fiscal year. Case files do not always follow this rule.

Data Base: A comprehensive file of information stored in a computer and organized for easy retrieval and analysis.

Data Base Management System: A computer program designed to enter, retrieve, manipulate and format information stored in a computer data base. The commands the user enters into the system are given through the use of a query language.

Decentralized Files: Records maintained in or near the offices that create and use them.

Degradation. In computers, refers to slowing of the response time of the system due to overloading.

Densitometer: A device used to measure the optical density of a microform image or base by measuring the amount of light reflected or transmitted.

Density: In micrographics, the light-absorbing or light-reflecting characteristics of a photographic image, filter, etc.

Diazo Material: A slow print film or paper, which generally produces nonreversed images; i.e., a positive image will produce a positive image and a negative image will produce a negative image. Used to create duplicate microforms.

Disaster Box: An initial supply of disaster recovery materials.

Disaster Plan: A written set of procedures that outlines and guides disaster recovery efforts.

Disaster Team: A working team of individuals who arrive at the disaster site knowing what to do and who are capable of working together to resolve the problems created by the disaster.

Disk: A high capacity, random access storage medium. Most disks are fixed, meaning that they are sealed inside the computer. Often referred to as a hard disk to differentiate it from a floppy diskette.

Dispersal: Sending copies of vital records to locations other than those where the originals are housed.

Disposal: The final removal, whether for destruction or formal transfer to another agency, of records that have reached the end of their retention period.

Disposition: Any means of changing the location or physical state of records. Includes retirement, destruction, microfilming, duplication or transfer.

Distributed Logic: Refers to a network of computers or intelligent terminals (each with its own microprocessor). These systems may share access to printers and storage media. However, they are not all dependent upon the same CPU.

Document Mark: An optical mark, usually rectangular, below (and/or above) the image on a roll of microfilm; used for counting images automatically.

Dot Matrix Printer: A high speed computer printer that uses a combination of dots to compose printed characters on typed pages. Operates at speeds of from 120 to 200 characters per second and up. The quality is not acceptable for most word processing applications. Also called a draft or high speed printer.

DP (Data Processing): The machine storage and manipulation of information.

Dry Processing: In micrographics, development of a latent image without wetting, usually accomplished by application of heat.

Electronic Spreadsheet: A program that defines rows and columns, as well as their mathematical relationships, on a computerized spreadsheet. Used to revise numeric calculations without reentering the mathematical formulae.

Electronic Typewriter: A word processor with limited storage that offers more sophisticated formatting, such as flush right and left margins, than is possible on a standard electric typewriter. Electronic typewriters may have a single line display, but they do not have true screens and do not permit simultaneous typing and printing.

Ephemera: Current material of temporary value. The term commonly includes pamphlets, brochures and photographs.

Field: In machine-readable records, an area or position in the record set aside for recording of a specific type of information. Also referred to as a data element.

File: 1) A file folder. 2) The records contained in it. 3) Groupings of folders or records, whether on paper, film or electronic media.

File Code: The standardized letters and numbers used to code records series listed in a files classification scheme.

File Integrity: Refers to the accuracy, completeness and original order of the records in a filing system.

Files Classification Scheme: A comprehensive listing of files classifications and their retention schedules in a files manual.

Files Classification System: A logical and systematic arrangement of files into subject groups or categories based on some definite scheme of natural relationships.

Files Coordinator: The person with specific and immediate responsibility for the records management program at a given files location.

Files Location Plan: A listing of all files held at a specific location. Includes folder label information in the proper order, including file code, title, years of coverage and retention code.

Finding Aid/List/Tool: A succinct list of records or books, with a very brief entry for each title.

Fiscal Value: The usefulness of records for documenting financial transactions.

Fixing: A processing step that makes a developed film image stable, by rendering it insensitive to light.

Floor Load: The capacity of a floor area to support a given weight, expressed in terms of weight per unit of area.

Floppy Diskette: A storage medium for word processors and computers. Consists of a round, flexible Mylar sheet stored in a paper sleeve. Typically used for storing 250 pages or less of text or data.

Format: The physical form in which material appears (books, slides, film, aperture card, recording, etc.).

FORTRAN: A high level computer programming language typically used for mathematical applications.

Freeze Drying: A technique used to dry water-damaged records. The damaged records are frozen and then dried in a vacuum chamber, during which process the frozen water passes from a solid state directly to a gaseous state.

Freezing: A holding technique for water-damaged records.

Front Projection: The process of creating an optical image on a reflective surface, so that the projector and the viewer are on the same side.

Full Cut: A folder with a tab running its full length.

Functional Filing: A method of organizing records by the subject or the function they serve. Like records are filed according to the same classification regardless of their organizational location.

Generation: Successive stages of reproduction of an original or a master.

Generic Programs: Computer programs that can be used by many types of businesses for many types of applications. Examples are data base management systems and electronic spreadsheets.

Guide Card: A heavyweight card with a caption tab used to subdivide the contents of a file drawer, as an aid to filing. When hanging folders are used, guide tabs on the folders take the place of guide cards.

Hardcopy: A record on paper, such as a computer printout, a photocopy or a typed sheet.

Hardware: The equipment and components included in a computer system.

Historical Value: The usefulness of records for documenting an organization's policies, key personnel, major transactions, processes, trademarks and events. Typically, about 5% of total records have historical value.

Hollinger Box: Officially, any one of a number of acid-neutral archives boxes manufactured by the Hollinger Corp. Used as a generic descripition of any archives box.

Image Rotation: The ability to rotate microfilm images in readers in order to allow projection of all images right side up and right reading on the screen.

Inactive Records: Records that do not have to be readily available, but which must be kept for legal or historical purposes. Typically, these are records referred to less than once per file drawer per month.

Index: A reference guide to a listing or file, most commonly used as a locator.

Interface: The juncture of two or more devices, systems, disciplines or fields, or the device which serves as link.

Interleaving: A technique used to speed up the drying of water-damaged paper. Sheets of dry, absorbent paper are placed between sheets of wet paper.

Interlibrary Loan: An arrangement by which one library may lend material to another, governed by a formal code.

Jacket: A flat, transparent, plastic carrier with single or multiple film channels made to hold single or multiple microfilm images. Synonymous with microfilm jacket.

Journal: 1) In libraries, a periodical issued by an institution, corporation, or learned society, containing current news and reports of activities and work in a particular field. 2) In accounting, a register of like transactions, such as sales or payroll, that are posted to the general ledger.

K: Kilo or thousand. Refers to bytes or characters of information.

Lateral Files: Files which are stored from left to right rather than from front to back. Includes side-opening filing cabinets and shelf filing equipment.

Legal Value: The usefulness of records as evidence supporting an organization's transactions, activities, claims and obligations.

Letter Quality Printer: A printer that uses fully formed characters on a printwheel to produce typed documents. Typically prints at 20 to 70 characters per second. Used for most word processing output.

Library Science: The knowledge and skill by which information is recognized, collected, organized and utilized.

Light Box: A device for inspecting film that provides diffused illumination evenly dispersed over the viewing area.

Local Area Network (LAN): Typically, a coaxial cable-based internal network that links word processors, computers, peripheral devices, copiers and other office equipment together. Depending upon the configuration, LANs can link different manufacturers' machines, and are capable of carrying text, data, image, voice and video communications.

Machine-readable Records: Records that require specialized equipment to read the information they contain; includes micrographics and magnetic media.

Magnetic Media: Tapes, disks and other formats used to store electronically generated information.

Matte: Dull, gloss-free surface finish. Also, the drafting surface on polyester films.

Mb: Megabyte, or a million bytes (or characters) of information.

Menu: A list displayed on a computer screen that identifies the functions the machine is ready to perform, such as a list of the available programs.

Methylene Blue: A chemical dye formed during the testing of archival permanence of processed microforms using the methylene blue method.

Microfiche: A transparent sheet of film with microimages arranged in a grid pattern. A heading or number large enough to be read without magnification normally appears at the top of the microfiche.

Microfilm: 1) A fine-grain, high-resolution film used to record images reduced in size from the original. 2) A microform consisting of strips of film on rolls that contain multiple microimages. 3) To record microphotographs on film.

Microfilm Jacket: *See* jacket.

Microform: A form, usually film, which contains microimages. *See also* aperture card, jacket, microfiche, roll microfilm.

Micrographics: Techniques associated with the production, handling and use of microforms.

Microprocessor: A computer on a chip. In other words, the CPU is on one chip, as opposed to being composed of many processors linked together. Mini- and mainframe computers use multiple processors.

Micropublishing: To issue new (not previously published) or reformatted information in microform for sale or distribution.

Modem: A device that converts digital information to analog signals and back for electronic transmission of data.

MS-DOS (Microsoft Disk Operating System): A trade name of Microsoft Corp. for an operating system used on many personal computers.

Multi-tasking: The ability of a computer to run more than one program for more than one user at a time. Typically a characteristic of large computers, although some personal computers offer this capability. Also referred to as multi-programming.

Multi-user: The ability of a computer to support several users, each at a different terminal, simultaneously.

Mylar Film: Trade name of the Du Pont Co. for a polyester-type film of high strength and dimensional stability, used for drafting films.

Mylar Sheets: Plastic sheets used in disaster recovery operations, to separate water-logged papers without tearing or damaging the wet paper.

Negative-appearing Image: An image in which the lines and characters appear light against a dark background.

Non-record Material: Material that does not need to be filed or that can be destroyed after a short retention. This includes drafts, worksheets, routine replies and extra copies of documents created for convenience.

Nonreproducible: Not intended for use as an intermediate master, and usually opaque. Generally blue or light violet in color.

Numerical File: A file in which the primary arrangement is numerical.

Object Code: The instructions for a particular program compiled into machine language.

OCR (Optical Character Recognition) Reader: A device that scans printed text and converts it into machine readable computer code.

Office of Record: The office assigned responsibility for custody and maintenance of specific records. Generally the office in which the records were originally created and filed.

Official Files: Originals, including official copies of outgoing correspondence, that document policy, operations, property, financial transactions, and legal obligations. Official records have the legally recognized and judicially enforceable quality of establishing some fact.

Offline: 1) The processing of a search by the computer after the user has logged off and is no longer interacting with a computer. Printed records are often generated after the user has logged off the system. 2) Pertaining to equipment or devices not under direct control of a computer.

Online: 1) Direct interactive communication between a user and a computer program. 2) Pertaining to equipment or devices under the control of a computer.

Open Shelf Filing: A method of filing records vertically on shelves instead of in conventional filing cabinets.

Operating Value: The usefulness of records in the conduct of an organization's regular business.

Optical Disk: A film-like storage medium that is created and read by a laser, and which has an exceptionally high storage capacity. Still in the developmental stages, owing to cost and the fact that information on disk cannot yet be updated.

Oral History: Recordings or transcripts of recordings with individuals regarded as relevant for inclusion in an archives. Oral interviews are usually based on previously known background materials and are an effort to gain information that is not otherwise documented or available.

Overlay: Transparent or translucent prints, which, when placed one on the other, form a composite picture.

Overlay Drafting: Separation of common images, such as electrical and plumbing components, onto several sheets of drafting film to allow multiple use of those images.

Packet Switching Network: A commercial telecommunications carrier that allows subscribers to share access to high speed data lines on a pay-as-you-use basis. Packet switching implies interleaving of message "packets," so that multiple transmissions can be carried simultaneously.

PBX/CBX: Private Branch Exchange, Computerized Branch Exchange. A computer-based, user-owned private telephone system, including the switch (the computer), all handsets, and cables and wiring. Connects with a telecommunications supplier such as the phone company only when calls originate outside of or leave the premises. Offers cost advantages, as well as advanced features not usually available on standard rental telephones.

Peripherals: Devices such as terminals and printers attached to a CPU.

Permanent Records: Records of indefinite, long-term value. Typically, about 5% of all records holdings.

Personal Computer: A computer based on a microprocessor, designed to be used by a person without a data processing background.

Planetary Camera: A type of microfilm camera in which the document and the film remain in a stationary position during the exposure. The document is on a plane surface at the time of filming.

Plotter: A device that uses a tracing pen to draw graphics under the control of a computer graphics program.

Primary Classifications: The most general categories under which records can be filed.

Processing: A series of steps involved in the treatment of exposed photographic material to make the latent image visible and ultimately usable, e.g., development, fixing, washing, drying.

Processor: 1) In micrographics, any machine that performs the various operations necessary to process photographic material, e.g., development, fixing, washing, etc. 2) In computers, the device that controls all operations and performs all functions.

Professional Computer: A personal computer with highly integrated software for word processing, information retrieval, electronic spreadsheet applications, graphics, program development and electronic communications. Typically uses exceptionally well-designed peripherals.

Program: The coded set of instructions that runs a computer.

Public Records: Records open by law or custom to public inspection.

Pulpit Ladder: A safety ladder having an extended top shelf, used for retrieving records stored on high shelves.

Query Language: A high level user language for using a computerized data base.

RAM (Random Access Memory): The CPU memory used to store and process programs and data. This is volatile memory, and is erased every time a new program is entered.

Reader: A device that enlarges microimages for viewing; usually consisting of a light source, illuminating optics, microform holder, lens and screen.

Reader-printer: A device that enlarges microimages for viewing and also has the capability of producing a hard copy of the enlarged image.

Reading Files: Copies of outgoing correspondence in chronological order. Also called chronological or day files.

Record Priorities: Disaster recovery priorities based on the value of the information the record contains, the intrinsic value of the record itself, and/or the vulnerability of the media and the type of damage incurred.

Records: Papers, correspondence, forms, books, photographs, films, sound recordings, maps, drawings or other documents, regardless of physical form or characteristics, and including all copies thereof, either originated or received by an organization.

Records Center: A low-cost facility or centralized area for the controlled maintenance, retrieval and disposal of inactive records.

Records Creation: The production or reproduction of any record.

Records Inventory: A physical inventory to identify the size, scope and complexity of an organization's records in order to evaluate, appraise and organize the collection.

Records Management: The systematic control of all records from their creation or receipt through processing, distribution, organization and retrieval to their ultimate preservation or disposition.

Records Manager: The person assigned primary responsibility for the records management program.

Records Processing: In word processing, refers to data base management systems integrated with WP software.

Records Retention Schedule: A comprehensive schedule of records series by department, indicating for each series the length of time it is to be maintained in office areas, records centers, and when and if such series may be microfilmed and/or destroyed.

Records Series: A group of identical or related records that are used, filed and disposed of in the same way.

Records Values: The determination of usefulness of records for operating, administrative, legal, fiscal and historical purposes.

Reduction Ratio: In micrographics, the relationship (ratio) between the dimensions of the original or master and the corresponding dimensions of the microimage; e.g., reduction ratio is expressed as 1:24, or 24X.

Reference Material: Published, publicly available information held for consultative or research purposes.

Repetitive Typing: Typing that involves the recurring use of the same text, such as paragraphs or whole documents, or format, such as forms and reports.

Retention Period: The period of time records must be kept, usually stated in terms of months or years, but sometimes expressed as contingent upon the occurrence of an event, such as employee termination, contract closure, statutory limitations period and the like.

Retrieval: Locating and delivering records for use.

Revision Typing: Typing that involves editing documents, which includes inserting, deleting and reordering text.

ROM (Read Only Memory): The part of the CPU used to store the computer's permanent programs. These are the internal operating systems used to read all other programs.

Scheduled Records: Records for which there is an official retention schedule.

Secondary Classifications: The second most general class of categories by which records can be filed.

Service Bureau: An organization that provides contract micrographic or data processing services to a number of users on a fee basis.

Shared Logic: Refers to a number of peripherals (terminals and printers) sharing the same CPU, as well as the same disk storage. As opposed to distributed logic.

Shared-resource System: Refers to a WP or DP system where a number of terminals share access to disk storage, printers or other peripherals. May be either shared or distributed logic.

Software: The programs that cause a computer to perform specific functions.

Source Code: Program code as written by the programmer. It must be compiled into object code before it can be executed.

Specification: A written outline of requirements for hardware and software. Used to solicit and evaluate vendor proposals, and to select the best fit with a given set of needs.

Stack: A series of bookcases, arranged for compact storage of a library collection. The term also refers to the area housing such a group of bookcases.

Standard Details: In drafting, design details such as electrical installations, elevator corridors and other items used in many different drawings and projects.

Step-and-repeat Camera: A microfilm camera that exposes a series of images on an area of film according to a predetermined format, usually in orderly rows and columns, e.g., microfiche.

Subject File: A file in which documents are arranged by subject. Distinguished from a case file.

Supporting Files: Includes duplicates of official records, working papers, ephemera and other records not covered under the definition of official records.

Suspense File: A file arranged chronologically by the date in which records or information will be referenced. A "tickler file" is one type.

Suspension Filing Equipment: Equipment in which records or file folders are suspended vertically. Used with file folders, printout binders and large documents such as engineering drawings. Often referred to as hanging files.

Tab: The portion of a folder or guide card that extends above the main part of a folder or guide to display a caption or label.

Tab Cut: The length of the tab in proportion to the width of the folder. For example, a one-third cut means a tab running along one third of the top of the folder.

Tape Drive: In computers, refers to the device for mounting tape storage media. Many computers use tape to back up large files, typically of 20Mb or more.

Terminal: A computer or word processing workstation consisting of a screen and a keyboard.

Terminal Digit Filing System: The arrangement of records in numerical order by final groups of digits (usually two digits per group), reading from right to left.

Tertiary Classifications: The most specific and least general categories under which records can be filed.

Tickler File: A suspense file. It reminds the user of future tasks and events.

Title Block: The space on a drawing set aside for an identifying legend.

Transfer: The change in physical custody of records from one organization or unit to another. For example, office records may be transferred to a records center.

Transitory File: Contains records valuable only for a short period of time.

Transitory Records: Routine correspondence with short-term records value. The retention period is limited to the interval required for completion of the action covered by the communication.

UNIX: An operating system developed by Bell Labs that runs on many personal computers. Also runs on some larger computers.

Updatable Microfilm: Microfilm that permits the addition of images after part of the film has already been exposed.

Vacuum Drying: A technique used to dry water-logged records by pulling the moisture from the records as a gas.

Vital Records: Records containing information essential for: the resumption of operations after a disaster; the reestablishment of the legal and financial status of the organization; and the determination of the rights and obligations of individuals and corporate bodies with respect to the organization.

WP (Word Processing): The automated storage, editing and formatting of narrative documents, correspondence, reports and other business communications.

X.25: A communications standard that permits different manufacturers' systems to send and receive information over a packet-switching network.

Bibliography and Information Resources

Periodicals

ARMA Records Management Quarterly. Association of Records Managers and Administrators, Bradford, RI (quarterly).

Auerbach Reports on the Electronic Office. Auerbach Publishers, Inc., Pennsauken, NJ (monthly).

Computer Decisions. Hayden Publishing Co., Rochelle Park, NJ (monthly).

Creative Computing. Creative Computing, Morristown, NJ (monthly).

Data Communications. McGraw-Hill, Inc., New York, NY (bimonthly).

Datamation. Technical Publishing Co., Greenwich, CT (monthly).

Desktop Computing. A Wayne Green Publication, Peterborough, NH (monthly).

The Guidelines Letter. Guidelines, Orinda, CA (monthly).

IMC Journal. International Micrographic Congress, Bethesda, MD (quarterly).

IRM. Information and Records Management, Inc., Hempstead, NY (13 issues/year).

Infosystems. Hitchcock Publishing Co., Wheaton, IL (monthly).

Journal of Micrographics. National Micrographics Association, Silver Spring, MD (bimonthly).

Office Administration and Automation. Geyer-McAllister Publications, Inc., New York, NY (monthly).

The Office. Office Publications, Inc., Stamford, CT (monthly).

The Seybold Report on Office Systems. Seybold Publications, Inc., Media, PA (monthly).

Books

Aschner, Katherine. *The Word Processing Handbook: A Step-by-Step Guide to Automating Your Office*. White Plains, NY: Knowledge Industry Publications, Inc., 1982.

Ashworth, Wilfred. *Special Librarianship*. Ridgewood, NJ: K.G. Saur, 1979.

Bakewell, K.G. *Library and Information Sciences for Management*. Hamden, CT: Shoe String Press, 1968.

Bohem, Hilda. *Disaster Prevention and Disaster Preparedness*. Berkeley, CA: University of California, Task Force on the Preservation of Library Materials, 1978.

Brooks, James and Draper, James. *Interior Design for Libraries*. Chicago, IL: American Library Association, 1979.

Closurdo, Janette S., ed. *Library Management*. New York: Special Libraries Association, 1980.

Cohen, Aaron and Cohen, Elaine. *Designing and Space Planning for Libraries: A Behavioral Guide*. Ann Arbor, MI: R.R. Bowker Co., 1979.

Costigan, Daniel M. *Micrographic Systems*. Silver Spring, MD: National Micrographics Association, 1975.

Dorfman, Harold. *Microfilm Shop Talk*. Whitestone, NY: Microfilm Control Co.

Eastman Kodak *Control Procedures in Microfilm Processing. D-17*. Rochester, NY: Eastman Kodak Co., 1976.

Eastman Kodak. *Preservation of Photographs*. Rochester, NY: Eastman Kodak Co., 1979.

Eastman Kodak. *Storage and Preservation of Microfilms*. Rochester, NY: Eastman Kodak Co., 1965.

Giachino, J.W. and Beukema, Henry J. *Engineering Technical Drafting & Graphics*. Chicago, IL: American Technical Society, 1978.

Gill, Suzanne L. *File Management and Information Retrieval Systems: A Manual for Managers and Technicians*. Littleton, CO: Libraries Unlimited, 1981.

Gracy, D.B. *An Introduction to Archives and Manuscripts*. New York: Special Libraries Association, 1981.

Hamilton, Beth A. and Ernst Jr., William. *Multitype Library Cooperation*. New York: R.R. Bowker Co., 1977.

Harvey, Joan M. *Specialized Information Centres*. Hamden, CT: Shoe String Press, 1976.

Hedlin, E. *Business Archives: An Introduction*. Chicago, IL: Society of American Archivists, 1978.

International Reprographic Association. *Pin Graphics Manual*. Franklin Park, IL: International Reprographic Association, 1980.

King, David E., ed. *Special Libraries: A Guide for Management*. 2nd ed. New York: Special Libraries Association, 1980.

Maedke, W.O.; Robek, Mary F.; and Brown, Gerald F. *Information and Records Management*. 2nd ed. Encino, CA: Glencoe Publishing Co., 1982.

Mitchell, Betty Jo, et al. *Cost Analysis of Library Functions: A Total System Approach*. Greenwich, CT: JAI Press, 1978.

Mitchell, William E. *Records Retention*. Evansville, IN: Ellsworth Publishing Co., 1976.

Mezher, Glenham C. and Turner, Jeffrey H. *Micrographic Film Technology*. Silver Spring, MD: National Micrographics Association, 1979.

Microfilm and the Courts: Reference Manual. Denver, CO: National Center for State Courts, 1976.

Microfilm Source Book. New Rochelle, NY: Microfilm Publishing, Inc., 1982. (Available from Knowledge Industry Publications, Inc., White Plains, NY.)

Mount, Ellis, ed. *Planning the Special Library*. New York: Special Libraries Association, 1972.

National Micrographics Association. *Glossary of Micrographics. TR2-1980*. Silver Spring, MD: NMA, 1980.

National Micrographics Association. *Guide to Micrographic Equipment. RS15-1979*. Silver Spring, MD: NMA, 1979.

National Micrographics Association. *An Introduction to Computer-Output-Microfilm*. Silver Spring, MD: NMA, 1981.

National Micrographic Association. *Micrographic Standards and Related Items. RR1*. Silver Spring, MD: NMA, 1981.

National Micrographics Association. *Practice for Operational Procedures/Inspection and Quality Control of First-Generation, Silver-Gelatin Microfilm of Documents. NMA MS23-1979*. Silver Spring, MD: NMA, 1979.

National Micrographics Association. *Practice for Operational Practices/Inspection and Quality Control for Alphanumeric Computer-output Microforms. NMA MS1-1980*. Silver Spring, MD: NMA, 1980.

National Micrographics Association. *Thermally Processed Silver Microfilm. T003*. Silver Spring, MD: NMA, 1982.

Payne, Majorie. *The Retention Book*. Chicago, IL: Records Controls, Inc., 1981.

Shera, Jesse H. *An Introduction to Library Science: Basic Elements of Library Services*. Littleton, CO: Libraries Unlimited, 1976.

Strable, Edward G., ed. *Special Libraries: A Guide for Management*. Rev. Ed. New York: Special Libraries Association, 1975.

Strauss, Lucille J., et al. *Scientific and Technical Libraries: Their Organization and Administration*. 2nd ed. New York: Wiley-Interscience, 1972.

Waters, Peter. *Procedures for Salvage of Water-Damaged Library Materials.* Stock #030-000-00105-2. Washington, DC: Superintendent of Documents, GPO, 1975.

Williams, Robert W., ed. *Legality of Microfilm: Admissibility in Evidence of Microfilm Records.* Chicago, IL: Cohasset Associates, 1980.

Young, Margaret L. and Harold C., eds. *Directory of Special Libraries & Information Centers.* 6th Ed. Detroit, MI: Gale Research, 1981.

Professional Associations

American Federation of Information Processing Societies, Inc. 1815 North Lynn St., Suite 800, Arlington, VA 22209

Association of Records Managers and Administrators, Inc. 4200 Somerset, Prairie Village, KS 66208

National Micrographics Association, 8719 Colesville Rd., Silver Spring, MD 20910

Special Libraries Association, 235 Park Ave. South, New York, NY 10003

Index

About the Authors

Katherine Aschner is president and founder of Arcadia Associates (Seattle), an office systems consulting firm serving government and private industry in the U.S., Canada and the Middle East. A graduate of the University of Wisconsin, she was the youngest regional director of the Records Management Division, U.S. General Services Administration. Her clients now include banks, utilities, labor unions and hospitals, as well as law, mining, manufacturing, aerospace, engineering and insurance firms. Ms. Aschner is the author of *The Word Processing Handbook: A Step-by-Step Guide to Automating Your Office.*

Frederick Klunder is King County (WA) records management officer, and was formerly vice president, Arcadia Associates. **Julia Niebuhr Eulenberg** is a records coordinator with Battelle Human Affairs Research Centers (Seattle). **Terence Murphy** is president of Curtis Archives (Seattle). **Jane Cargill** is a principal of Information Design (Edmonds, WA), an information management consulting firm.

Other Titles from
Knowledge Industry Publications....

The Word Processing Handbook: A Step-by-Step Guide to Automating Your Office
by Katherine Aschner

| 191 pages | hardcover | $32.95 |
| | softcover | $22.95 |

Electronic Mail: A Revolution in Business Communications
by Stephen Connell and Ian A. Galbraith

| 141 pages | hardcover | $32.95 |
| | softcover | $22.95 |

Office Automation: A Glossary and Guide
edited by Nancy MacLellan Edwards

| 275 pages | hardcover | $59.50 |

Information Technology: An Introduction
by Peter Zorkoczy

| 140 pages | hardcover | $29.95 |

The Future of Videotext
by Efrem Sigel, et al.

| 194 pages | hardcover | $34.95 |

Electronic Mail Executives Directory
compiled by International Resource Development, Inc.

| 176 pages | softcover | $95.00 |

Online Search Strategies
edited by Ryan E. Hoover

| 345 pages | hardcover | $37.50 |
| | softcover | $29.50 |

The Teleconferencing Handbook: A Guide to Cost-Effective Communication
by Ellen A. Lazer, Martin C.J. Elton, James W. Johnson, et al.

| 219 pages | hardcover | $34.95 |

Computer-Readable Databases: A Directory and Data Sourcebook, 1982
edited by Martha E. Williams

| 1472 pages | softcover | $120.00 |

Available from Knowledge Industry Publications, Inc. 701 Westchester Avenue White Plains, NY 10604.

DATE DUE

18 Apr 86			